JUST SCHOOLING

JUST SCHOOLING

Explorations in the cultural
politics of teaching

Trevor Gale and **Kathleen Densmore**

Open University Press

Open University Press
McGraw-Hill Education
McGraw-Hill House
Shoppenhangers Road
Maidenhead
Berkshire
SL6 2QL
United Kingdom

email: enquires@openup.co.uk
World wide web: www.openup.co.uk

and
Two Penn Plaza
New York, NY 10121-2289, USA

First Published 2000
Reprinted 2001, 2002, 2004

Copyright © Trevor Gale and Kathleen Densmore, 2000

A catalogue record of this book is available from the British Library

ISBN   0335 20322 1 (pb)   0335 20323 X (hb)

Library of Congress Cataloging-in-Publication Data
Gale, Trevor, 1956-
    Just schooling : exploration in the cultural politics of teaching / Trevor Gale
and Kathleen Densmore.
        p. cm.
    Includes bibliographical references (p.) and index.
    ISBN 0-335-20323-X (hb) – ISBN 0-335-20322-1 (pbk.)
    1. Critical pedagogy. 2. Teaching-Social aspects.   3. Multicultural
education.   4. Language and education–Social aspects.   I. Densmore, Kathleen
Mary. II.Title.
LC196.G35 2000
371.3–dc21   99-086748

Typeset by Graphicraft Limited, Hong Kong
Printed and bound in Great Britain by Biddles Ltd,

Contents

Foreword

This book's title is a play on words asking three questions: about whether and how schooling still matters, about whether and how it can be made more just, and about whether and how schooling is still political in new conditions.

The first question: *Just Schooling* asks whether schooling is a diminished force in contemporary societies and cultures, whether it has become 'merely schooling'. This is not just a rhetorical question but one that the teachers who worked with Trevor Gale and Kathleen Densmore confront everyday. The connectedness of what is done in classrooms to new worlds of work and technology, new cultures and identities likely is *the* key dilemma facing teachers, schools and governments – especially and particularly for those who are not aware that such a dilemma exists. It is worth noting that even the cinematic accounts of teaching that Gale and Densmore discuss here are rooted in very traditional assumptions about the knowledge and value, discourse and practice that schools might dispense.

A legacy from the last century of educational theory and policy has been to treat schooling as if it were *the* principal source of children's and adolescents' life knowledge, as if it were both the main archive and pedagogical place for learning. In schools one was supposed to encounter all one needed to know about everything from Egyptian history to the biosphere. In schools one was supposed to learn how to 'be' and appear a literate and aesthetic, rational and civilized person. Schooling must now find its place – perhaps a new and different place – in worlds where space and time are compressed and redefined continuously, where community geographies and school demographies shift semester by semester, where information, discourses and images – spurious, redundant, critical, canonical, marginal, dominant – rupture, blend and expand exponentially beyond government, corporation, community or school control.

The second question: *Just Schooling* asks whether it is possible to have a 'socially just' educational system. If so, Gale and Densmore ask, upon which philosophic principles should such a system be based? How might these principles inform teachers' work and common sense, and how we shape students' lives and literacies?

In any dictionary of educational policy, the term 'social justice' would have multiple entries, each mapped against a different national and regional policy context. For many American readers, the goals of schooling typically have been defined in terms of 'equality of opportunity'. That is, 'justice' in a meritocracy is taken as equal access to compete for unequal educational outcomes and life pathways. For many Australian, Canadian and UK readers the term is likely to have a different morphology, with a focus on what Gale and Densmore here describe as 'redistributive justice'. There state schooling has taken on a commitment to redistribute educational and social outcomes towards those communities at the economic and social margins. In Australia, the latter concept of social justice has shifted from an emphasis on 'equality of access' to a search for actual 'equality of outcomes'. This involves the risky and elusive tasks of defining and assessing academic and social outcomes, discourse and material consequences of schooling, and of understanding how these blend with students' and communities' other social and economic capital.

For those reading this book from the vantage point of indigenous, cultural and linguistic minority communities, and for those working from the perspectives of feminist and postcolonial studies, critical legal and race studies, *Just Schooling* raises once again issues of inclusion and exclusion. There are running debates over which kinds of difference are actually named and recognized in educational policies and practices, the degree to which historically marginalized communities, their knowledges, histories and aspirations are actually recognized and 'included' by schooling and educational systems. Here teachers and schools face the everyday challenges of the critique and reconstruction of what might be a 'common curriculum', the development of culturally appropriate and enabling pedagogies, and the reconstruction of school/community relationships.

The third question: *Just Schooling* asks, persistently and yet again, whether and how education is a domain of cultural politics. The title itself plays with the name of a major book by the philosopher Jean Francois Lyotard, *Just Gaming*. Lyotard, an architect of postmodern social theory, would ask whether the normative goals of truth, justice, and power so focal to our discussion here actually have any real value in new social and cultural conditions. His alternative is to see the formation of ideologies and institutions as language games, genres and strategies with varying and often unpredictable consequences in local contexts.

Clearly, Gale and Densmore would not have us dismiss issues of equity, value and justice as mere games, the task of teaching as mere gaming. Rather their aim is to reintroduce the fundamentally moral and political dimension of the tasks facing beginning and practising teachers. At the same time, their invitation to a 'cultural politics' sees schooling and education as necessarily involved in matters of discourse, text and representation. By their account, schooling is a discourse practice on several complex levels:

- Schooling is regulated through policy discourse: as in current neoliberal and technicist educational policies;

- Schooling is constructed as mythology through narrative discourse: as in the influential cinematic representations of schooling examined here; and
- Schooling is itself an institutional device for regulating access to and use of discourses: as in the instances of classroom practice and the agendas for literacy education and curriculum reform taken up here.

In this way, Gale and Densmore are concerned with educational policies as discourses, as institutional practices that effect teachers' work and students' life futures. They also propose, following on from Australian work on genre and critical literacy, the mastery and critique of discourses as the central strategy for redistributive and recognitive justice.

Many readers of this book will be student teachers and students of educational research. *Just Schooling* sets out to reframe teachers' common sense about difference, about justice, and about the possibilities of a just educational system. Gale and Densmore tell us that this book is a hybrid: part textbook and part research study, part essay and part narrative, and, no doubt, part science and part story. As you read, you will probably be composing a kind of counter-text about your particular local, regional or state educational system – weighing and discussing what might be possible, and indeed what might be 'just'.

What might a socially just school look like? Is it engaged in the redistribution and reconstruction of discourse and texts? Which discourses and texts? How are these optimally engaged with by students and teachers? The test for *Just Schooling* will be its local application and sustainability in the classrooms and schools where you work.

Allan Luke

Acknowledgements

The possibility that this collection of ideas might form the basis for a book was first raised by Stephen May in our discussions over the search for an appropriate textbook for students, although it was Nick Burbules who introduced us as potential co-authors. Both gave us that initial encouragement to turn an idea into a proposal and for this we thank them. We are also grateful for the wonders (and traumas) of email without which we might never have 'met' and this book might never have been written. Indeed, this entire project was completed without us ever meeting in a traditional sense, although we have discovered, nevertheless, a great deal of compatibility in our interests and commitments. We would also like to thank those whose interest and encouragement contributed more directly to the production of this work. They include: the staff at Open University Press, who were so obliging and patient with us; Bob Lingard, John Knight and Carl Padover for their friendship and intellectual guidance; Pam Gale and Carmen Mills, who generously attended to many of the technical and tedious matters of preparing a manuscript; and, most importantly, those with whom we share the intimacies of our lives and whom we love dearly, Pam and David. We would be remiss if we did not also thank Allan Luke for writing the Foreword during a particularly taxing period in which he was actively engaged in rethinking and reworking systems of just schooling. Finally, portions of this book have appeared elsewhere in different forms and have been reworked for inclusion here. We would like to thank the publishers for permission to make use of the following materials: a version of Chapter 2 originally appeared in Gale, T. (2000) Rethinking social justice in schools: How will we recognise it when we see it? *International Journal of Inclusive Education*, 4(2); Chapter 3 in Gale, T. (2000) Are we raising the standards of language use or just playing games? *Melbourne Studies in Education*, 41(1); and Chapter 6 in Gale, T. and Densmore, K. (2001) Questions of (re)production and legitimation: A second screening of teacher–student relations, *Journal of Curriculum Studies*, 33(5)

Introduction: just to put you in the picture

Just schooling

This book is not just about schooling; it is about *just* schooling. More specific-ally, it explores what it means for teachers to act justly in classrooms and towards their students. It is written at the beginning of a new millennium in which there remains 'widespread homelessness, joblessness, illiteracy, crime, disease (including AIDS), hunger, poverty, drug addiction, alcoholism as well as the various habits of ill health, [youth suicide] and the destruction of the environment' (Wallace 1991: 6). All of these have spawned 'a temper of distrust, disillusionment, and despair' (McLaren 1997: 520) in many areas of western societies, including within and about their systems of schooling. We mention this at the outset because we do not want readers to disassociate the book's discussions from the abject material conditions experienced by many real students and their families. Also, we want to argue that issues of social justice are particularly pertinent for contemporary capitalist societies and their citizens. But we do not want that argument to be reduced to 'textual disagreement and discourse wars' (McLaren 1997: 522) even though we will engage in aspects of this 'war' ourselves as a way of addressing people's adverse experiences.

When it comes to theorizing and practising social justice not everyone agrees about how students should be treated and what 'playing fair' means for teachers. Sometimes it is easy for us to regard these matters as self-evident and, therefore, as not worthy of prolonged discussion. It is as if we are convinced of the simplicity of statements like Justinian's who commented in the sixth century that 'justice is the constant and perpetual will to render to everyone their due' (quoted in Isaacs 1996: 42). But the problem is, even among those who have the will, not everyone agrees on what they are due and how it should be rendered. Tripp (1993: 58), for example, has identified at least 12 different ways of understanding what it means to act fairly. Many writers have attempted to address this complex array of opinions about what is socially just (and what is not). Our categorization of these various perspectives in Chapter 2 as *distributive, retributive* and *recognitive* is informed by several of these discussions and we have recommended some of them at the end of that chapter for further reading. In our account of social justice we particularly emphasize a more recent politics of recognition that, among other things, gives prominence to the meanings and material consequences associated with words and actions.

What follows is an overview of the book's content and how it is organized; how we go about addressing the issues these comments raise. From the book's title and the paragraphs above, you would already be aware that we are concerned with social justice and its relevance for teaching. This is a theme that underlies many of the chapters, including discussions of popular issues such as gender, race and social class. In addition, there are other related themes that will be of particular interest for those who are, and/or want to be, teachers; themes that encourage exploration of what is meant by concepts central to schooling, but are often taken for granted, such as language, education and diversity. Throughout the following chapters these and other issues are explored and examined, with successive themes drawing on previous discussions for their explanation.

The book draws on the voices of teachers in combination with understandings from the academic literature. Throughout, three teachers 'speak' more frequently than others and their particulars are outlined below. In writing about these teachers and their work we have not aimed for a textbook or for a research monograph in their traditional and separate senses. Rather, our intention has been to produce a text that might sit comfortably in both camps. This is not simply in recognition of 'the politics of the textbook' (Apple and Christian-Smith 1991) and the performativity criteria introduced by research monitors, but also a concern to address the dichotomies that such politics create. To these ends we have drawn on relevant academic scholarship to illuminate theoretical discussions of issues related to just schooling and we have also drawn on research data to confirm, challenge and rework these explanations in ways that we hope will contribute to academic understandings. Rather than this being a discussion between two seemingly opposite positions, our approach is dialectic. That is, we employ theory to 'talk' to the world of practice *and* we implore practice to 'talk' to the world of theory. In fact, we do not see these as necessarily separate worlds and so do not see their separation as particularly helpful in understanding and challenging schooling.

An approach to research and its presentation

The theoretical and methodological orientation of this book is perhaps best described as socially critical and post-structural. By 'critical' we do not mean that we take a negative stance on social matters irrespective of what they entail and by 'post-structural' we do not want to suggest that there are no stories of value about the social world. Nor do we necessarily regard being critical and being post-structural as being at odds with each other and/or as separated respectively into modern and postmodern camps as some would have them. Instead, we tend to think of our post-structuralism as (re)informing our social critique, which has long 'assume[d] that it is the task of social scientists to take things apart' (Kogan 1979: 5). Our deconstructive efforts are informed by particular social and methodological orientations. As critical researchers, these very broadly involve five interrelated commitments: first, to investigate matters beyond their 'surface appearances' (L. Harvey 1990: 19); second, to 'stand apart from the prevailing order of the world and ask how that order came about' (Cox 1980: 129); third, to take little for granted, asking 'whose interests are being served and how' (Tripp 1998: 37) in the arrangements we find; and fourth, given that this assumes that 'we live in a world of unequal distribution of resources and power', to understand how socially critical researchers can 'work towards a more just social order' (Lenzo 1995: 17). Added to these is a commitment to reflexive conversations at all levels of the research endeavour, achieved through 'a constant shuttling backwards and forwards' (L. Harvey 1990: 29) between such things as theory and data.

In keeping with our intent to write a textbook *and* a research monograph, we tend to canvass a variety of theoretical positions on any given issue, although, clearly, we hold particular theoretical preferences and this is often evident in our exploration of these issues. Also fighting to be heard in this theory-work are evidences of teaching practice, and in particular, interviews conducted as part of our research (discussed more fully below) with those directly involved in schooling students. These resources are supplemented by observations of teachers at work with students, often represented as critical incidents (see Tripp 1993), and academic literature that pertain to the substantive issues. A further data source, specifically utilized in Chapter 6, is the interactions between three 'onscreen' teachers and their students, who appear in the films *Dangerous Minds* (1995), *Kindergarten Cop* (1990) and *Dead Poets Society* (1989). But to reiterate, our work is not solely driven by theory or data. Instead, it attempts to give prominence to both as dialectically related.

There are two main research projects on which this book draws. The first includes in-depth and extended interviews with three teachers, one from each of three levels of schooling: David, a primary/elementary school teacher; Michelle, a secondary/high school teacher; and Carl, a post-secondary technical college teacher. Although they are actual people, for reasons of confidentiality their real names have not been used, nor any detail that might identify them or their specific schools. Their interviews extend across a range of issues with a central interest in exploring how teachers' implicit and explicit views on language, education and diversity influence the schooling that students receive. More explicit research questions are revealed in the chapters that follow. We introduce these three teachers more formally below and hope that they will become familiar companions as you read their views on issues examined throughout this book.

A second project involved over 20 semi-structured interviews with parents, teachers and school administrators associated with government

primary/elementary and secondary/high schools. The interviews were aug-
mented by observations in classrooms, although over fairly limited durations
and contexts and, hence, these should be seen more as supplementary sources.
A major aspect of the research focused on the nature of and the extent to
which actors at the level of schools mediate government and departmental
policy (in this case, policy concerning students with learning difficulties/
disabilities), thereby influencing students' schooling. Other aspects of the
research considered the ways in which students (with difficulties/disabilit-
ies) are conceived within schools and the language that is involved in this
construction. Again, more specific research questions appear in the following chapters along with the data used.

Interviews from these projects were audiotaped and later transcribed.
However, in writing this book it was possible to include only a fraction of
the 240,000 words of interview text that this collection produced. Indeed,
many of the interviewees and participants who contributed data in this way
are not quoted directly even though their contributions are reflected in the
book's more general comments and analyses. Sometimes data are sacrificed
for theoretical explanation but there remains a clear intention to include the
voices of teachers and other relevant actors alongside our more theoretical
accounts, and for those accounts of theory and practice to converse with each
other. To maintain confidences, names of interviewees have been changed
and other material that might identify specific individuals, institutions and/
or geographical areas have been altered or omitted. What is worth acknowledging is that contributors are drawn from western democracies in which
English is the medium of instruction. One convention followed throughout
is that where conversations from the data are directly quoted, the voices of
teachers and parents appear in plain text while other speakers (interviewers,
students, and so on) are represented by italicized text. A second convention
involves referencing these speakers. Comments drawn from the first research
project are referenced to David, Michelle or Carl, whereas those from the
second project are referenced to indicate the interviewee's status as a teacher
(T) or parent (P) and are numbered (T1, T2, P1, P2, and so forth) to distinguish
one interviewee from another.

Now to some more personal introductions. Throughout this book we
have included the voices of three teachers more frequently than others. Our
intention is for readers to gain a picture of who these teachers are, what
they think about a range of issues we raise and how these views influence
their teaching practices. We do not expect that readers will be able to identify with our three teachers in all respects but we trust that there will be
aspects of their identities and/or circumstances with which some resonances
may be found. It is our hope that in recognizing familiar ideas and circumstances in their comments, this might provide non-threatening opportunities for readers to rehearse and examine their own ideas as they (re)negotiate
their position on just schooling. We are grateful for the willingness of these
teachers to reveal themselves to us through our research. We have found
them to be well intentioned and dedicated to their students, highly regarded

by their peers, and easy to work with. We trust that readers will similarly enjoy their company and the honesty with which they talk about themselves and their work.

David: access to resources, good career prospects

David is a primary/elementary schoolteacher with over 15 years' experience. He works in a government school with recently established facilities, a population of around 600 students, and which is surrounded by modern detached housing located in an urban area. David claims that this population is 'not homogenous' but he acknowledges that there are very few students who have non-English-speaking backgrounds or who belong to racial minorities. Most of the students' parents are middle-income earners and both parents tend to be in paid employment. There are a few single-parent families but they do not represent a sizeable group. 'Something I should have mentioned, I guess, is that we have a very high proportion of children with disabilities of one kind or another' (David). These students are catered for within the school by a special unit that attracts both supplementary government funding and students with various intellectual and physical disabilities, totalling approximately 10 per cent of the student population. David is one of seven male teachers at his school. At the time of interview, he was enrolled in a Masters programme at a nearby university.

Michelle: travelled, varied but short career, facing new challenges

Michelle is a health and physical education teacher in a secondary/high school, although she also teaches classes in social and political studies. She has over five years of teaching experience, several in overseas countries in inner city schools as well as in private schools in her home country, and has recently commenced working at her current teaching appointment, a small government school of approximately 200 students set in a rural town surrounded by agricultural farming. The main school building has a heritage facade but its interior has been refurbished and its good facilities are complemented by newer buildings. Just under one-third of the school's students live in outlying areas, the rest live in town. The town once had a thriving industry but this has since closed. Most of the town students are from families whose main source of income is from some form of welfare payment. The students have various living arrangements: many live with both parents, some live in one-parent families, others live with relatives such as an aunt or an older sibling, and a few are self-supporting. Up to 30 per cent of the student population is drawn from one racial minority group. Michelle comments: 'my little welcome to the school from the principal [head teacher] was "teaching is a challenge"'.

Carl: an 'alternative' career, confronting others' 'failures'

Carl is a teacher in an inner city technical college located in a large regional city and has over 15 years of experience in various alternative secondary/high school and college settings. At the technical college he teaches mathematics to adult learners whose past school performances in these areas have been poor. He also conducts preparatory classes in media studies for adults returning to study after long periods of unemployment, sickness, or childcare and who are seeking entry into university or other institutions and courses that offer a recognized qualification. 'I know it sounds terrible, but you are dealing with second chance education, you are dealing with the failures of the formal institutions' (Carl). As many as 90 per cent of students are drawn from the local community and range in age from 18 to 65 years. 'There is no real archetype' (Carl) – in some years the majority of students are males aged between 25 and 35, in other years the majority are young and often single mothers – but there are at least two recurring characteristics. The students are overwhelmingly located 'at the lower end of the socio-economic scale' (Carl) and they largely belong to one racial minority group.

Organization and content

The chapters in this book focus on issues of social justice, language, education and diversity. There is a sense in which each chapter sets the scene for those that follow but it is equally possible for readers to move back and forth between them according to their needs and interests. At the very least we hope that readers will want to revisit parts they have found particularly helpful and to make internal comparisons to allow some parts of the book to inform their understandings of others. Most chapters include Guiding questions and end with Questions for discussion/research and Suggested readings. The Questions for discussion/research are provided for readers as a way of stimulating and extending discussion and/or further research in relation to the issues raised in each chapter. Whether utilized for discussion or research, the questions should be seen as starting points from which other questions may be added or developed. By including such questioning in relation to our work we hope to create spaces for its critique, not just reinforcement of our own ideas. The suggested readings are for those seeking further insights into the issues raised in each chapter. Some engage with specific issues in greater depth and/or add to the overall discussion, while others question, and, at some points, provide quite different accounts of these issues. It should be noted that the lists are far from exhaustive. Other possible sources can be found in the reference section. As noted above, several chapters also include comments by teachers and others involved in the schooling of students, and relate theory to practice in a more explicit way.

Chapter 2 outlines what is meant by social justice, arguing in favour of a recognitive approach, and relating these debates to students and schooling.

Chapter 3 explores these issues of justice within theories of language use – a central domain of schooling – identifying four different perspectives and advocating a critical disposition that challenges notions of language as simply involving matters of technique. Informed by such critique, Chapter 4 moves beyond language rules to consider language strategies; a shift, we argue, that requires an understanding of a metalanguage characterized by the term 'discourse' and centrally related to 'text' and 'ideology'.

Chapter 5 begins by canvassing various ideological positions on what it means to get an education, arguing that a socially democratic view of education is more in keeping with a recognitive approach to social justice. Continuing this focus on ideologies and their implications for the schooling students receive, Chapter 6 analyses the onscreen relations between teachers and students represented in three Hollywood films. The chapter deconstructs the discourses of these classrooms to reveal the ideas, beliefs and values that inform them and the commitments they are missing for more authentic and radical democratic versions of schooling.

Issues of diversity implicit in this account are taken up more explicitly in Chapters 7 and 8. Specifically, Chapter 7 examines inclusive and exclusive discourses mobilized by teachers to explain students' academic successes and failures, particularly those explanations that draw on old nature–nurture debates but also those informed by a more recent politics of difference. Chapter 8 continues this discussion by confronting the negative discrimination in schools often associated with issues of gender, race and social class. It argues further, that the separation of these matters into categories of difference can sometimes serve to hide their similarities and points of overlap and that a more fruitful analysis might be pursued by considering the forms of oppression that these discourses engender.

Chapter 9 concludes the book by drawing together suggestions throughout earlier chapters for (re)constructing teacher practices and outlines a framework for just relations in schooling. Drawing on Giddens (1994), the chapter argues for the democratization of teacher–student relations in four connected arenas, ever widening contexts characterized by personal, group, institutional and community life.

Playing fair: who gets what and why?

Introduction

The beginning of a new decade often entices politicians, bureaucrats, educators and interested others to rethink schooling; how it should be arranged to address perceived changes and future needs of society. The beginning of a new century and a new millennium is no exception, especially given continued racial oppression, sex discrimination and a tremendous growth in wealth accompanied by ever increasing impoverishment for the majority of the world's population. Education systems in many parts of the world – and the western world in particular – are currently involved in reflecting on and projecting a future for schooling in new times.

Broadly, those who have interests in these systems seek answers to what it means to go to school in the twenty-first century and what purposes schooling serves. For example, at one level, the dazzling pace of scientific and technological advances suggest that there is a greater need than ever to increase the level of education for the population in general, in order to provide highly educated technical workers. At the same time, many urban schools still 'warehouse' students, excluded by the school system, from promising employment.

There are a multitude of responses to these issues, too many to adequately address here. Still, there are some that we think warrant specific attention and which have the potential to impact on all areas of society: namely, issues that regulate who gets what and why, and what it means to play fair. Some commentators are unconvinced that these are issues schooling can do much about, others are unsure that it should even try. We do not belong to either of these camps but neither do we think that schooling is the primary or sole domain in which to promote just social arrangements.

So, what does social justice have to do with teachers and schooling? In our view, Connell (1993: 11–15) provides three very good answers. First, when it comes to the distribution of society's resources, education systems lay claim to a large share of the financial cake. Many governments with a legislative responsibility for education allocate up to a quarter of their budgets on this area, sometimes more. On its own, this is reason enough for us to examine how this large sum of money is distributed and to consider what it might mean to face the fact that this distribution is socially unjust, given that it disproportionably favours the upper levels of education systems (universities, colleges and the latter years of secondary/high school) in which there are fewer numbers of students and when it seems to favour those distinguishable by particular social indicators, such as their gender, race and social class.

Second, education has a significant and growing influence within society. It is often positioned as central to a nation's economic viability, providing societies with a particular kind of skilled workforce and informed citizenry and, more recently, has been positioned as a financial enterprise in itself. This shift in the kinds of knowledge now valued by education systems and its commodification are also accompanied by significant changes to the ways in which knowledge is organized and accessed, largely influenced by re-cent advances in information technologies that are unequally available to stu-dents. However, what warrants our attention is not just that school curricula and pedagogy are experiencing change. Also significant in social justice terms is that education is gaining increasing importance in determining people's access to employment. As Connell (1993) expresses it:

> more and more jobs in all kinds of fields have become credentialed . . . [the] 'professional' model is spreading . . . it becomes more and more difficult to get a job as a sport coach, camp director, company manager, etc. without the corresponding degree. The education system becomes more and more important as a gatekeeper.
>
> (Connell 1993: 14)

Third, and following on from these first two observations, Connell contem-plates what it means to educate, suggesting that it constitutes more than a simple algorithm of resources plus curriculum plus pedagogy. Drawing atten-tion to the nature of schooling's hidden curriculum, Connell argues that the various ways in which systems and teachers deal with students can be just as much an affront to the socially just provision of education. Not all students are alike and their differences may well be cause for different treatment, not only in the distribution of educational products but also in the institutional processes involved in educating students. In this context, Connell highlights the importance of education as a moral trade, concerned as it is with what is to be valued by society and how this is to be played out in the allocation of responsibilities and the distribution of resources. Connell claims that systems that privilege one group of students over another – that provide some students and not others with access to social and/or economic goods – degrade the quality of education for all, not just for those who miss out on this privilege.

Guiding questions

Understanding Connell's meaning – that students miss out on something even when they are privileged through their schooling – necessarily requires an understanding of what he regards as social justice. This is the intent of this chapter: to canvass the various perspectives on social justice and to think through what they mean for schooling and for teachers' practices in particular. We also want to argue in favour of an expanded view of social justice that addresses the shortcomings of perspectives exclusively focused on issues of distribution and the minimal regulation of actions, and to explore how their expansion might help teachers to rethink issues of fair play. The questions, then, that guide this chapter are:

- What are the various ways in which social justice is understood?
- What do these definitions look like when put into practice by teachers?
- How can teachers move beyond the shortcomings of these practices?

A teachers' guide to playing fair

Justinian, whose definition of justice we briefly commented on in Chapter 1, was not the only philosopher in the classical era to be concerned with the meaning of justice. You will recall his definition that 'justice is the constant and perpetual will to render to everyone their due' (quoted in Isaacs 1996: 42). The problems of determining what everyone is due (their rights) and how this should be rendered (distributed) to them, reflect the themes of two distinct yet related meanings for justice that continue to find expression today.

The first of these concerns was rehearsed in Plato's *The Republic* (see Ryan 1993) where a just action was portrayed as one that is right, good or desirable. Two things are implied by this definition. First, what is right is determined by a society's prevailing morality and ethics and, by implication, this 'rightness' changes over time as does its corresponding morality and ethics. Hence, 'the search for social justice arises from the meeting of a particular kind of authority with particular aspirations that are located in particular historical circumstances' (MacIntyre 1985: 112). For example, 'the idea that human beings share the same intellectual faculties and potential, regardless of sex, race or class, is a comparatively recent one' (Preston and Symes 1992: 102). Second, what is good involves determining the extent to which actions produce or intend to produce beneficial consequences. This is one reading of social justice that informs the current vocationalization of education (discussed more fully in Chapter 5), which is claimed to have beneficial consequences for employers as well as employees.

A second view of justice is attributed to Aristotle who argued, among other things, that a just action is one that is fair in its distributions of social and material goods. This view recognizes that what is right and/or good may not be entirely achievable (at least not in the foreseeable future) and that just actions are those that are distributed in proportion to the entirety of what everyone is due. So, an action can be fair without being entirely right or good but it is never these without being fair. This is what Aristotle meant when he claimed that 'the just is proportional' (in Ryan 1993: 36); fairness is everything, it legitimizes the distribution (and/or withholding) of portions of what people are due, particularly when the whole is not available. Someone trying to apply this reasoning today might ponder the situation that a computer for every student might be a reality for students in some schools whereas students in other schools have limited or no access. If access to computers is to be just, their distribution among students needs to be in proportion to what society determines is right and good. The problems of Aristotle's time, however, were qualitatively different from the problems of today. Namely, whereas Aristotle lived in times of scarce resources, many in western democracies live in times of abundance. While Aristotle acknowledged the dilemma of how to construct fair criteria for distributions that account for the 'relative difference' between people, he was speaking of equal distributions without changing the existing social structure. Over time there have been many attempts (some outlined below) to explore these questions of fair distribution, including considerations of needs, rights, deserts, merit and hereditary status.

These two meanings for justice – as right, good and fair – are abstract ideas, divorced from socio-historical contexts. Moreover, while they find expression in contemporary understandings, they are not necessarily separate ideas and are not utilized without considerable disagreement over the meanings assigned to them. In and out of schools, for example, fairness is regarded as synonymous with actions that are right and good; 'that's not fair' is a popular expression utilized to identify and claim some wrongdoing, some act of injustice. Others recognize a greater diversity of meanings for justice and tend to arrange these differences in manageable perspectives. In our explorations below, we follow this strategy by classifying explanations of social justice as *distributive, retributive* and *recognitive*. From the outset it is important to appreciate that, at times, the differences between these categories can be minimal while the differences within them can be great. That is, the divisions we adopt can seem arbitrary but in our view they offer plausible and useful accounts that warrant their representation in this way.

Two final matters before we consider these perspectives. Even though social justice implies a comparison – you cannot determine if an action is just unless it is compared with another action and/or with principles for guiding action – such comparisons can be conducted at the level of individuals (where social groups are understood simply as collections of disassociated individuals) or at the level of groups (in which individuals share an identity that differs from other social groups). As will become apparent, this difference at the level of comparison accounts for quite different understandings of social justice. Another related matter concerns distinctions (generally made by economists) among different kinds of social goods, particularly public goods and private goods. Put simply, public goods 'are goods that are non-rival (one person's use does not reduce their value to someone else) and non-excludable (where it is impossible to get anyone to pay). [However] Education is an example of a [social] good that is rival and could be excludable'

(Corry 1998: 79) but since the introduction of mass schooling it has been maintained as a public good because of its perceived benefits to society as a whole (see Taylor *et al.* 1997: 126). More recently, there is a tendency to reposition education as a private good because it is seen to reap more of an individual than a common benefit, particularly in the post-compulsory years, and because its benefit is regarded as primarily economic. This, too, makes a difference to one's perspective on social justice in education, as we will encounter in the following discussions.

Distributive justice

One well-known perspective on issues of social justice is commonly referred to as *distributive* justice. Distributive conceptions of social justice implicitly begin from the premise that individuals have an intrinsic value and worth. This valuing of people is the primary rationale that justifies the (re)distribution of goods and resources among them. One of the most famous modern authors on these matters is John Rawls (1971) who thought his way through issues of social justice by imagining how people would respond if their starting or 'original positions' in life were equal and they had no prior knowledge (but possessed what he called 'a veil of ignorance') concerning the positions they would later attain. How would they determine, for example, the dissection of a cake with no inkling of which piece they were to get? Most likely, the pieces would be equally weighted and would equal the number of persons. According to Rawls, this is because such division is the only way for individuals to maximize their eventual shares. Drawing on such hypothetical accounts, Rawls argued that social justice involves two main principles: liberty, or individual freedom (to the extent that this is compatible with the freedoms of others); and the equal distribution of material and social goods (except where an unequal distribution would contribute to the well-being of those who have unfavourable starting positions).

These principles, and particularly their caveats, have often led social theorists to ponder the freedoms and the (minimum) material and social goods that individuals need, as a basis for determining and justifying any unequal distribution. There are two ways in which this justification problem has been addressed by social theorists and by social actors more broadly. The first of these involves a liberal-democratic form of distributive justice – sometimes negatively referred to as a *deficit model* of social justice – which is premised on 'simple equality' (Walzer 1983): an idea that regards all individuals as having the same basic needs, which is a fiction in view of distinct individual circumstances. The liberal-democratic solution to an equality imbalance is to compensate (or normalize) disadvantaged individuals by supplying them with basic material and social goods that meet their (dominantly determined) needs. Equality in this sense is a baseline measure. In education contexts, this is the rationale behind the provision of remedial classes for students who lack certain basic skills; often those skills associated with such things as reading, writing and mathematics (rarely sport, social studies, art, and so on) as well as skills related to behaviour and citizenry. From this perspective, the disadvantaged are those who lack what society deems to be the educational, social and cultural basics.

This last point is important for understanding how a liberal-democratic position differs from a social-democratic or *difference model* of social justice. Characterized by 'complex equality' (Walzer 1983), which theorizes that people do not have the same needs or the same resources at their disposal to meet those needs, the social-democratic position argues not just for unequal distributions of social goods but for the distribution of different social goods for different people. These distinctions have given rise to the adoption of the term *equity* (that is, positive differentiation) as a justified deviation from *equality* and to register social justice as different from 'sameness'. Moreover, social-democrats have attempted to address (the logistics as well as the logic of) the 'relevant difference' problem identified by Aristotle and raised by the principle of different distributions to different people, through references to social groups rather than to disassociated individuals. Low socio-economic groups, for example, might need access to additional financial resources in order to benefit from education whereas girls as a group might require access to educational opportunities previously denied them. Equality of opportunity, then, extends the notion of access to material goods to include access to opportunities to acquire those goods.

These different ways of understanding distributive justice provide competing guidelines for practice, as the secondary/high school teacher in the following interview extract demonstrates. Michelle, a participant in our research discussed in Chapter 1, is caught between a desire for generalizable principles that are fair because of their applicability to all and an (apologetic) admission that fairness needs to account for her students' unequal starting positions. In exploring these issues with Michelle, we asked her how her appreciation for differences in 'normal' student behaviour influenced her teaching practices:

What effect does that have on your teaching? What do you do differently?

I think this is wrong in most instances. I have certainly been guilty of doing it and I probably still am guilty until I pull myself out of it. If one student, for example, said to me, 'Ah shut-up miss', and then another student said to me, 'Shut-up miss', the student that I know has problems at home and that behaviour would be accepted at home, I wouldn't come down as hard on them as I would on the other person whom I knew came from a fairly stable background. In a sense I know that is very unfair, but that's probably something I'm still learning about.

What does fair mean? Does it mean treating every child the same? Does it mean treating every child according to what they need?

Well, that's the thing. I mean students will always say to you, 'Miss, he didn't get in trouble, and I've just done it and I've got in trouble for it'. They'll always pick you up on it and they will always throw it at you. I think you have to have a consistent set of rules where everybody has to abide by those rules, such as swearing or being dangerous in a physical education class, or being mobile in a class, that sort of thing. I think they are consistent rules and they are covered in school rules, and, of course, in your own classroom rules. But I think when it comes to different behaviours and different attitudes and tones in voices, it's more individualized and you have to look behind why they're doing what they're doing.

In many ways, Michelle's comments indicate that she holds to a deficit model of social justice, even though she is willing to acknowledge that similar student behaviours may require her to make different responses for different students. We see this deficit view when Michelle refers to one student, to whom she gives her strongest response, as coming from 'a fairly stable background' while her other student is associated with 'problems at home'. In other words, Michelle's conception of difference with respect to these students' backgrounds and how these influence their behaviour, is understood in terms of stability and instability. To be fair to Michelle, such either/or alternatives might not be how she sees all students and their backgrounds. She does, after all, suggest that decisions regarding her responses need to take into account each student's individual background. But there is still some sense of a hierarchy of student backgrounds and her 'look behind the scenes' is also revealing of her liberal-democratic view of social justice that recognizes difference at the level of individuals and not at the level of social groupings. Michelle's feelings of guilt concerning her indiscretions in not treating all her students according to one set of rules also indicate that she generally subscribes to the view that individuals share a common set of needs. Her guilt is compounded by the schooling system within which she works that requires 'a consistent set of rules where everybody has to abide by those rules' (Michelle) and by her students who remind her of these institutional expectations.

Retributive justice

Other theorists have attempted to address these dilemmas for (teaching) practice by reworking their understandings of social justice in ways that privilege liberty and freedom in social interactions over the distribution of social goods. This is in response to what Nozick (1976) sees as Rawls' (1971) overemphasis on the social goods individuals possess and his underemphasis on the processes by which individuals produce and acquire these goods. In his critique, Nozick (1976) reasons that individuals *deserve* and/or are *entitled* to differential rewards in accordance with their differential contributions to productive and competitive processes. Hence, social justice is primarily concerned with fairness in the competition for goods (presumably, capitalist markets provide the quintessential example) and is not a matter of equalizing possessions. These similarities with the logic of markets have prompted some writers to dub this conception of social justice as 'market-individualism' (Rizvi and Lingard 1996; Taylor *et al.* 1997). In education contexts, desert and entitlement are often discussed in terms of academic *merit:* the notion that students can be individually ranked according to their academic performances (a function of their talents and efforts) and that they should be similarly rewarded (often through entry to privileged positions in schooling, employment and within society generally).

What is seen by Nozick (1976) as unfair, then, are measures that both limit individuals' freedoms to exercise their talents and efforts and those that limit the rewards individuals receive from them. Nozick supports rules and laws that protect an individual's life, property and freedom of movement but is critical of those that interfere with an individual's activities and possessions beyond this. Isaiah Berlin (1969) has referred to such views of social justice as indicative of a 'negative liberty' that not only shuns regulation (particularly from governments) but also requires rules or laws to protect the just entitlements or rights of (self-determining) individuals to act 'without interference'. Some writers have claimed that there is also a sense of a narrow liberty in this perspective given that it favours 'property rights' over 'person rights'. Apple (1989) uses these terms to argue that in a market economy the extent to which individuals have power in social relations is a function of their property holdings rather than of their general membership of society, with emphasis on the former narrowing the number of individuals who can participate. Schools are replete with rules that limit the activities of students, ostensibly for the purposes of promoting students' talents and efforts and protecting their freedom to exercise them. Copying, for example, is outlawed and punished in many classrooms because it is seen as representing as one's own the intellectual property of others. This is despite the fact that when such behaviour is termed 'modelling' it is interpreted as a very useful approach to learning. These observations do not condone copying *per se* but offer a reminder to look behind the names given to actions to consider who benefits and who is harmed by the meanings they are ascribed. (See Tripp (1993: 46–8) for a brief discussion of this questioning approach and how he relates this to similar issues.)

Carr and Hartnett (1996: 28) refer to this negative influence on social justice as *retributive:* 'a means of punishing those who illegitimately infringe the rights and freedoms of others'. We also think that retributive justice is useful in naming the perspective's implicit legitimation of the retribution metered out to individuals who possess limited property rights and, therefore, limited power to participate in decision-making processes, as they are currently arranged. Despite claims of fairness in market competition (the fictitious virtue of 'the level playing field'), the narrow liberties of market relations ensure that there are 'distortions of the market: it is not a fair market in talent and effort if it is not talent and effort that determine the outcome' (Commission on Social Justice 1998: 48). In the private sector, for example, company directors' 'salaries and bonuses are often quite unrelated to the performance of the company concerned, and are sometimes actually inversely correlated with company performance' (Commission on Social Justice 1998: 47).

There are at least two reasons for also making this claim about the relationships between performances and rewards in educational contexts. First, there are the statistics that indicate that individuals from advantaged social groups hold disproportionate amounts of society's goods. If talent and effort are truly the criteria upon which individuals' succeed, then we should expect to find 'success' evenly distributed across social groups and the rewards of talent and effort redistributed (through schooling) with every new generation (Conant 1940: 598). The reality is very different. Many researchers have noted that in western capitalist societies the gap between rich and poor is growing and the inverse relationship between poverty and academic success is so strong that 'the best advice we can give to a poor child keen to get ahead through education is to choose richer parents' (Connell 1993: 22). Contrary to popular belief, talent and effort are not always fairly rewarded in schools and in society generally. Moreover, some suggest that talent is overrated and does not warrant the rewards it is offered. These commentators argue that 'a person's talents, and his or her capacity to make productive use of those talents, are very much matters of luck [that is, acquired at birth and, therefore, out of his/her control] and are also, in some part, the product of society. Nobody . . . *deserves* his or her (natural) talents' (Commission on Social Justice 1998: 45, emphasis in original).

Second, there are problems with trying to identify and justify talent. Schools, it seems, are characterized by a particular organizing logic that is compatible with the dispositions of some students (typically those from the dominant groups in society) and not others. In such circumstances the talents of students whose dispositions are most like those of schools are lauded and rewarded; their similar dispositions can even be (mis)taken for talent. But as for other students, 'the supposed fairness of meritocracy does not exist because the schooling system frequently fails to see the potential of those who do not inherit the language, culture, and values of the upper classes' (Brint 1998: 183). Talent, and the lack of it, are also difficult to justify, not least because of their connections with the social contexts in which they are expressed. In short, 'it is not possible to completely isolate measured "intelligence" from social background. Even if we accept IQ scores as good measures of intelligence – something that many leading scientists no longer do . . . – we find that IQ scores are substantially conditioned by the social environment' (Brint 1998: 191).

Several of these issues find expression in the comments of teachers in our own research. For example, in responding to questions about how teachers adjust their teaching to accommodate students with learning difficulties, one primary/elementary school teacher (T8) explained:

> You have to understand that the level we're talking about is that they're not independent learners. The first thing you experience as a teacher is the need to be prepared. I've had educational psychologists say this to

me but I'd just love them to show me how to do it. To get these kids integrated you have a little – we photocopy a little book and bind it and it looks really cute and the kid can colour in the pictures. The kid can't read the instructions and that's your first problem. You open up the book and it's useless because the kid doesn't know what to do. You then have to come back and read the instructions for that child while there are twenty-odd others hanging around. Then, of course, the kid probably has a very short concentration span or a short term memory problem and can't stay on task anyway. Then you resolve that by sitting with the child, tapping at the desk while you're marking sixteen other things with the kids in a line over here. Not that you're servicing your other children because you're sitting there trying to keep one child on task, and the twenty others can be doing what they like. The child can't mark it, they can't self correct it, etc.

(T8)

In analysing these comments and others like them we do not want to suggest that teachers are unsympathetic to the well-being of their students and, in particular, to students with difficulties such as the one described here. But what is interesting in this teacher's comments is her belief in the right of 'the twenty others' to equal teacher time, even though she recognizes that her practice suggests otherwise. Students are entitled to equal 'servicing', as she puts it, a revealing comment given that education is increasingly portrayed in market terms. More revealing is the teacher's discourse that frames the issues as those of talent and focuses attention on the struggling student rather than on the classroom's curricula and pedagogy. The classroom, it would seem, is organized to accommodate independent learners: students who can follow written instructions, who have extended concentration and memory spans, who can complete tasks independently of others and who are self-correcting. Those who fail this test of isolation from other students and, to a lesser degree, from their teacher are regarded as lacking talent. However, what is not recognized is that this organization of learning is not independent from broader cultural norms. Classroom lessons are social constructions informed by particular views of education (see Chapter 5), themselves embedded in the values of dominant social groups. Given a different organization of curricula and pedagogy in the teacher's classroom – of collective study groups with genuine input into what is to be learnt, for example – this student might not feature as a problem.

Recognitive justice

A third group of theorists and activists advocate a somewhat different view of social justice that attempts to insert these procedural issues back into the discussion. This difference should not be taken to mean that all things previously learnt are discarded. There are differences in this third account but it also incorporates aspects of those already considered. Indeed, this is an important reading of difference within the perspective itself, which recognizes differences *and* areas of commonality among cultural groups. Informed by the work of theorists such as Iris Marion Young (1990) and Nancy Fraser (1995), we refer to this perspective as *recognitive justice* because of its insistence not only to *rethink* what we mean by social justice but also to *acknowledge* the place of social groups within this. These two meanings for recognition form the broad parameters for an expanded view of justice.

The recognitive imperative to rethink social justice begins with its root meanings. Lummis (1996: 24–6) writes in this way about *Radical Democracy*; the adjective, 'radical', is purposefully chosen to intensify rather than to modify the noun, to draw attention to the thing itself and to suggest motion. Advocates of recognitive justice think similarly about social justice, that a radical response is required to redress its restrictive conceptions. Their intent is to increase the potency of social justice, to emphasize issues that promote its achievement, particularly those that draw attention to actions and not simply to the outcomes of those actions. In this radical vein, you will recall that we began by referring to social justice as 'the constant and perpetual will to render to everyone their due' (Justinian, quoted in Isaacs 1996: 42). Throughout, we have assumed that this rests on 'the equal moral worth of all persons' (Young 1990: 37), although readings of historical and contemporary contexts suggest that these assumptions are not universally valued. Of course, political will is a necessary requirement for social justice but it can also be subverted through a narrow understanding of what it should encompass.

Distributive and retributive conceptions of social justice share at least three characteristics that serve to narrow their foci in this way. First, they tend to be concerned with people's assets (or lack thereof) and only minimally with social processes and procedures that (re)produce those assets. Some even regard a regulatory focus on these actions as evidence of injustices. Second, and relatedly, this static emphasis on material goods – dubiously extended to include social goods such as opportunity, position, power, and so on – limits concern to the socially just distribution of goods and services, typically patterned on statistical models: $x spent on each student in the education system, x per cent of women represented among principals and head teachers, and so forth. Third, this 'impartial' treatment at best regards all people as the same – an appeal to hegemony that Lummis (1996: 26) likens to the illusion of the emperor's new clothes – and at worst serves to hide the assimilation of group differences by the dominant. As Young expresses it, 'the ideal of impartiality encourages the universalization of the particular' (1990: 205). In short, the criticism of distributive and retributive justice perspectives is that they tend to confine their interests to economic spheres and ignore the cultural politics of social institutions, such as schools.

Lummis' approach to rethinking democracy has the potential to address these criticisms. Democracy, Lummis (1996: 22) notes, can be translated from its Greek origins *demos* and *kratia* as 'people power'. But, like social justice, 'it describes an ideal, not a method of achieving it'. Hence, the democratic struggle involves addressing such issues as, 'Who are the people? What is power?' These are important questions for those who also struggle for social justice and, as the criticisms above imply, require answers that recognize the validity of social groups and address institutional processes. Informed by these acknowledgements, recognitive justice – or 'positive liberty', to rework Berlin's (1969) earlier phrase – advocates three necessary conditions for social justice: the fostering of respect for different social groups through their self-identification; opportunities for their self-development and self-expression; and the participation of groups in making decisions that directly concern them, through their representation on determining bodies. Following Justinian's insight (in Isaacs 1996: 42) that our desire for social justice needs to be 'constant and perpetual', recognitive justice moves beyond 'an approach to social justice that gives primacy to *having* [to] one that gives primacy to *doing*' (Young 1990: 8, emphasis added).

Conditions of self-identity and self-respect

How, then, do teachers who subscribe to recognitive justice acknowledge the equal moral worth of their students? How can they foster self-respect in their students and facilitate positive self-identities for students from different social groups? In researching these issues, we asked parents about the ways in which their children are identified by teachers within their classrooms. We were interested in both how these identifications reflect broader institutional arrangements and how they found expression within the academic language of schooling. Among several responses, one parent (P6) commented on the ways in which academic assessments are linked with student identities and how these identities are often assigned to students rather than developed from positive images of themselves. This was in response to our inquiries about her daughter's assessment as having a Level Six disability – the highest level of disability on the school's assessment scale – and how this featured in teachers' understandings of who her daughter was and her placement in their classes:

> If your child is a [Level] Six the teachers go into the next room and say, 'Okay who is going to take this Level Six?' or the 'nice' ones say, 'Who is going to take this child, she is a Level Six?' That is what they see. They don't see who the child is.

> *If they said, 'Who is going to take Cindy?', that would be a different matter?*

> That's right. If they put up Cindy's name they might say, 'Oh yes, I know Cindy. She's all right'. I know they ask who would like to take this child because they tell me that's what they do. It is pretty awful, but I understand that.

> *Is it much better to have teachers who want your child in their class?*

> Yes. I'd much rather have a teacher with the right attitude; if it is a teacher that says, 'I'll take Cindy', rather than, 'I'll take the Level Six'.

Some people have a noble attitude of, 'I'll take the [Level] Six', and that really gets up my nose. This charitable person.

If I was able to ask Cindy, 'What does it mean to be disabled?', what do you think she'd say?

She knows that she has got Down's syndrome. It is hard to know what she thinks, [although] she is aware that she can't do some things that the other kids do and she is very conscious that her language is not as good as other kids. Her friends accept her but around other people she is really conscious [of her differences] and that is why she doesn't talk to strangers very much. Whether she considers herself as having a disability, I couldn't say. Her [older] sister [Naomi] is the same [in her understanding of these things]. She asked me the other day, 'Does Cindy have a disability?' She knows that she has Down's syndrome. I said, 'Some people in society would say that she has'. She said, 'Oh! I thought it was just people who were in wheel chairs'. That is the concept that kids have . . . I would hate her [Cindy] even knowing that [others label her as disabled]. She just thinks that she's Naomi's sister and our daughter and this is her school. All of this disability stuff and the fact that she might be excluded – she's only 6 [years old] so it is above her head. Her and her sister are the same [in the way they understand these things]. I think that if she [Cindy] went to a Special School or Unit it would be just incomprehensible [for both of them].

(P6)

Having Down's syndrome is clearly different from the 'disadvantages' of being female, being poor or belonging to a racial minority – although these are not mutually exclusive groups. But the issues discussed above are not particular to Down's syndrome. They are more broadly illustrative of the ways in which assigned group identities tend to ensure that 'only the oppressed and excluded groups are defined as different' (Young 1990: 170). Within a recognitive justice perspective, difference is differently valued. It 'does not imply that there are not overlapping experiences, or that two groups have nothing in common' (Young 1990: 171). While Cindy's dis/abilities were assessed at Level Six, this also became her identity assigned by the school. It is an identity that serves to accentuate her differences from her peers while her similarities are silenced. In this respect, Cindy's story is not unlike that of students with gendered, raced and classed identities of social disadvantage. The story teller is generally someone else, which belies just conditions for self-identity and self-respect that require starting points for thinking about social arrangements other than the vantage points of the dominant.

   Some would claim equality in that the story teller is the same for all groups. That is, the school's assessment procedures operate under the banner of equality since everyone is subjected to the same measures even if everyone does not measure up equally. But as Beilharz (1989: 93) notes, 'to argue in this way is necessarily to introduce the logic of charity; and the language of the "needy", for there are citizens, and there are those outside the city gates, who are deserving compassion' – sentiments echoed by Cindy's mother. This form of charity – the well-intentioned but dominant orientations of teachers – threatens Cindy's self-worth by concentrating on her disabilities and displacing her view of her own identity formed within her family unit. Cindy herself is aware of her differences but they are interpreted through an appreciation for relations and processes. Recognitive justice, then, is a view of social justice that begins from the standpoint of the least advantaged; an 'approach [that] attempts to *generalise* the point of view of the disadvantaged rather than separate it off' (Connell 1993: 52, emphasis in original) and thereby change everybody's sense of self (Fraser 1995).

Conditions of self-development and self-expression

As oppressed groups recognize and identify themselves in a positive way, they acquire the potential to resist their oppression. New energy is created when people begin to believe in themselves and take more control over their own lives. Teachers, however, who favour recognitive justice must also address oppressive institutional processes that inhibit the development of their students. As Young (1990) explains,

> oppression consists in systematic institutional processes which prevent some people from learning and using satisfying and expansive skills in socially recognized settings, or institutionalized social processes which inhibit people's ability to play and communicate with others or to express their feelings and perspective on social life in contexts where others can listen.
>
> (Young 1990: 38)

In our research we were specifically interested in examining the institutional processes of schooling within classroom settings and school contexts. We wanted to know how teachers were implicated in these processes. What can and do teachers do, for example, to promote the development of their students' abilities and to encourage student expressions of their experiences?

Two teachers who collaboratively taught a class of 50 primary/elementary school students related the following account of their efforts to redress the injustices of their schooling system; injustices meted out to one particular student (Andrew) through procedures that largely prevented him from developing and utilizing his skills and which inhibited his expression of his feelings. Again, it is an illustration of a student with a disability – severe cerebral palsy – and some might be tempted to think that oppression of students from such groups is more likely given the extent of their reliance on others or at least the extent to which they are portrayed as more reliant. Certainly, the particular oppression experienced by this student is related to his disability and the context in which he is located. We imagine that for others, oppression would take different forms and substance. However, the following interview extract should be read first as an example of institutional constraint on a student exercising his capacities and expressing his experiences and then as illustrative of institutional constraints on particular student capacities and experiences. This in mind, we asked these teachers about their experiences of schooling as a constraining influence on student development. One of them (T11) began by relating her and her colleague's struggle with their institution and its administration to create the conditions necessary for Andrew's self-development and self-expression:

> We felt that this child had every right to communicate with us if he could do so and he should be given that opportunity. At that stage, all he could do was give us a yes/no response with his mouth, by the shape of his mouth. We were knocked back everywhere we went [in our efforts to help him communicate] and we ended up putting in [funding] submissions ourselves to various commissions and clubs to get this child a computer – and the paraphernalia that went with it – so that he could start communicating. That was quite successful [but] it was a lot of work . . . [Before that] we had screaming for hours because that was his only way of saying 'I'm angry' . . . We actually got the first computer from a different part of the school. It was in the library . . . [I] got myself into quite a bit of trouble . . . [I was told by an accomplice within the system's administration] that if we wished to get the equipment that this child needed that we had to set ourselves up and learn to be disliked . . . [and] that we were going to create some friction.

Why?

> Well, because you have [challenged] a basic principle. We had one child who was going to tie up a computer. That computer was in the library and was accessed by however many hundreds of children. At that time it was the only Apple Mac[intosh computer] in the school so there was software that could only be used on that particular computer. When it was brought up into our room it meant that the access went from 500 down to 50 – we did use it for other children as well at that time. It caused friction. It did cause friction and there was a mentality, and there still is I think, that questioned, 'Why should all of that money be spent for one child when you have x number of children in the school?' I can see where that kind of thinking comes from. I have no trouble identifying with that but at the same time we had a child here that we felt had the ability to communicate and [he] wasn't being given the opportunity to do so. We had a duty of care to him to let him try to say, 'Hey, I'm feeling really sick', or 'Just leave me alone, give me some time out'. Once we got that [computer] going he actually voiced those feelings for the first time in his life.

(T11)

One of the first things these comments illustrate is how distributive accounts of social justice – particularly liberal-democratic versions – fall short of delivering justice for Andrew. For example, equal opportunity to communicate with and learn alongside his peers was not facilitated simply by his inclusion in the same classroom; access does not automatically deliver equality. The absurdity of thinking otherwise is stark in this particular situation and in others has fuelled arguments against inclusive school practices for similar students with disabilities, errantly in our view. Illustrated more generally is that students, whatever their differences, do not enter classrooms with the same capacities to communicate and that classrooms and schooling systems of themselves do not take account of these differences. Except for 'those outside the city gates, who are deserving compassion' (Beilharz 1989: 93), such arrangements appear quite fair to those who hold to market conceptions of social justice and classroom interactions 'based on the assumptions of homogeneity and uniformity' (Taylor *et al.* 1997: 151).

A second and related matter that this interview extract raises is the way in which individuals and institutions utilize social justice discourse, notably liberal-democratic versions of distributive justice, to maintain unjust social arrangements. It is not fair, it is argued, to deny the entire school population access to its library computer for the sake of one student and a few of his peers; the latter, a concession the teachers offer to dilute the strength of this distributive argument. Neither is it fair, it seems, to spend disproportionate amounts of money on resources specifically for the use of one student. Certainly, material aspects of social justice are important but they should reflect the outcomes of socially just practices, not drive them. One could just as readily inquire about the utilization and redeployment of other resources in the school, although this, too, tends to draw attention to who has what rather than what is being done to redress the institutional oppression of students. This raises a third observation, that recognitive justice primarily finds expression in processes. Lummis (1996: 160) writes similarly about democracy: 'the actuality of democracy itself – the people's power – exists while the performance is taking place'. Clearly, these teachers are active in their pursuit of social justice, not simply in their efforts to acquire needed resources but more broadly in their 'constant and perpetual' struggle to secure the conditions for their student's self-development and self-expression. This is how they measure justice, not in whether Andrew has access to the classroom and to a particular computer, even though these serve the processes of his development.

Conditions of self-determination

What is evident here is that students' self-development and self-expression require their participation in the educational process. However, what is also clear is that the participation envisaged by recognitive justice is more than simply accessing opportunities to learn and engage in tasks determined by others. There is nothing intrinsically libratory in such participation. Rather, what counts in social justice terms is how participation is determined; through processes that take account of the interests of all participants or those that serve the interests of dominant groups? According to Young (1990: 38), 'domination consists in institutional conditions which inhibit or prevent people from participating in determining their actions or the conditions of their actions'. What is required to address such domination are levels of involvement that are premised on self-determination and that facilitate the representation of affected interest groups in decision-making processes.

Knight (1998) has written in these terms about dominating institutional processes waged against one secondary/high school and its struggle to 'participate in decisions defining important educational knowledge' (Knight 1998: 295) within its community. The school, itself committed to the involvement of its constituents in curriculum decisions of this kind, was shut out of government decision-making that resolved to withdraw financial support and to close the school. The government's decision was met with considerable opposition; delaying tactics, temporary accommodation provided by the local community, instruction delivered by volunteer teachers, but also student and community participation in the legal system's broader decision-making processes. As Knight (1998: 295) explains, 'the school and local community sought to expand the concept of accountability as defined by the State'. It was these struggles in broader contexts that finally secured the official reopening of the school, the law courts ruling that through the school's closure the government had discriminated against its minority group students.

Parents of students with disabilities interviewed in our research experienced similar problems with school policies regulating the placement of their children in particular classes; guidelines for practice that seemed at odds with government discrimination laws. For parents faced with these decisions, 'what is annoying is that you have to fight' (P4); the weight of evidence and research concerning the benefits of inclusive teaching practices not always enough to secure the involvement of parents (and students) alongside teachers in determinations within schools and classrooms. In the end:

> They can pull the carpet out [from under my feet] and the only thing supporting me would be the Disability Act saying that you can't discriminate on the basis of the disability. That is the only thing that we've got to fight with at this stage. I would use it if I had to. I haven't had to yet. I would use my research as a weapon. You wouldn't use that [legal avenue] until you really had to, but I find that most people, once they learn what you know, they're willing to change.
>
> (P4)

This is consistent with commentaries that represent many teachers as unaware of social justice matters and which suggest that 'differential privilege of members of different . . . groups is perpetuated in part by the process of schooling . . . [For example,] many if not most teachers unconsciously behave differently towards Blacks or Latinos than they behave toward whites' (Young 1990: 154). Hence, we were particularly interested in the educative attempts or 'strategies of consciousness raising' (Young 1990: 155) employed by parents to secure meaningful participation in school processes that affected their children, especially where these students were not representative of dominant groups. One parent (P3) we interviewed, a leader of a self-help group for parents of children with disabilities, provided the following account of her educative project with teachers:

> It is not easy because the teachers are still going through this change as well. They're not used to teaching kids who are different and [determining] how they're supposed to do it. I can handle that, it doesn't bother me. If the teachers are willing to learn, you can sit down together. That's what we have done at our school. It wasn't easy to start with but we have got this communication going that teachers can come up with good ideas for [enabling] children [who are different] to be included [in classrooms]. What scares me is . . . having to start again with the new teacher. The Special Education teacher has been quite cooperative even though she hasn't understood where I am coming from and if she goes I'll get a new one and the battle will start over again. There's no consistency in the [schooling system] about what we're doing . . .

> *What kind of relationship do you think your fellow parents have with teachers?*

> It is really hard because what normally happens is that parents have got this idea of what they want. If they know about inclusion and that's what they've decided [to pursue], that's what they want. Most teachers haven't heard of it [inclusion]. No, I shouldn't say [they] haven't heard of it, [rather, they] may not agree with it or they'll do what the special education teacher tells them and they've only been taught [how to teach in] one way. It can get really confusing and therefore there is an automatic clash and that usually happens with everyone [every parent] I know. They've had that happen to them. You've got to be a very good communicator to get past that and what I tell parents is that you can't do it alone. I can go and support another parent and I can feel very confident I know what I'm talking about. But when it comes to my child I just break down and cry. It is such an emotional thing and that's why you need that support there when you're talking to teachers. They'll come up with all of this jargon and the other thing that they do too is have one or two extra educators there. If they know that you're going to bring three, they'll take four. It is a power game: 'If we can get more people on side then we'll convince them'. These are the games that we're talking about. That is what has helped me get to where I am. Most parents say, 'I can't do this', and give up and then they do whatever the [schooling system] wants. It is easier for them and that's what it boils down to.

> (P3)

There are at least two matters in these comments that warrant our attention. First, self-determination does not mean *separate* determination. In both this account and the one related by Knight (1998), dominated groups struggled to rework not to abandon institutional processes. What should also be understood is that it is unlikely for the dominant to magnanimously grant self-determination to minority groups. As Frederick Douglas, an American slave, once said, power concedes nothing without a struggle. Even if we agree that the imperative of social justice is 'to *generalise* the point of view of the disadvantaged rather than separate it off' (Connell 1993: 52, emphasis in original), we still have to confront issues of how this might be realized. Part of what is required is communication and dialogue. This dialogue is both a precondition for and outcome of the kinds of participatory processes required in a democracy. It includes the mutual recognition of diverse individuals in public and private forums where different individuals and groups of people sit down together, however difficult that may be at times and however different their voices may sound. (See Burbules (1993) on communicative rationalization as part of a multicultural democratic citizenship.) Self-determination is, in part, a collaborative and an educative exercise.

This leads to a second and related observation: socially just processes – ones that foster self-determination – are necessarily democratic ones. Indeed, 'democracy is both an element and a condition of social justice' (Young 1990: 91). Lummis (1996: 37) records the political virtues of democracy as 'the commitment to, knowledge of, and ability to stand for the whole'. None of these include the stand-over tactics or power games employed in the above examples, which include the use of exclusive language, professional status or the weight of numbers. In relation to the latter, some may wonder whether democratic processes that rely on the principle of 'one person one vote' – often championed by democrats – can ever deliver social justice for minority groups. What this deceptive individualization of the democratic process hides is the way it works to promote the common interests of dominant groups. But recognitive justice requires the interests of groups to be represented – not simply the interests of atomized individuals – and for their views to be seriously engaged within decision-making processes. This is not just important for the disadvantaged:

> Having and exercising the opportunity to participate in making collective decisions that affect one's actions or the conditions of one's actions fosters the development of capacities for thinking about one's own needs in relation to the needs of others, taking an interest in the relation of others to social institutions, reasoning and being articulate and persuasive, and so on.
>
> (Young 1990: 92)

All people benefit from such educative processes that maximize the knowledge and perspectives that contribute to decisions about possible future actions.

Conclusion

Table 1 provides a summary of the three social justice perspectives canvassed in this chapter. Its structure is based on Justinian's definition of justice, each perspective offering an interpretation and elaboration of his

Table 1 Perspectives on social justice

Justice:	the will . . .	. . . to render . . .	. . . to everyone . . .	. . . their due
	What should social justice desire? Whose desire?	How should social justice be achieved?	Who should social justice benefit?	What should social justice deliver?
Distributive justice	Freedom, social cooperation and compensation for those who lack the basics Individuals/ groups, represented by government authorities	Through proportional distributions to individuals/ groups	Disadvantaged individuals/ groups	Material and social goods/ opportunities basic to social life
Retributive justice	Liberty, protection of rights and punishment for those who infringe these rights Individuals, displayed in their free interactions (e.g. in the marketplace)	Through open competition and (gov) protection of life and property	Individuals who contribute to society	Material and social goods/ opportunities commensurate with talent and effort
Recognitive justice	Provision of the means for all people to exercise their capabilities and determine their actions All people, expressed within and among their social groups	Through democratic processes that generalize the interests of the least advantaged	All people, differently experienced within and among different social groups	Positive self-identity; self-development; self-determination

references to 'the will', 'to render', 'to everyone', 'their due'. As implied above, there are also similarities here – in style and substance – with Lummis' questioning of democracy, about which he asks: 'Who are the people? What is power? Should the people have the power? How could such a situation be arranged? By what set of institutions could it be guaranteed?' (Lummis

1996: 22). There is not necessarily a direct one-to-one correspondence between these questions and those represented in the table, although Lummis' concerns can be answered by reading across the columns. Note that the second column is headed by two questions and, therefore, two answers are offered by each perspective in response.

Throughout, we have argued in favour of the third perspective for its expanded understanding of social justice, which includes a positive regard for social difference and the centrality of socially democratic processes in working towards its achievement. Yet, in choosing this position we want to avoid suggesting that material conditions and distributive matters are unrelated to or are unimportant in defining and practising social justice. Nor do we want to underestimate the considerable gains that have been made through advocating the equal treatment of individuals. Clearly, these matters are important in delivering social justice but they are only part of the project with which we are concerned. That is, shifting 'from a focus on distributive patterns to procedural issues of participation in deliberation and decision making' (Young 1990: 34) does not mean abandoning our interest in 'who has what'. The problems of schools are directly connected to societal dysfunctions. Efforts to improve our schools are, therefore, likely to be most effective when they come in the context of broader social movements that redress social inequities. One place to focus, nonetheless, is on certain unjust practices carried out in schools and classrooms. Within the school arena, like other arenas both personal and encompassing, we find the potential to create and enhance all-inclusive processes of participation where individuals and groups contribute to creating new meanings and more democratic practices. (See Raymond Williams (1989) here for his concept of a common culture.)

How these matters play out in contexts of schools and classrooms has been a concern of our discussions so far. Our intention has been for these examples to illustrate as well as contribute to an understanding of what social justice looks like from various perspectives. In the chapters that follow we pursue these matters more fully, particularly the implications of a recognitive justice framework for schooling and teacher practices. While other issues fall within these parameters, this book focuses on those that influence teachers' conceptions and expressions of language, education and diversity. Often this requires us to rethink our understandings in order to determine those that give adequate acknowledgement to issues of social justice.

Questions for discussion/research

- What purposes should schooling serve in contemporary times?
- What criteria should teachers use to respond differently to different students?
- How can teachers arrange their teaching to serve the interests of all students?
- What are socially just conditions for learning?
- Who should determine what is learnt in schools?

Suggested readings

Christensen, C. and Rizvi, F. (eds) (1996) *Disability and the Dilemmas of Education and Justice*. Buckingham: Open University Press, Chapter 1.

Lummis, C.D. (1996) *Radical Democracy*. Ithaca, NY: Cornell University Press, Chapter 1.

Ryan, A. (ed.) (1993) *Justice*. Oxford: Oxford University Press, Introduction.

Taylor, S., Rizvi, F., Lingard, B. and Henry, M. (1997) *Educational Policy and the Politics of Change*. London: Routledge, Chapter 7.

Troyna, B. and Vincent, C. (1995) The discourses of social justice in education, *Discourse: Studies in the Cultural Politics of Education*, 16(2): 149–66.

_____ *three* _____

Language games: what are the rules? Whose rules?

Introduction

There is a sense in which language is universal; most, if not all, of us use it in one form or another in our interactions with others as well as using it just for ourselves. Yet, it is apparent that not all language forms are universally (well) used and nor are they universally (well) known. Still, when we enter a school, we tend not to think about this much; that we are entering an environment in which certain forms of language are used and valued more than others and that individuals within that environment differentially use and value these (and other) language forms. Even when we do think about these things, we tend to regard them as matters of technique; that because of the very purposes of these institutions as sites for student instruction, individuals within schools are engaged in processes of learning various standard language skills, including when it is appropriate to use (and not use) them.

Certainly, there is a technical element to language use but in this chapter we specifically focus on how language is used to advance political agendas. Indeed, we regard the technical as political when it comes to language use in schooling, and most other activities engaged within the social world for that matter. Our purposes, then, are to draw attention to the politics inherent in language use and to raise questions about its role in schooling; questions that might otherwise go unasked. We contend that to focus exclusively (and narrowly) on technical issues in language is to miss the point of what these techniques are designed to achieve. In this narrow frame of mind, for example, there is danger in not thinking about *who* determines the techniques associated with various forms of language and *when* and *where* it is appropriate to use them. Again, if we do think about these things, we tend not to follow this through to consider *who benefits* (and who does not) from standard determinations regarding language use. There is, then, a critical and recognitive agenda in this political account of school language.

By *politics*, we mean to include the 'struggle [by individuals and groups] over the resources and arrangements that set the basic terms of our practical and passionate relations. Pre-eminent among these arrangements is the formative institutional and imaginative context of social life' (Unger 1987: 145) and pre-eminent and formative within this context is schooling. Further, we assume in this and subsequent chapters that language, given its centrality in the educative process, is a major site of struggle within schools. We have known for some time that 'language is inextricably bound up with *all* the learning that goes on in school' (Barnes *et al.* 1971: 160, emphasis added), not just that which occurs in the English classroom and/or what appears in official school curricula.[1] This is because 'meanings reside not only in words, but in people, and language is part of the system, or set of systems, whereby people in society exchange meanings' (Hodge 1981: 137). How meanings are expressed in society are an important part of school relations, not least because 'students' and teachers' use of language, to request and obtain action and information, is central to teaching and learning in the classroom' (Wilkinson 1982: 85). More broadly, we are of the view that there is evidence of a way of using language that is particular to schooling – a particular cultural and linguistic capital (Bourdieu and Passeron 1977; Bourdieu 1984; Bourdieu 1997) – which acts as a major and effective arbiter of (academic) achievement in schools operating beyond the bounds of merit and, more to the point, which governs the boundaries of merit.

Guiding questions

We follow this line of thinking through the examination of four broad approaches to understanding language use, each with its own view of what language is, how it should be used and what this means for students' schooling. Even though each approach can be associated with specific historical epochs and recognized as dominating the thinking on language use during these times, several are also evident during other periods, are variable across contexts and have a way of (re)surging in interest and dominance. The chapter, then, is not so much a linguistic history as a political and social critique. We are aware, for example, that there are gaps and discontinuities hidden by our mapping of the political character of language use in schools, both between the approaches we canvass as well as within them. Nonetheless, we believe there are helpful and illuminating arguments in their representations that warrant attention, particularly given our dispositions for just schooling.

The four language perspectives that we consider can be described respectively as traditional, structural, functional and critical and we draw on the comments of teachers – particularly David, Michelle and Carl and other participants in our research outlined in Chapter 1 of this book – to illustrate and critique what each looks like in practice. In doing so, we seek answers to the following:

• What are the rules of language use?
• Whose rules are they?
• Whom do they serve?
• Who wins and who loses because of them?

We have named the approaches implied by these questions after games children play and invite the reader to play along as we explore what these 'language games' (Wittgenstein 1953) mean for students. Where it is specifically addressed, we take 'literacy' to mean the use of language in accordance with the rules of the game. To the extent that each game advocates different rules for language, literacy is also differently understood within each of them; the chapter progresses from narrow to broader conceptions as it moves through its analysis of these games. We are also cognizant of the work of Green (1997) who, in arguing for 'a more adequate, comprehensive conceptualisation of literacy', proposes that 'literacy involves, fundamentally, the articulation of language and technology' and 'the integration of text and information'. From time to time you might like to refer back to the 'teachers' guide to playing fair' outlined in Chapter 2, as a way of evaluating the merits of the traditional, structural, functional and critical literacies we examine. Following this order, we have dubbed these approaches 'join the dots', 'blind man's bluff', 'who am I?' and 'snakes and ladders'. So, let the games begin!

Join the dots

Traditionally, language is viewed as a regulated system comprised of categories of words that perform certain functions in a sentence: a noun names an object, a verb indicates action, an adjective provides added description of a noun, and so on. Rules of grammar organize these into sentences while other rules relate to its representation, involving such things as punctuation, spelling and even handwriting. The emphasis in these rules tends to be on the *mechanics* of language use rather than on its *meanings*. This is not to suggest that meanings are unimportant to traditionalists but that the path to understanding language is seen to be via a technical understanding of its constituent parts. The rationale is that mastery of a set of prescribed elements, individually acquired, leads to mastery of language in its entirety, a kind of 'join the dots' approach that identifies and organizes language parts into some coherent whole.[2] The only problems that language users experience in relation to meanings, then, are in having the technical skills to be able to send and receive them.

This traditional disposition towards language use, and the abstract laws that inform it, is often exclusively concerned with what is written and, therefore, sent. This is evident in such rules as a sentence should not end with a preposition, a predicate must agree in number and case with its head noun, *i* before *e*, except after *c*, and so forth. Yet rules of this kind can be inappropriate when applied to spoken language, to many dialects or even to colloquial language use. Consider the following parody of grammatical rules, each drawing on generally accepted language use in everyday speech:

A preposition is something you should never end a sentence *with*.
It is wrong *to* carelessly *split* infinitives.
And you should never begin a sentence with a conjunction.

Notice that all three rules are broken in the sentences that convey them, even though this does not interfere with their meanings. The prescriptive rules of traditional grammar can also obscure rather than enhance communication; a point that is well illustrated in Winston Churchill's well-known and grammatically correct remonstration: 'This is an errant pedantry up with which I will not put!'

What is evident in these brief examples is that even though the traditional approach to language employs rules to assist the sending and receiving of meanings, there are times when these same rules are, at best, meaningless (they do not appreciably contribute to sending/receiving meanings) and, at worst, obstructionist (they frustrate and obscure meanings in the sending/ receiving process). This is quite apart from an appreciation for meanings as problematic themselves, issues we return to below and in Chapter 4. Again, the analogy of 'dots' – this time imagined a little differently – is useful here in understanding traditional conceptions of language as a technical process of transmitting information. To paint the picture, the perspective implies that using language is much like using Morse code where production of the correct number of dots (and dashes) ensures delivery of the correct message.[3] There are connections here between this traditional approach to language and the period in which it first came to prominence. In Samuel Morse's time, western societies were also interested in processes of a different kind; namely, those that related to the production of economic goods on the factory floor and, later, the conveyor belt. In these factories, workers turned raw materials into marketable products. Like traditional language use, the process was often segmented with different workers performing different tasks and it was governed by rules to ensure that the overall process functioned despite its staccato and repetitive routines.

There are at least two more dots to join in relation to these matters. First, characterization of the industrial revolution as rule-orientated has some similarities with contemporary revolutions in information (Lyotard 1984), image (Baudrillard 1981) and capital accumulation (Jameson 1983), even if the rules of these latter revolutions appear more arbitrary. The technologies that service these revolutions – computers, electronic processors and the like – require a certain precision in their utilization. The threat of the millennium bug, for example, was indicative of a failure to appreciate the pervasiveness of these rules. We should not be surprised, therefore, to witness the revival of a basics rhetoric for schooling with a technical vision for literate students during this current period, partly as an expression of a conservative restoration movement but also in response to the ascendancy of neo-liberalism in contemporary societies. Conservatism and liberalism are (sometimes uncomfortable) allies of contemporary 'new right' politics. The resurgence in a traditional approach to education, language and literacy that appeals to external and universal standards, then, is also being driven by imperatives to legitimize or give account of how efficiently the educational dollar is being spent and to demonstrate the effectiveness of schooling in delivering productive individuals. Within this accounting process, the illegitimacy/illiteracy of 'disadvantaged' groups is being addressed, once more, through tests and target programmes (see Luke *et al.* 2000, for an excellent discussion of these issues).

Second, the period of industrial revolution in western countries also witnessed the introduction of mass compulsory schooling, informed by traditional rules of language use. As several authors have noted, 'there is a very real sense . . . in which English teaching as a distinctive curriculum domain is linked specifically and directly to the emergence and consolidation of public, mass compulsory, "popular" education and schooling' (Green 1998: 177).[4] The rules that informed language teaching in schools at the time, and which persist today, have their origins in Latin. When applied to English schooling, they offered not only status but also a model for instruction. In this sense, language rules were more than just a way of governing language use but also a way of governing language users. Schooling itself took on this rule orientation as a way of instructing and governing students in ways that reinforced the dominance of dominant groups; the appearance of grammar schools providing one example of the centrality of language rules to schooling. But none of this should be very surprising; 'people learn to give rules to others because rules provide a rapid way of helping – or forcing – another person to make specific responses which are reinforcing to the rule giver' (Baldwin and Baldwin 1990: 205).

The schooling of Eliza Doolittle in the musical *My Fair Lady*, based on Shaw's *Pygmalion*, is a good illustration of this traditional way of thinking about language and other forms of behaviour often associated with high culture. Even her name – Doolittle – gives an indication of the perception we (as the audience) are to have of Eliza who lacks 'proper' language and social skills. Indeed, the play and film project the view that once Eliza can 'talk proper' she will also acquire associated ways of acting, a belief that continues to find currency in schooling. Consider, for example, the following extract from our conversations with Michelle. Earlier in the interview, Michelle had referred to her secondary/high school as a place for students to learn 'how to behave properly' and we were interested to know what 'proper' meant in that context:

'Proper' is what I have learnt growing up, what I accept as being correct, and what I think most of the school accepts as being correct . . .

How, then, do you deal with students from different cultural backgrounds who have different understandings of what is proper?

You just have to try and take that into account sometimes. And I know in my first few years of teaching it was difficult for me. A classic example – [when I was teaching] overseas – the kids would say, 'What?' To me, that is rude, and I'd say, 'It's not, "What?" It's "Pardon". It sounds better'. 'Oh, sorry Miss, "Pardon"'. But after a while I began to understand that that is their language, that is their culture. They say, 'What?' and that's not being rude and that took me, maybe, two schools to realize. The first couple of times when I used to say, 'Excuse me, it's "pardon", not "what"', they looked at me as if to say, 'Who are you?'.

(Michelle)

Notice the positive correlation between language and behaviour with the implication that incorrect language use comes from rude language users who are 'without culture, learning, or refinement' and whose speech is 'harsh to the ear' (Delbridge and Bernard 1994: 868). The importance given to appearances, behavioural and linguistic, is a prominent feature of conservative ideologies that, as we have already noted, focus on an adherence to strict sets of rules. Even so, there is some acceptance in Michelle's comments of different language use, although somewhat reluctantly and, we suspect, to the detriment of standards as she sees them. In this overseas environment Michelle was 'the odd one out' (Michelle) and resigned herself to accept what she could not change. Still, the point is well made: language instruction is a central feature of schooling, and teachers – who bring to school understandings of proper language from their predominantly middle class upbringings – utilize it as a means of control over more than how students speak and write. In this vein, consider the following exchange between a teacher (T5) and student observed in a primary/elementary school classroom during a formal 'show and tell' or 'sharing time' session; its form typical in character of what genrists refer to as a recount:

Guess what? Me dad got me this horse bridle yesterday.

'My dad', not 'me dad', Sam. Yes, I see he did. That's quite smart, isn't it? What is on the side?

Dunno.

Now, that's, 'I don't know', Sam. I think you do. It's like this thing on my belt.

Umm . . . (shrugs shoulders)

It's called a 'buckle'. Remember we learnt that in spelling last week? Buckle. And what do you use it for?

Me dad said that you gotta . . . umm (long pause) . . . so the bridle won't fall off the horse.

Tighten it. Your dad said that you must tighten it?

Yeah – and he said that you gotta make sure it's not real tight, 'cause if it is, it'd hurt the horse.

That's 'got to', Sam, and at school we don't say, 'yeah'. What do we say?

Yes.

Good boy.

(T5)

Students participate in sharing times like the one above on the pretext that they can 'speak on a self-chosen topic that does not have to meet criteria of relevance to previous discourse' (Cazden 1988: 8) and in these respects it is itself a speech-event more in keeping with the child-centred approach to schooling outlined below. In a traditional classroom, however, students are aware that their 'sharing of out-of-school experiences . . . is often the only time when they are considered relevant in school' (Cazden 1988: 8). There is also another level of sharing in these classrooms that reflects what Bourdieu (in Thompson 1991: 62) refers to as a tendency of the middle classes towards 'hypercorrection'. Note in the above example that correct language is interpreted as the language of the school and is clearly articulated in the teacher's correction: 'at school we don't say . . .'. Note, too, that Sam's sharing is given status because of its relationship to the school's curriculum; 'buckle' is one of the words on the class spelling list.

However, what is even more revealing of Sam's schooling is the way in which the teacher directs the conversation to foreground the school's activities and importance. The buckle on Sam's bridle becomes part of the conversation because the teacher makes it so, a 'linguistic turn' that is informed by more than just interest in what Sam has brought to show his teacher and class. More cogently, it represents an attempt to demonstrate the relevance of the school curriculum to students' everyday lives and to superimpose that curriculum over the activities of their lives. In effect, school knowledge becomes the point of reference from which to understand and appraise all (other) activity. Sam, for example, becomes a 'good boy' when his language use falls into line with this way of seeing the world, a moral and intellectual disciplining that we return to shortly. In the above verbal equivalent of dotting the *i*'s and crossing the *t*'s, it is clear that 'one pervasive feature of the content of teacher talk is the expression of control – control of behaviour and of talk itself' (Cazden 1988: 160). These are the same controls that traditional teachers exercise over student compositions: required student writing with the express purpose of demonstrating to teachers their students' technical language skills. 'Drills and skills' exercises and formal written examinations are typical of this traditional approach to language use, yet what teachers who subscribe to these pedagogies fail to understand is that:

> Since test developers use standards of correctness in language rather than criteria of appropriateness as benchmarks when putting together their instruments, test norms based uncritically on the standard in this way will always disadvantage non-standard users.
>
> (Corson 1993: 120)

There is a second aspect of this traditional approach that relates to our earlier observation regarding the importance of meanings. Certainly, there is a strong emphasis on language techniques within traditional language usage but there is also evidence of a literature-based or literary strand – similar to the classics – that involves the study of poetry, drama, the novel, the short story, and so on. At first glance these two interests seem unrelated and, undoubtedly, the interests of grammarians appear the more dominant and widespread of the two. However, if we understand that their common concern is with the management of behaviour towards common ends, then the connection becomes more readily apparent. Traditional language rules attempt an external control of language use (and users) whereas literary pedagogies focus on internal controls; a form of moral instruction that sanctions particular readings or interpretations of human experiences, socializing students into the dominant culture of schooling and society. Interestingly, 'it is only in relatively recent times that the specific disciplinary effects of literary pedagogy . . . has been extended to primary schooling' (Green 1998: 184). We had this confirmed for us in our research when we asked David about what he meant by equipping his students 'to become informed citizens . . . by dealing, say, with literature'. It became apparent that

> even just dealing with picture books with kids, there are any number now. Children's literature has just come along in leaps and bounds in recent years. It really has. There is much more literature in primary school libraries which is multidimensional. There are whole things that are parodies of quite serious issues and also things that you can deal with at a superficial level as well if you wish, but if you wish to read between the lines you are not imposing another interpretation. It is there and intended. Now, even with primary school children, the opportunity is there to at least lead them to that awareness that this isn't sort of talking about a coloured bird, or whatever the particular thing may be, but it's an analogy of a real life and a human situation. And the point I make with the children is that we can read this just superficially. And, yes, it's a nice, quaint, little story and that's good and you get something, but if you can see this other thing to it as well, if you think and you can see those things, then it is much richer. And from that you transfer the idea to the children that thinking, and being able to think, and enjoying thinking, leads to a much richer life. There are all these things that are there for you if you realize it.
>
> (David)

David relates this 'richer' literary world to traditional grammar, observing that 'it seems to me that you reach a point [after technical mastery] where learning from that point on is aesthetic' (David). This seems to contradict King's (1983, in Green 1998: 185) claim that literary pedagogy in traditional contexts constructs an 'ascetic life'. One reading of David's comments could produce such an interpretation, given his advocacy for the 'monastic' and hermeneutic discipline of reading between the lines to find 'this other thing' and the richer discovery that 'all these things . . . are there for you'. Yet this also points to an alternative interpretation of a pedagogy concerned with 'language and personal growth' (Dixon 1975, in Green 1998: 187), features of a second perspective on language use to which we now turn.

Blind man's bluff

The 1960s and 1970s are often characterized as a period of protest against the moral and behavioural constraints of a previous era. The dominant imperatives of the time were to do what comes naturally, to give open expression to individual rights and personal freedoms and, not surprisingly, these found currency in the teaching of language and schooling more broadly. During this period, Noam Chomsky – author and protagonist of a structural view of language – began to question the need to teach language rules to students. His argument was that children were able to master the total and unique aspects of a particular language system and to use this system productively and creatively before they reached school, without even knowing what a noun, verb or adjective was. Based on this and similar observations, Chomsky (1966, 1972) hypothesized that people were born with an ability, which he called a language acquisition device (LAD), to generate language forms beyond what their experiences suggested possible. Students' errors in using language outside of their experiences, then, were simply a misapplication of innate language rules. Indeed, the misuse of 'teached' instead of 'taught', for example, was evidence, Chomsky reasoned, of the existence of this underlying language structure acquired at birth.

From this perspective, students overcome language errors through their immersion into the world of language use and its users, utilizing this environment to test their understandings of language structure, which they then modify according to the feedback they receive. Thus, the more exposure to varied language experiences, the more refined that students' knowledge of language structure becomes. Chomsky speculated that this interaction between students' environments and their innate capacities for language was evidence of a transformational or universal grammar: a two-level surface and deep language structure. In brief, the argument is that students' knowledge of grammar is developed at the deep structural level and is transformed into or used to generate surface level language. Chomsky likened this language process to the way in which children learn to walk, that is, 'naturally'. In taking their first steps, children are often assisted by their environments – a helping hand from an adult, a table that can be grabbed, and so on – yet much of the work is seen to be done by children themselves. While they might initially stumble and fall, in much the same way that students use 'incorrect' language forms, they generally persist through trial and error to the point where they can manage the task without too many complications.

Similar in some ways to the story of the blind men and the elephant,[5] there is a certain blind faith required of teachers (and students) to think about language as more than what can be seen and appreciated first hand (the surface features), particularly when that which is hidden from view (the deep structural level) commands so much authority. Still, such faith spawned what is known as a whole language approach to teaching English, informed by holistic notions of the whole being greater than its parts.[6]

Whole language pedagogies also advocated a process approach to language use in response to the traditional segmentation of the curriculum; hence, the development of such teaching-learning activities as 'process writing'. Other characterizations refer to a 'child-centred' or 'progressive' view (Lawton 1984) and emphasize intrinsically rewarding experiences, personal development and self-expression.

At its broadest level, then, the conversion from a traditional to a structural view of language displaced students from the 'monastic' life to the 'mystic'. Green (1998: 187–90) notes that the shift also entailed changes in emphasis: from writing to speech (albeit, often written as narratives); from the transmission of information to its interpretation; and, more generally, from high culture to popular culture, in keeping with the optimistic and popular-democratic impulses of the time. Worth noting, too, is that this social wave of freedoms and 'naturalness' experienced in western countries was fuelled by their post-war economic booms and an accompanying Keynesian view of economics; itself, a kind of blind faith. In brief, Keynesian economics is what informs government policy to respond with increased government expenditure, secured against future earnings, to increasing demands made on government. As in the economy, this new emphasis in schooling repositioned students from language producers to language consumers.

There is a (false) sense of security in believing in the naturalness of students' abilities to develop their language use largely by themselves – a matter we return to shortly – and it requires teachers to rethink their roles within the educative process. Again, Green (1998) notes that the shift of emphasis from teaching to learning had significant consequences for teacher–student relations. For teachers, it involved greater emphasis on their contributions as models (of language use) rather than as authoritarians, removing the (textual) barriers that previously separated students from their teacher as person(able). In our research, David succinctly encapsulates this new vision for teachers: 'I think this business of the teacher being a focus and setting the agenda for the children is very real and I think they respond the way you respond' (David). This is in stark contrast to the personality that Michelle was instructed to adopt during her training: 'Come across really hard when you start . . . show them who is boss' (Michelle). Teachers also shifted from their positions as instructors to those of facilitators, 'one who simply attends to the learner learning, or guides him or her toward cultural and personal understandings' (Green 1998: 191), a stance that has resonance with contemporary depictions of teachers in some quarters, typically those organized around new information-based technologies.

This structural view of language and its implications for teaching also have significant consequences for students. In brief, the notion that students learn to use language naturally is the ultimate denial of the cultural and contextual differences associated with language and its users. Not only are teachers bluffed or deceived by this separation of (language) techniques and meanings, but also the linguistic capital of students from marginalized groups is devalued and they are unwittingly denied explicit instruction in the language (and morality) rewarded by schooling. Blindfolded in this way, 'the difficulty for the newcomer is that so much of the "meaning" of what its [dominant] members say derives from this "history" and is therefore assumed by them to be self-evident' (Doughty *et al.* 1972: 88). In the following interview extract from our research, Carl reveals something of the consequences for students from non-dominant groups who are (re)positioned by pedagogies associated with universal grammar:

> *You mentioned earlier that this institution offers a second chance for a lot of its students. What does it mean to be a 'second chance' institution?*

Well, I guess what I'm talking about there is that people have gone through what we might call a first chance education, what we as white people would accept as our long and continued process of education, where we are expected to go to school . . . [and] play by the rules quite readily all the way through the compulsory years . . .

> *How do you think people know what the rules are? Whose rules are they?*

Well, I guess they're our rules and I mean 'ours' in the sense of mainstream society . . . I think the rules are learnt through the processes of socialization that we go through, both in our family situation and in social situations such as schools. I mean, we adapt to a bureaucratic society, whether we agree with that [society] or not. We're quite good at adapting to a bureaucratic society. I guess [marginalized people of colour] don't know the rules. They don't know what the bureaucratic society is. They don't know what the whole process of socialization is, what its purpose is.

> *Why do you think they don't know the rules?*

Well, I think the first part of this is the position of the family, the social position, how cohesive that family that you come from is and what the morals and the ideals of that group are. Say the parents were a doctor and a lawyer. Then they will have a whole series of aspirations for their children and, I guess, they instil [in them] certain rules on how they got through. I don't like the term, but jumping through hoops, being shown how to jump through hoops.

> *I wonder if those doctors and lawyers make that explicit to their children?*

I think they do, yes. To me it was . . . I can't actually say that I had a cherished upbringing, but I certainly had a good upbringing. My parents were not well educated but the anticipation was that we would all be better educated than them.

(Carl)

What is proposed here is that schooling in western societies creates its own failures by excluding students from access to its rules of operation: the expectations, morals and aspirations of white middle classes. Moreover, those who succeed, those who know how to 'jump through the hoops', do so because they arrive at school already equipped with this knowledge of what to do and how to 'be'. In short, if you do not know the rules you cannot play the game, which makes winning all the more difficult! As Corson (1993) notes:

> the special language demands that conventional schooling places on children from marginalised social groups and minorities unfairly requires them to show competence in what the school demands, while not equipping them with that competence or even justifying the demands.
>
> (Corson 1993: 110–11)

Who am I?

Enter the functional approach to language use and Michael Halliday, one of its best known advocates. Halliday and others who argue in favour of applying this approach in schools (for example, Martin 1985; Christie 1990; Derewianka 1990), contend that the language of schooling is not as naturally acquired as structuralists suggest. In particular, Halliday claims that grammar is the last aspect of language that children develop, in response to their growing perception of the usefulness of particular language forms in particular contexts. As Halliday (1973: 10) puts it, 'the child knows what language is because he [*sic*] knows what language does'.

Halliday's (1973, 1975) observations of children and the use they make of language led him to describe seven language purposes or functions: the instrumental (to satisfy wants); the regulatory (to control others' behaviour); the interactional (to establish and define social relations); the personal (to express feelings and opinions); the imaginative (to express fantasy); the heuristic (to explore, investigate, acquire knowledge and understanding); and the informative (to report facts, conclusions, information). Halliday further suggested that with experience a child's single-purpose language develops a multipurpose character with a multiplicity of uses or 'macro-functions'. These he identified as the experiential (for learning); the interpersonal (for interacting with others); and the textual (for creating written or spoken texts). While regarding these purposes and functions as shared among language users, functionalists argue that what is not universal, but socially constructed, are the rules regulating their expression. Thus, students whose home language already matches the language of the school have an advantage. The long-term rewards for using language according to these rules are access to the 'best' of society's goods: wealth, status, professional occupations and the like. Yet for students whose language use varies from the norm, the penalties for using 'inappropriate' language can include restricted access and/or exclusion from these goods.

The functionalists' solution to these problems lies in making explicit to students the implicit knowledge concerning society's dominant language use. This includes teaching students technical aspects of language favoured by dominant groups but in the context of purposeful and powerful texts and in combination with instruction on their schematic structures. Teachers of this functional persuasion refer to these ways of constructing and representing texts as genres (categories of texts with similar purposes and features), including text types such as recounts, narratives, information reports, explanations, instructions (procedures) and arguments (expositions) (see Derewianka 1990). Genres vary from one another not only in the purposes they address but also according to their experiential, interpersonal and textual functions. In redressing the exclusion of non-dominant students from using these powerful texts, what is envisaged is an apprenticeship model for teaching and learning language in which teachers provide students with model texts for examination and with demonstrations of how to construct them. In turn, students replicate these models, often in partnership with others, and are provided with opportunities to (re)turn to teaching models for revision and further guidance.

As noted, the importance of the technical aspects of language in this approach is related to their functionality. Grammar, for example, is seen as useful because it serves the broader function of a text, which is invested with the purposes of the language user in a particular context. Technical features of language represent that investment, but they are not the investment itself; we return to these matters in Chapter 4. This way of thinking about language led to the development of functional or systemic grammar that describes the use of textual features according to descriptors such as 'processes', 'participants' and 'modifiers' (of circumstance and attribute). To the extent that all grammar 'regulate[s] the possibilities of how a particular practice might be recognised or interpreted' (Rizvi 1993: 136), Green (1998: 192) sees little difference between functional grammar and its traditional and transformational predecessors. That is, the 'discipleship' inherent in genre pedagogies is just as regulatory of language users as other 'monastic' and 'mystic' teaching-learning systems discussed above.

Still, functional grammar advances a significantly different position for the technical aspects of language than those advocated by traditionalists and structuralists. As David explains:

> The surface features are the things that tend to be the most resistant to change – so that [language] usage will change, spelling will change, but the punctuation won't. It's very hard to make sense of text without full stops or periods and without capital letters. It's not very receptive to those sorts of changes. So I mean the point is that they are crucial. The reason that the language won't accept those changes is because that has great impact on the meaning, otherwise it wouldn't mind more of it being changed. Spelling doesn't change the meaning . . . That is why I value punctuation, not just for the sake of being pedantic and accuracy is somehow sacrosanct. It's just the idea that it's through that that [students] communicate precisely what they want to say.

The value, then, of these things like correct grammar, or correct punctuation, correct spelling, is their ability to convey meanings accurately or as accurately as possible?

Yes, they have no other function as far as I'm concerned. That's it.

(David)

Apart from arguing that language techniques are subservient to meanings, David's comments also hint at matters for which functionalists have been criticized. Notice the way in which language is seen to be homogeneous and its author hidden, such that '*the language* won't accept those changes' (emphasis added). The point here is that dominant individuals and groups make decisions about the rules of language use, not language itself. Even though functionalists reveal the rules – and, by association, the rule-makers – of powerful language and encourage their students to develop their abilities in its use, they perpetuate the subordination of marginalized groups by encouraging them to adopt the language of the dominant.[7] It is this dominance that remains hidden in a functionalist approach, much like it is in David's account of which language rules are resistant to change and which are not. Similar to Delgado-Gaitan's (1990) critique, the empowerment intended and claimed by such an approach is often little more than 'the act of showing people how to work within a system from the perspective of people in power' (Delgado-Gaitan 1990: 2). That these people of power are able to establish their view of the world and their way of acting within it as the most valued or even as the norm, is evidence of their 'symbolic domination' (Bourdieu and Passeron 1977).

There are several respects in which this functional view of language is reminiscent of child-like riddles that begin with the question, 'Who am I?', followed by a series of clues upon which listeners are to base their response. Some, like the riddle posed by the Sphinx,[8] have severe consequences for those who fail to unravel them, with similarities to the adverse effects faced by students who fail to acquire the language of the dominant. To avoid these adversities, students from marginalized groups are shown and have explained to them a series of clues to help them solve the riddle of powerful genres. At its core – like 'Who am I?' riddles – it involves a particular kind of 'identity work' (Green 1995: 394), which David explains as 'if you want to be a "this", then you need to speak the language of "that" . . . every discipline has its own particular jargon'. Hence, 'if you want to work as a geologist then you need the language of a geologist; if you want to work as a plumber then you need the language of a plumber' (David). Yet, as Fairclough notes:

> In no actual speech community do all members always behave in accordance with a shared sense of which language varieties are appropriate for which contexts and purposes. Yet such a perfectly ordered world is set up as an ideal by those who wish to impose their own social order upon society in the realm of language.

(Fairclough 1992a: 34)

In effect, functionalists, and genrists in particular, perpetuate – albeit, naively – a disciplining of students that favours certain ways of being and engaging the world. Certainly, students are introduced to a 'who's who' of dominant genres but they are (mis)led to believe in these as *the* standard for language use, that it is beyond critique. Thus, teachers do not simply provide students with introductions to appropriate ways of expressing who they are, but also who it is appropriate to be. That is, power is spoken in and through particular genres from (dominantly) designated positions. As David remarks, although perhaps without the sympathies of this critique, 'the language is the education'. If they were not so well schooled in such language use, students from subordinate groups might be encouraged to ask: 'Who am I?', 'Where am I represented in these genres?', 'How do they represent me?' and 'What have/ do I become by using them?'

These are critical matters that we discuss more fully below, but it is worth pursuing for the moment what this dominant language can do for students who utilize it or at least what it claims to be able to achieve for them. This is important in a context where language users who are unable to use the language of the dominant remain subjected to a 'disarray which leaves them "speechless", "tongue-tied", "at a loss for words", as if they were suddenly dispossessed of their own language' (Bourdieu, quoted in Thompson 1991: 52). Along these lines, consider Michelle's explicit instruction to her students concerning the language used by the physiological and medical disciplines to describe the human backbone: 'we call it the vertebral column because that's technically correct. It's not a spine. A spine is something else'. The constraints on students' language use are clear but there are also potential benefits in adopting this more disciplined language. As Michelle illustrated to us in our conversations with her:

I said to the kids today – a lot of them who are keen footballers – 'If you are going to be a nurse or a fitness trainer or even a professional sportsperson, it is to your advantage to know this sort of terminology', which it is. 'If you have to describe a joint or if you have to describe something, if you know the words, that will make it easier, that's why you learn'.

Would you go to a doctor and use this terminology to talk about your vertebral column?

Yes. You can say, 'Look my third vertebrae down in the thoracic region of my vertebral column is sore. And my *latissimus dorsi* is giving me a bit of trouble'. Not that you would do that too often.

How do you think a doctor would react to that?

Well, I have done it before just for the reaction. [And the reaction] I've got [has been], 'Oh, are you a doctor?' I just say, 'No, I am a PE [physical education] teacher'. I know all the words, but I think it's something personal too . . . I am very inquisitive and if I go to a doctor, I want to know everything. 'What's my heart rate? What's my blood pressure? What's this? What's that? Where was that pain?' I had kidney stones, and the doctor tried to pull the wool over my eyes and I looked at the X-ray and I said, 'Well, there it is. My Bowman's capsules, they're dilated'. I only said that because he was giving me the run-around, saying, 'There is nothing wrong with you'. It was there in black and white and I'm sure he was thinking, 'Well, she doesn't know any of this stuff'.

How did he respond?

He said, 'Oh, how do you know about that? Where do you work?' I said, 'I'm a PE teacher, and I know the kidneys'. And he said, 'Oh, well, yes, there could have been a stone there, but we aren't sure any more'.

(Michelle)

It is revealing that Michelle connects 'knowing the words' with who she is as a person, particularly given our discussion above on these issues. What also is apparent is a strong sense of the functionality of language, of using it to get what one wants. In the doctor's surgery, Michelle uses her knowledge of a particular and privileged way of talking about her body to gain respect, to secure a position from which to speak with her doctor on equal terms, and as a precursor to acquiring knowledge about her physical condition. Foucault (1980) has referred to this use of language in terms of 'power/ knowledge' relations; we return to these issues in Chapter 4. One insight from these references is that power and knowledge (and powerful language) is not something that people possess as much as it is something that they use. Power is evident, then, to the extent that this use generates control (however temporary) over others. Thus, if we take

> language use, as an example, in three specific contexts where there is an inherent [im]balance of power: doctors' surgeries, courtrooms and classrooms. Each of them illustrate the fact that power is not necessarily exercised in the *amount* of talk or even of silence, but rather in the management and style of talk.
>
> (Mayor and Pugh 1987: 145, emphasis in original)

Understood from this perspective, the genre approach offers a particular way of managing language use and language users. It is also indicative of a broader corporate management style prominent in the 1980s and 1990s; times of economic recession and recovery in western societies in which the struggle to maintain (affluent) living standards concentrated the efforts of dominant groups on ensuring that, at worst, their way of life became sustainable and, at best, it delivered profitable outcomes. Such management entailed a shift from Keynesian economics to a neo-classical economic approach whereby governments, unable or unwilling to match increasing social demands with more resources, sought to redirect that demand into areas they considered themselves better equipped to address or areas they found more legitimacy in addressing. The more recent rechannelling of the aspirations of Australian secondary/high school leavers for university study into other more manageable areas is a case in point (see Gale 1999a).

In this economic climate, schooling was called on to be more responsive to these global changes. It was required not only to tighten its fiscal belt but also to graduate (a certain number of students) who could make a productive contribution to society and who held certain corporate values (such as, loyalty to the market). At one level, the student as language user becomes a producer of texts that are useful to students preparing to become future workers (notice the many references by genrists to the language of occupations) and useful to society seeking skilled workers of a particular genre. At another level, students continue to be consumers of texts, using them to acquire certain social goods in a way that resembles their positioning as consumers of economic goods, which in turn contributes to the operation of western economies.

Snakes and ladders

There is another perspective on language use that informs the above critique of traditional, structural and functional perspectives and which seeks to use language in ways that avoid their dominance and oppression of certain social and cultural groups. Similar to Agger's (1992) definition of critical cultural studies,[9] this critical view of language is distinguishable by its political disposition and the dialectical relations or dialogue it establishes not only between a text and its context or, as some describe it, the word and the world, but also between reading and writing or, more broadly, (language) analysis and (language) practice. In short, a critical perspective explicitly addresses ways of 'being in (and with) the world' (Roberts 1998: 112) as this is embodied in language use. Thus, teachers focus on 'teach[ing] students how to learn through the text of mathematics [for example] or through the text of HPE [health and physical education]' (Michelle). What is envisaged is not only 'knowing *about* language' but also 'knowing *through* language' (Lankshear 1997: 44, emphasis in original).

In terms of their politics, critical language theorists are of the view that material and social goods are inequitably distributed within society and that these distributions have more to do with political struggle (see Unger 1987) than with 'natural' explanations of 'the way things are' or 'always have been'. That is, 'critical theory rejects as illusionary the effort to construct a universal normative system insulated from a particular society' (Young 1990: 5). Further, this critical explanation of inequality suggests that many individuals and social groups suffer from oppressive practices (including language practices) as the dominant in society seek to establish and maintain their influence and subsequent rewards. Indeed, such dominance can be achieved with the consent of those dominated, as illustrated above in functionalists' modelling of powerful genres, a form of dominance that Gramsci (1971) describes as 'hegemonic'.

These understandings draw attention to why students from particular social groups who are proficient language users and why students from other groups who are not, do not look very different across traditional, structural and functional accounts of language use. The fortunes of students subjected to these (political) arrangements take on the appearance of 'winners and losers' (MacIntyre 1985) or a language game resembling 'snakes and ladders' in which 'annual "league tables of school achievement" continue to reflect long-standing, and by now thoroughly familiar patterns of institutionalized "success" and "failure"' (Lankshear *et al.* 1997: 4). That is, the same types of students tend to climb up the ladders and the same ones tend to slide down the snakes. Moreover, it seems that in the new work order of contemporary societies there are fewer winners, an outcome regulated by providing fewer ladders and, by comparison, more snakes. Drawing on Harris (1979) and Gee *et al.* (1996), Lankshear *et al.* (1997) confirm this restricted and restrictive vision for language users by arguing that global economies desire a relatively small proportion of knowledge workers with high order language skills. Hence, it is not surprising, they argue, that language use for the vast majority of students should remain at the level of basic competence and technique. The role of schooling, then, is to produce and legitimize this differential skilling of future workers in ways that appear 'tolerably fair and explicable' (Lankshear *et al.* 1997: 5).

It is not the dice nor the players' skill, then, that determine winners and losers in this game, even though both of these myths, 'like most myths, . . . rest on a substratum of fact' (MacIntyre 1985: 97). A more cogent explanation lies in what Pierre Bourdieu refers to as 'cultural capital', of which 'linguistic capital' represents one form. As Bourdieu (1997) explains, and which we discuss in more detail in Chapter 6, cultural capital 'is what makes the games of society – not least, the economic game – something other than simple games of chance offering at every moment the possibility of a miracle' (Bourdieu 1997: 46). Representing the accumulation of knowledge, skills and dispositions, differentially accessed by individuals from various social groups, cultural capital provides a way of explaining how the hegemony of dominant groups is perpetuated. It makes it

> possible to explain the unequal scholastic achievement of children originating from the different social classes by relating academic success, i.e. the specific profits which children from different classes and class fractions can obtain in the academic market, to the distribution of cultural capital between the classes and class fractions.
>
> (Bourdieu 1997: 47)

Because the cultural capital associated with schooling reflects that of the dominant, it is necessarily unevenly distributed across students according to their social groups. In short, the dice are loaded! Despite this, schools continue to treat the cultural capital of dominant groups as if all students had equal access to it. Hence, those students who are positioned as culturally and linguistically bankrupt by this definition come to believe that their failure to succeed in schooling is a result of their lack of giftedness and often adjust their expectations of education, and life generally, downwards. Such analysis is the point from which critical language analysts and teachers develop different pedagogical game plans, ones that expose students to the language and culture of the dominant but also provide students with ways of reading through that dominance and constructing alternative linguistic and cultural forms. Paulo Freire (1972) provides such an example in his work among the poor and illiterate in Latin America. Reacting against a banking concept of (language) education that 'extends only as far as receiving, filing, and storing the deposits' (1972: 46), Freire sought to expose his students to the tools of critique, as well as technique, which would enable them to 'say their *own* words' (emphasis in original) and to '[re]name the world'. Freire's notion was that 'the dead weight of history' bears down on those whose 'voices have been silenced', limiting their possibilities to work together collectively to create a brighter future.

Jennifer O'Brien, a primary/elementary schoolteacher featured by Comber *et al.* (1994), similarly reflects these characteristics of a critical language pedagogy in the questions she encourages her students to ask themselves as they encounter the language around them. For O'Brien, all language is 'fair game for discussion and analysis', not just school texts but also those associated with students' broader social relations, including such things as Mother's Day catalogues, television programmes and commercials, supermarket books and the usual children's literature and reference material found in schools.

O'Brien's teaching attempts to *provoke* her students to adopt a *critical stance* in their analysis of this use of language. This involves reading texts not only to decode the print and its surface level or literal meanings – what Guppy and Hughes (1998) refer to as 'reading the lines' – but also to discern the broader assumptions embedded in the language, to read between and 'beyond the lines'. Readings such as these are accessed through questioning: 'Does the world have to be like this? Is the world [really] like this? How does this text relate to my experience?' (O'Brien, in Comber *et al.* 1994). O'Brien also attempts to *invoke* within her students a *critical praxis*. What is intended is an approach to constructing or writing texts that has a social and cultural agenda in mind, encouraged by questions that ask: 'Can I change it? Can I take a different position on these things? Can I look at the world differently?' (O'Brien, in Comber *et al.* 1994).

We also found evidence of critical approaches to language use in our own research. The comments of two teachers in particular are worth discussing here, although we begin with a third interview extract as a way of illustrating how being critical can be reduced – much like empowerment discussed above – to a point where it seems to have 'too little meaning' (Lankshear *et al.* 1997: 40). Michelle had previously spoken about her concern for the adverse representations of women and her efforts to redress this through her teaching and use of language. In response to our questions of clarification, she reflected on her gender and

> especially being a PE teacher . . . at certain times it annoys me that the criteria for girls is different than it is for boys. But then, of course, I

come back to physiological differences for girls – there is a huge physiological difference, so therefore the criteria must be different. But I am
a big one for gender equity in the way we use words. For example, I
had a little boy in my class the other day – he was only in Grade 8 and
it wasn't even in a HPE class, it was in a social studies class – and he
said something like 'sportsperson'. So I said, 'Well done, James. Good
on you. You actually used the term "sportsperson". You didn't give a
gender at all. You didn't give the thing any gender. You just said
sportsperson. You didn't say man or woman. Good on you. You probably didn't even think about it did you?' And he said, 'Oh, yes, I did
Miss. I thought about it.' And I said, 'Well done. It was good'. So yes, I
do try to encourage terms like that. And probably being female, a
sporting female, it's probably more pronounced. That would be a classic
example, talking about sport and not trying to 'genderize' it, if there is
such a word. But not just sport. 'Policeperson' is another example that
another student has used in my class.

(Michelle)

Michelle's regard for gender equity and its implications for action are more
reminiscent of what Ball (1994) refers to as 'first order effects'. Analysing
schooling policies and their possibility for promoting change, he writes that
'first order effects are changes in practice and structure (which are evident
in particular sites and across the system as a whole), and second order
effects are the impact of these changes on patterns of social access, opportunity and social justice' (Ball 1994: 25–6). The effects of Michelle's narrow
focus on her students' language use are of this first order. In themselves, the
words 'sportsperson' and 'policeperson' represent superficial dealings with
critical matters that may result in changes to the way language is practised
by students and how their interactions are literally structured, but this does
little to address the underlying dominance of social relations by particular
groups. Certainly, there is an appeal to an 'outside' reference point – the
female sporting body – and a (vague) appreciation for its subservience, but
there is little recognition of how this and the rules that govern it are socially
and culturally constructed. In the end, there is little qualitative change.

It is to more 'second order effects' of critical language use that we now
turn, through brief analyses of the (language) pedagogies of two Australian
teachers in our research, although we do not want necessarily to represent
their teaching practices as ideal. Like all teachers, their pedagogies are not
beyond critique but they provide evidence of this critical way of thinking in
action and it is these critical practices and their consequences for students
that we want to focus on here. The first of these teachers (T2) works with
primary/elementary school students and begins by discussing the analytical
thinking he seeks to develop in these students to inform their reading and
construction of social studies texts:

The analysis level usually involves some sort of comparison, so if the
student is, let's say, comparing Germany to Australia, they'll select a lot

of features to compare them on population, resources and all that sort
of thing. I can remember a student recently presenting [a project on]
how long Australia's been settled. And, of course, she said Germany
was settled eight thousand years ago or something and Australia [had
been settled] since 1788. And I made a point of it by saying, 'Why did
you represent Australia's settlement in this way? We know that
Aboriginal people were here before then, so that's a deliberate decision
you've made to choose that as the date of Australia's settlement'. I did
not accept from her that that could just be something unconsidered.
'You've made a deliberate decision there. Why have you decided that?'
I don't just say, 'Oh, but Aboriginal people were here' . . . she knows
that . . . and I'm not going to treat her as if she didn't know that and
say, 'Oh, look you've got to think about *x, y,* or *z*', you know. I would
just expect that she would have thought about that and, therefore, she
had made a decision and so I feel entitled to ask what was her reason
for it . . . I think that when you reach for those levels of understanding,
when you're taking these decisions as a given with the class, then
through that I think I show them the importance of examining their
own assumptions . . . I think that's a significant shift, to put the responsibility on them to think through their taken-for-granted assumptions.

(T2)

There has been considerable dispute within Australia over the representation of British claims to sovereignty as matters of Australian 'settlement' or
'invasion', depending on whether one considers Australia in 1788 to have
been *terra nullus* (no one's land) or whether the Aboriginal inhabitants at
the time were its custodians and, therefore, have 'native title' rights. Highlighting his student's representation of the year of Australia's settlement, the
teacher also draws attention to this wider debate with which the student is
familiar. This is not a (superficially) semantic argument about using one word
in place of another, as if they are synonymous or have equal validity. Nor is
it about using words in ways that simply avoid offending non-dominant
groups by not naming existing social relations, a criticism we levelled at
Michelle's celebration of gender-neutral terms. Here the teacher encourages
his student to venture 'behind the lines' of settlement and invasion, to make
text–context connections between these words and various ways of understanding the world, and to consider their likely effects for various individuals
and groups. Moreover, the teacher invites the student to speak from this
world view, to explain the rationale that informed her selection of 'settlement' as an appropriate term.

The underlying propositions for critical language use are these. First, to be
informed by words, to know what they mean in a critical sense, readers
must also read and know the world or at least know that it is about the
world that words speak. Similarly, to produce words, to write and act critically, involves an understanding of the world view that produces them or
the ideas 'out there' that are grasped by writers, even if the owners of these

ideas are not completely known to writers. Second, knowing these things and acting in these ways requires a degree of self-consciousness that leads to a questioning disposition directed at finding out about what is not known. The teacher above 'did not accept from [his student] that that [choice of words] could just be something unconsidered' and so felt 'entitled to ask what was her reason for [choosing] it'. In other words, critical language users do not accept that only explicit assumptions should be subjected to analysis (see Young 1990: 148–51). Readers are not blamed for their semi-consciousness but have a responsibility to consider more than what is in print; indeed, without doing so, 'reading cannot become an act of *knowing*' (Roberts 1998: 111, emphasis in original).

This leads to a third proposition concerning the political nature of these arrangements, that things hidden often serve dominant interests and that these are often uncovered by analysing language from the standpoint of the non-dominant. It is in relation to this alternative standpoint that the following secondary/high schoolteacher (T10) comments. The challenge, as he sees it, is not just to read texts in this way but to use the knowledge gained from such reading to inform future writing and action. Of course, there are dangers – particularly for students from non-dominant groups – in pursuing such an approach. For example:

> *Aren't the more formal aspects of language a consideration if you are thinking along these lines, if you are hoping that your students will go on to university and succeed in those contexts? Aren't they contexts in which those kinds of things are highly regarded?*

> Yes, but I think that whole notion needs to be challenged as well. I mean, I challenged this several years ago. We had two young girls who came down from [a remote] Island [in the Torres Strait, north of Australia] and, as I said before, they were people with English as their fourth language. When it came time for them to do assignments at university [as part of a bridging course], they had to present a particular [written] piece, and my suggestion was 'write it in your first language and present it. I mean, the subject is "Introduction to Communication". If the lecturer can't come to your level to communicate, then there is something wrong with the philosophy that they are espousing'.

> (T10)

What this teacher demonstrates so well are the clear and inescapable connections between text and context, matters which we take up more fully in Chapter 4. What he identifies so clearly is the connection between how 'the philosophy' or the ideas that dominate certain contexts, in this case universities and schooling more generally, demand that language users produce certain types of texts. Writing a very different text, one that is potentially inaccessible to the guardians of dominant education systems, confronts this dominance by claiming a legitimacy for the construction of different texts and, ultimately, different political arrangements for language users. In this case, what is acceptable and what is not acceptable language use is challenged in a way that steps outside of the realm of the technical into that of the critical. What makes this all the more poignant is that it is played out within the particular arena of an academic subject concerned with communication; itself implicated in broader relations of language and power. In brief, the above students' language challenges both what communication is and who holds legitimate knowledge with respect to it; in this case, repositioning teacher and student in ways that might cause us to ask, who is giving whom an introduction to communication?

Conclusion

Freebody and Luke (1990: 7) suggest four related roles for language users: 'code breaker (how do I crack this?), text participant (what does this mean?), text user (what do I do with this, here and now?), and text analyst (what does all this do to me?)'. In one sense, these more or less reflect the respective emphases in the above four perspectives on language use. In another sense, and in combination, they are also consistent with a critical view of language use. Critical language users, then, do not seek to do away with matters of technique. These are important but they should not be all encompassing, dominating the use of language to the exclusion of all other interests. Neither should language techniques be teachers' and students' only priority. Both of these approaches separate technique from critique; dangerous games as we have illustrated. Rather, critique and technique are dialectically related within a critical approach to language.

What are envisaged are powerful language users. In Lankshear's characterization:

> The powerfully literate reader can contest texts, resisting meanings and positions these would otherwise 'impose' ... As a writer of texts the powerfully literate person develops 'powerful competencies' with a range of genres and techniques which may be employed in pursuit of personal, ethical and political purposes.
>
> (Lankshear *et al.* 1997: 78)

Chapter 4 takes up these power–knowledge relations, introducing and relating concepts of text, discourse and ideology; a metalanguage or language to talk about language that includes 'a set of meta-words, meta-values [and] meta-beliefs' (Gee 1990: 153).

Questions for discussion/research

- What view of language informs contemporary schooling?
- How can teachers ensure that their (language) pedagogies are inflected with critique?

- What might form the grounds for critique of a critical view of language?
- Does the structure of language inherently contain ideas of domination?

Suggested readings

Comber, B., Nixon, H., Badger, L. and Hill, S. (1994) *Literacy, Diversity and Schooling.* Adelaide, SA: University of South Australia, Module 3 (video).

Lankshear, C., with Gee, J., Knobel, M. and Searle, C. (1997) *Changing Literacies.* Buckingham: Open University Press, Chapter 2.

Popkewitz, T. and Brennan, M. (eds) (1998) *Foucault's Challenge: Discourse, Knowledge and Power in Education.* New York: Teachers College Press, Chapter 7.

Roberts, P. (1997) The consequences and value of literacy: a critical reappraisal, *Journal of Educational Thought,* 31(1): 45–67.

four

Language strategies: how to play the game

Introduction

It is one thing to know the rules of the game, whose rules they are and, by implication, whose game. It is another to know how to play the game, that is, what strategies to adopt: first, what to do when the rules give no clear directions to players, and second, how to get the most out of the game by stretching the rules to their limits.[1] These are matters that we described in Chapter 3 as 'gaps' in our account of language use, although hints of game plans that go beyond the rules were evident, particularly in our outline of critical language perspectives. What we intend in this chapter, then, is to continue our discussion of language but shift from a focus on *literacy* (using language in accordance with the rules) to matters of *strategy* (how language is used to advantage its users) or what Lyotard (1984: 10) describes as 'a "move" in a game'. This is not to suggest an absolute distinction between these two interests; language rules can be used strategically, for example, and critical conceptions of literacy often include knowledge of the strategies we discuss below. Focusing explicitly on language strategies, however, allows us to explore more fully the hidden aspects of language use implicit in the ways that advantages (and disadvantages) are secured and maintained through language practices.

This is what Lankshear *et al.* (1997: 72, emphasis in original) refer to when they comment that 'knowing *about* [language] . . . is more than merely knowing *how*' to use it. The difference is something akin to being a seasoned player and a novice; often novices are yet to acquire a feel for the game whereas seasoned players are able to mobilize their *know-how* to 'us[e] the "right" language in the "right" ways' (Lankshear *et al.* 1997: 67). Carl, a post-secondary technical college teacher in our research, describes the differences between 'knowing how' and 'knowing about' in this way:

I did a year of calculus at university. I didn't have a clue what I was doing, but I passed. I got a Credit for it at the end of the year and still walked out of there not understanding much about it, but I learned the rules; I knew the process, I knew what the words meant. I didn't

know why. I didn't know what I was going to do with it, but I knew
the rules.

(Carl)

Uncovering the 'meta-knowledge' (Lankshear *et al.* 1997: 72) informing these
rules requires the use of a 'second language' or a language to talk about
language, often recognizable by its use of the term *discourse*. Just as literacy
is discussed across different fields of study, many of the social sciences and
the arts now utilize this term, including those associated with social psychology and linguistics, and literary and cultural theories. In this chapter we
avoid reviewing the ways in which discourse is differently understood within
these fields. Rather, our interests lie within critical cultural studies, although
insights from other areas are also addressed at various points.

Two further matters need to be made clear in relation to our position and
which draw attention to our study of things cultural and critical. First, while
Foucault's understandings of discourse are frequently cited within cultural
studies, there are other cultural theorists who also have contributed significantly to how the term is variously understood (Macdonnell 1986). Moreover,
Foucault does not utilize discourse in ways that suggest only one meaning,
as he himself acknowledges (see Foucault 1972: 80). Thus, pinning down
what discourse means is difficult work and our efforts to do so in this chapter
should be read as one attempt among many, even though it has connections
with the work of other (critical) cultural theorists (see, for example, Thompson
1984; Fairclough 1992b) and even though it could be regarded as offering a
plausible and useful account of the strategic manoeuvres of language users.

Second, one of the things that makes our account critical is its attempt to
reinsert issues of ideology back into the discussion.[2] Discursive analyses first
appeared in reaction to what was perceived as the shortcomings of ideological analyses, at a time when there was some discontent with the latter's
ability to suggest ways of acting against and questioning the prevailing conservative politics (Mills 1997: 29–32). Our purposes in conjoining discourse
and ideology are related to the critical account of language use we began in
Chapter 3 and our desire for 'a politically inflected form of analysis' (Mills
1997: 158), which is not always ascribed to Foucault's work even though it
was evident in his activism. With similar intentions, others have chosen to
reinterpret Marx's writings on ideology to produce a form of ideological
analysis that accounts for 'the actualities of people's social relations' (D. Smith
1990: 37). Still others regard the discursive turn as 'trendy rhetoric that
when unpacked often says some pretty commonsensical things that reflexive
educators have known and done for years' (Apple 1996: x–xi).

The relationships we envisage among ideology, discourse and text, and
which we outline in this chapter, are represented in Figure 1.[3] As illustrated,
there is no one simple directional flow although, clearly, discourse is centrally
positioned in relation to ideology and text. Focusing on this position, the
diagram suggests that discourses produce texts as well as interpret them and
that they appeal to ideologies while also being informed by them. More

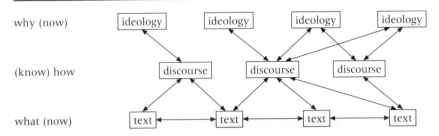

Figure 1   Language as text, discourse and ideology

broadly, one discourse does not necessarily produce and/or interpret text to the exclusion of all others and neither are discourses captive to particular ideologies. The devolution of control over schooling, for example, is not indebted to one ideological view but, as Rizvi (1994) has argued, has been variously influenced by the strictures of social democracy, market individualism and corporate managerialism.

While 'the point is not to grant autonomy to these moments' (Frow 1991: 139) of ideology, discourse and text, their analytic separation provides a way of questioning language and other social practices on a number of levels, namely: *What* is the character of texts? *How* are they selected and organized? *Why* are they important?[4] Three similar questions, more cognizant of 'horizontal' interactions (as depicted in the diagram), are also possible: *Why now*, what makes these issues important at this time? *Know-how*, in what ways are these issues mobilized? *What now*, what can we expect from these arrangements?[5] These two sets of questions represent bottom-up and top-down approaches to analysis, in keeping with the respective trajectories of post/modernity and post/modernism (see Giddens 1990: 45–53; D. Harvey 1990); one beginning from a concern with local *affects* and the other from a concern with global *effects*.[6] Others (see, for example, Featherstone 1989; Frow 1991) also write about post/modernization as a process that produces and/or interprets things as post/modern. In the model, we represent these processes as the work of discourse. It might also be helpful to understand relations between ideology, discourse and text in terms of Saussurean semiotics (Saussure 1983) – even though its elaborations have tended to serve structuralist understandings – in which signifier (read 'text') and signified (read 'ideology') are related through processes of signification (read 'discourse').

Guiding questions

These are the relationships we seek to explain in this chapter, Figure 1 representing our intended end point. What follows is an attempt to unpack this particular alignment of ideology, discourse and text, in order to make explicit the understandings that inform its construction. We have framed such deconstruction and reconstruction in terms of three broad questions:

- What are text, discourse and ideology?
- How are they related?
- How do they reveal matters of strategy?

As implied, our account positions discourse in relation to ideology and text and as the avenue through which the social world is engaged, both analytically and productively. It remains 'tied to knowledge on the one hand . . . and practice on the other' (Bowe *et al.* 1992: 13). Hence, while we begin with explanations of text (the affective or sensual domain) and follow this with an account of ideology (the effective or conceptual domain), these are never completely separate discussions from matters of discourse, even though we assign it a separate section below. It is to the first of these three domains that we now turn and interrogate in relation to matters of strategy.

Making sense of text

There are at least four senses in which a text can be defined: first, as discernible through the senses; second, as having a sense or meaning that can be attributed to it; third, as being separately identifiable or self-contained in one sense; and, in another, as reliant on other texts (and discourses) to ascribe sense to it. In many respects it is difficult to sustain these separations for too long as they constitute different aspects of the one social reality. It is a bit like comparing the different facets of a diamond and recognizing its various shades of colour; each is evident momentarily but the changing light means that its colours are difficult to isolate. Explanations of text are like this, descriptive of some parts at one point and then of others. Reading text, then, involves a dialectical interaction between sensing and making sense of text. As Figure 1 illustrates, it is both a 'horizontal' (text-to-text) and 'vertical' (text-discourse-ideology) exercise. Our focus in this section on texts may appear to suggest a purely horizontal account but a closer reading should reveal that these textual understandings also require an understanding of their vertical relations.

The first thing to notice about our definition of text is that it implies a much larger range of texts than simply the wording (from the Latin *textus*) represented by speech or print. The second thing to notice is that texts are where meanings reside. These two observations draw attention to the *extent* and *content* of texts, which come together when we appreciate that texts are identifiable through the senses: in what people see, hear, feel, smell and taste. Consider, for example, the sights, smells and tastes associated with cafés. The texts that inhabit these sites – the smells and tastes of coffee, for example – evoke distinctive meanings, perhaps similar to those sensed elsewhere but collectively recognizable nonetheless in a generic sense. They help us to recognize a café when we happen across one, even if we have never been to that particular café before.

Similarly, we know what is meant when we hear the national anthem played at school, at the football, or at the Olympics. Yet national anthems can mean different things to different people and different things according to the contexts in which they are heard. We use the term 'connotation' to indicate that a particular text (such as a national anthem) can have more than one meaning in a particular context or across contexts and 'denotation' to suggest that in a given context there is only one plausible or meaningful interpretation of a text, or that from a number of connotations a particular meaning is more likely or 'correct'. The humour of much parody and satire, for example, relies on connotations and denotations; that is, texts can appear amusing because they carry a double meaning or because they appear out of place. Further, it is the perceived legitimacy of some meanings – that they denote certain meanings and not others – that encourages some to believe in the ultimate authority of dictionary definitions, for example; that the words found therein have no other legitimate meanings than those it provides. However, such reasoning fails to recognize the socially constructed nature of words and their meanings, and their variations in different contexts.

Understanding national anthems (and other sensory material, including words) as texts with various meanings is also an important step in acquiring the second language we mentioned above. It necessarily requires narrow definitions of texts to be 'extended beyond literary texts to the sphere of social action, by virtue of certain features which are shared by action and texts' (Thompson 1984: 174), namely, their ability to convey meaning and for that meaning to be divorced from its author's intentions.[7] A teacher can call out a student's name, for example, and mean one thing by it but this meaning does not necessarily travel with this speech-act and ensure that it is read only in the way intended. In fact, teachers can mean several things by such practices. So, speech can be defined as text, because it conjures up recognizable meanings, but 'like the speech-act, the action-event (if we may coin this analogical expression) develops a similar dialectic between its temporal status as an appearing and disappearing event, and its logical status of having such-and-such identifiable meaning or "sense-content"' (Ricoeur 1981: 205).

Again, text is not confined to what is in print and nor is print the only text discerned by what we see. Teachers' actions can speak just as loudly as their words. What does it mean, for example, when teachers stand at the front of the classroom? How do we know which is the front (and which is the back)? Answers to this second question rely on a familiarity with classrooms, including knowledge of the positioning of such things as blackboards, whiteboards, teachers' desks, raised platforms, large carpet squares, televisions, overhead screens, the direction in which students' chairs and desks face, and so on. These, too, are texts that convey meanings. Teachers new to this classroom, for example, but generally familiar with traditional classrooms would have little trouble in reading its texts and knowing where to stand, if the front of the classroom was a position they wanted to occupy and if the arrangement of classroom texts supported this traditional positioning.[8]

All of these texts are signs that convey meanings. Readers familiar with Saussurean semiotics, however, may have noticed our preference for using the term 'text' rather than 'sign' and our antipathy for definitions that regard text as a collection of signs. While we have little difficulty in conceiving of texts *as* signs, the boundaries constructed by semiotics around signs that supposedly mark them out as different from texts – on the pretence that they are smaller – can appear arbitrary. In our view, these boundaries are better managed by regarding sign and text as synonymous and viewing 'text' in a similar fashion to how we understand the linguistic dimensions of the word 'fish', as having meanings that are both singular and plural. As noted above, text embodies both content and extent; it can refer to one meaningful element or to a collection of meaningful elements. Comparisons between the words text and fish are also useful in understanding the differences between text (used in a plural sense) and texts (also plural). This dual way of indicating plurality is similar to how marine biologists use 'fish' to refer to a collection of one species and 'fishes' to refer to a collection of several species. The analogy also extends to comparisons between schools of fish and con-texts, issues which we address shortly.

Intertextuality: comparing texts

Already in our explanations we have relied on comparisons among texts or what is often referred to as *intertextuality*, a term first coined by Kristeva (1986) in her account of Mikhail Bakhtin's work. Intertextuality involves the idea that the meaning or character of a text – its textuality or 'texture' (Halliday and Hasan 1976) – is negotiated through a dialectical process of comparing a text with its surrounding texts. In short, texts do not stand alone; they cannot be read in isolation but require comparison with other texts in order to determine their meanings. This is how we interpret Foucault's (1972: 98) comments that 'there can be no statement that in one way or another does not reactualize others'. It is discourse that is mobilized in this comparative work but for the moment we will concentrate more overtly on the various comparisons that they produce, specifically, antonyms, synonyms and metonyms.[9] It is important to recognize that the strategic purpose of these comparisons is to reduce the possible meanings attributable to a text – to redefine a text's connotations as denotations – and to insert more certainty for writers and readers into how texts are (to be) interpreted.

One common comparison occurs between two texts or collections of texts in ways that suggest they have opposite meanings. These *binaries* or dichotomies are often represented as having a natural validity; black and white, east and west, girl and boy, rich and poor, are all related in this way, each meaningful because of our understanding of the other. Schooling, for example, is often separated into private and public institutions.[10] This strategy of 'othering' includes implicit judgements of texts that render them good or bad, clever or dumb, and so on. It is also important to recognize that binaries are often imposed rather than existing naturally. A boy, for example, is not necessarily everything that a girl is not, biologically or otherwise, even though this is what is suggested when they are represented in binary relations. Consider also the relations between teacher and student. Are teachers never students and students never teachers? Are there never moments when one exhibits qualities of both?

Binaries can also be present even when a text's opposite is not explicitly mentioned. Students who are described as disabled provide a good example of such comparisons. Those who are not disabled are rarely described as 'able' as a matter of course, yet we know them to be so or at least that is how they are portrayed in the dichotomy signalled by the prefix 'dis'. In short, the strategic intent of binaries is to represent texts in either/or relations and to suggest that one is better and more desirable than the other. Indeed, undesirable aspects of one half of the binary serve to accentuate the desirable aspects of the other half.

We found several examples of this strategy in our research. Consider, for example, the following primary/elementary school teacher's (T8) explanation of how she and her colleague represent the different groups of students in their combined class:

> At the moment we have all the good kids up this end, not good kids but the ones who don't have difficulties, and down the other end we have the ones who have difficulties: the ones who have fallen into the [learning difficulties] net, the ones who are going down to [the] learning support [centre for extra help], all of the intellectually disabled kids, are all down that end . . . If they were up here and mixed around, they wouldn't be listening to you because you'd be catering for the majority of the kids . . . No, it is not inclusion, but we're living in the real world and that's the difference . . . It is not like these kids are getting something better than those kids. Those kids are getting more than they'd be getting if they were mixed in with the others.
>
> (T8)

What is clear here is the way in which 'these kids' and 'those kids' are related in binary terms and how this in turn impacts on the schooling each receives. Binaries that serve to perpetuate social injustices have been called into question in recent years but unless they are addressed beyond superficial levels (see our critique of Michelle's comments in Chapter 3), they will continue to be used to direct benefits to some and not others. As Howe (1996: 57) notes, 'mere inclusion, . . . physically including children with disabilities in regular classrooms but otherwise excluding them from meaningful participation, can do little to promote equality of educational opportunity'.

While the strategy of constructing binaries is to position two texts in opposition (as antonyms), thereby rendering one more desirable than another, another form of comparison is to suggest that two (or more) texts exhibit similarities (that they are synonymous). The strategy attributes positive or negative value to texts in two ways: first, by focusing attention on certain characteristics that the texts share, thereby excluding other characteristics, and second, by transferring characteristics of one text to another text under comparison, even though these might not initially form the basis of the analogy. So, when John Kimble, in the movie *Kindergarten Cop* (discussed in Chapter 6), is advised by one of his colleagues that 'kindergarten is like the ocean. You don't want to turn your back on it', the analogy draws our attention to characteristics common to both texts: their underestimated strength, their unpredictability, and so on. But the analogy also transfers other characteristics to kindergartens – for example, that kindergarten students, like the ocean, cannot be tamed – even though these associations might not be justifiable.

Technically, the ocean–kindergarten comparison is a *simile*, suggesting that one text is *like* another. Teachers often make such comparisons between siblings, for example, when observing 'you're just like your brother/sister', or between students from similar social groupings, when claiming 'you're just like all the others'. At other times, comparisons take the form of *metaphors* that suggest one text is *the same as* another. It is metaphor that Carl uses when talking about how he perceives his work as a teacher: 'I guess I see myself a couple of rungs up on the ladder, not far off the bottom where I can still reach down and help people behind me get up past me' (Carl). An important feature of similes and metaphors is that they utilize imagery as the vehicle to transfer meanings between texts. Used strategically, analogies such as these enable 'writers' to gain greater control over the meanings ascribed to their texts by 'readers', ensuring that their texts are, as Barthes (1972) suggests, more 'writerly' or less open to alternative interpretations.

A third form of textual comparison represents one text as part of another (whole) text. Known as metonymy, the nature of the comparison is such that the part is read as if it is the whole or vice versa. That is, one takes on the character of the other, which leads to the conflation or fusion of texts. For example, school principals or head teachers might describe a telephone call as coming from 'the Department', the 'Board of Education' or 'the Local Education Authority' rather than name the individual on the telephone, such as the Director. We might similarly remark that 'Michael Jordan is basketball' or even *Toys 'R' Us*, as one store that trades exclusively in children's toys is known.

When the *whole* takes on the character of the *part*, as in these examples, the effect can be to add authority or greater legitimacy to texts by masking their partiality. Bourdieu (1997) writes similarly about delegates who embody the concentrated social capital of their group (issues discussed in more detail in Chapter 6). Metonyms can also involve *parts* taking on the character of the *whole*. Such comparisons can be disempowering, particularly when applied by others, as when a Black student is asked to speak on behalf of all Black students or a girl is asked to speak for all girls. But it is also the basis of what Lummis describes as one of the political virtues of democracy: the 'ability [of a part] to stand for the whole' (Lummis 1996: 37), issues that we introduced in Chapter 2 and revisit in Chapter 9. As a strategy, metonyms are typically evident in what have become known as grand narratives: stories about the world that interpret particular texts as generally representative.

In determining its meaning, any given text can be compared with any other text. However, given that the work of comparing texts is directed and informed by discourse and that different discourses compare texts differently, texts tend to be compared with some texts and not others and in certain ways, as outlined above. We refer to the products of these typical textual comparisons as stereotypes: standardized combinations of texts and standardized methods for their comparison, which provide shorthand ways of discerning a text's meaning. 'Writers' and 'readers' generally find stereotypes useful in that they enable meanings to be conveyed quickly and without prolonged and repeated comparisons. Yet the standardized character of stereotypes means that if a writer uses a text to mean something other than what is considered to be the standard and/or if a reader is not familiar with the standard or has other standards, meanings can be distorted. By way of illustration, many people in western societies now mobilize discourses concerning gender that render obsolete previous stereotypes concerning the employment women should undertake; the 'nurturing' occupations (such as teaching), for example, if they engage in paid employment at all. To take another example, in the past, teachers (who are often women) have been typecast as glorified childminders (particularly those who teach younger students) who enjoy a short working day and long holiday periods.

Context: connecting texts

Implicit in this discussion of intertextuality and the comparison of texts is the issue of text connections or *contexts*; a collective noun with similarities to that of 'schools of fish' considered above. Con-texts, as the prefix implies, are 'forms of' texts or, to draw on its Latin origins *(contextus)*, are texts that are 'woven together' to form 'connections'. It is these connections between texts that allow us to recognize them as contexts. Consider the example we used above that connected such texts as blackboards, whiteboards, chairs, desks, raised platforms, large carpet squares, televisions, overhead screens, and so on. Woven together, these texts (along with others) constitute one form of the context often referred to as a classroom. Classrooms and schools provide examples of what Halliday and Hasan (1985: 46) refer to as 'contexts of situation', the immediate texts that give meaning to a text. But to fully understand classrooms and schools we also need to be cognizant of 'contexts of culture' or broader and backgrounded texts that ascribe meanings to particular texts. An important issue here is that contexts are not just collections of texts but that the collection itself has a particular character. Hence, classrooms and schools in one situational context might be quite different from another, even though they are broadly similar in their intentions.

The characteristics of contexts are subject to the same comparative strategies outlined above, given that they are forms of texts. However, it is also important to recognize the collective qualities of contexts. In brief, contexts are constituted by how their texts are selected (to form *paradigms* or sets) and how they are ordered (their *syntagms* or associations). Again, it is discourse that does the work of selecting texts and ordering them, with standardized selections and orderings referred to as genres (see Chapter 3 and below). The point here is that contexts and social institutions (such as schools, families, and so forth) – contexts with familiar and recognizable purposes and text collections – are regulated by particular grammars.

The names given to texts – for example, whether copying is associated with cheating or with learning and named modelling – also play an important part in the formation of contexts with implications for how texts are ordered and selected. This is well illustrated in our discussions concerning Cindy in Chapter 2. There we observed that Cindy's Down's syndrome was characterized by her school as a disability and that her identification or naming as a 'Level Six' had considerable influence over her selection by teachers into their classrooms. As noted above, issues of students' inclusion and exclusion are not simply confined to physical arrangements in schools. Yet, the desire of Cindy's mother for teachers at the school to select her daughter for who she is – that is, Cindy – is not a denial of where Cindy stood in the school's ordering of student abilities. Cindy herself was aware of the relations and processes of schooling that positioned her within her classroom but she still felt as if she belonged because of her personal attributes (see Chapter 9).

A critical conception of ideology

Much of the discussion so far has implicitly made reference to ideologies: collections of ideas, beliefs and values concerning the physical and social world, organized (selected and ordered) according to a particular logic. Thompson (1984) suggests that there are two dominant connotations for ideology. One tends to be negative and draws on its initial uses: first, as a term of abuse directed at ideologues who, following the French Revolution, continued to advocate revolutionary doctrines that were seen (by Napoleon) as detrimental to the welfare of France, and second, as the subject of critique by Marx and Engels (1976) in relation to a German idealism, seen by them to have no connection with the material conditions of social life. They characterized this aspect of ideology as 'false consciousness'. While this is not the same thing as believing that individuals are duped into holding particular beliefs and values, many Marxists or neo-Marxists have referred to ideology in this sense.

Gramsci (1971) similarly wrote about cultural hegemony, meaning the process by which dominant ideology, or the ideas of the ruling class, come to control intellectual life. In hegemonic relations there is general acceptance of dominant ideology and consensus on what this means for social life, including cultural leadership by the powerful and resignation to subservient positions by others who effectively participate in their own oppression. Like Marx and Engels, Gramsci saw the clash between dominant ideas and competing definitions and meanings of social life as a form of class struggle.

A second meaning for ideology tends to be neutral or 'domesticated' (Thompson 1984: 1). In this sense, ideology is 'purely a descriptive term: one speaks of "systems of thought", of "systems of belief", of "symbolic practices" which pertain to social action [read "text"] or political projects [read "discourse"] . . . No attempt is made . . . to distinguish between the kinds of action or projects which ideology animates' (Thompson 1984: 4). Ideologies simply express an individual's or group's account of why things are the way they are. This is similar to how many liberals interpret Kuhn's (1970) account of different scientific theories or research paradigms: as various and distinct collections of ideas about science and how the physical and social world can be known. But this is quite a different conception of the relations between ideology and science envisaged by Marx and Engels.

While we acknowledge that there are multiple ideologies and that the critique of ideology is itself engaged from ideological positions, we want to retain a 'critical conception of ideology' (Thompson 1984). That is, we reject the concept of (separations between) 'false' and 'true' consciousness as representative respectively of ideology and (objective) critique, and argue that the important issue is that ideology ultimately springs from social relations, conditioned by one's role in the productive process. Like Thompson (1984: 130–1), we think that 'to study ideology is to study the ways in which meaning (signification) serves to sustain relations of domination' in class societies. Resistance to domination is likewise part of this research agenda. Processes of signification involve discourse in strategies of domination, like metonymy, which 'cause the signifier to take the place of the signified' (Bourdieu 1997: 53), translating text into symbols of ideology and rendering them 'common sense'.

In Thompson's (1984) terms, and elaborating on the vertical (text-discourse-ideology) relations in Figure 1, 'ideology operates, not so much as a coherent system of statements imposed on a population from above, but rather through a complex series of mechanisms whereby meaning is mobilized, in the discursive practices of everyday life, for the maintenance of relations of domination' (Thompson 1984: 63). The ways in which ideological domination is attempted and achieved is through discourse but the intention to dominate is informed by ideology. As systems of domination and not simply belief, ideologies provide parameters or 'orders of discourse' (Fairclough 1992b) for particular strategic intentions; namely, those of legitimation, dissimulation and reification (Thompson 1984). Moreover, their practice is often interrelated, 'such that reification legitimates and legitimation dissimulates' (Thompson 1984: 131).

Interrelationships of this kind were evident in our research, particularly in our conversations with teachers on the nature of and rationale for schooling. On one occasion, for example, Michelle commented:

I think it's just a whole process of learning, not just academically, but socially and spiritually and physically learning.

Wouldn't students learn those things anyway? Do they really need a school to learn those things?

Yes, of course they need school for that.

Schools keep you in a job and they keep me in a job, but can't students learn without them?

They can learn certain things without schools, certainly. But there are things which some students, especially somebody who has a very bad home life, just can't learn without school: how to behave properly, how to sit properly in a class, how to concentrate for two minutes, how to play sport, or how to ask nicely at the school shop.

(Michelle)

That our questioning of the legitimacy of schooling as an appropriate mechanism for socializing students into society should spark such a rebuke from Michelle, demonstrates the extent to which such issues have been dissimulated and reified in her thinking. There is little recognition, for example, that these socialization processes may be detrimental to some students and advantageous to others or even that such arrangements require legitimation. Indeed, Michelle's account represents a good example of the 'tricks' of ideology (D. Smith 1990: 43) that separate the empirical conditions of students' lives, whose voices have legitimacy in their description, and how they are described. There is also much that these comments say about the purposes of schooling – issues that we address in Chapter 5 – but our point here is to illustrate that strategies of legitimation, dissimulation and reification, which contribute to the parameters of ideological domination, are not isolated from each other, even though at times, for analytical purposes, we might want to treat them as such.

Discursive practices

Thompson's (1984) comments on how ideology operates also point to the centrality of discursive practices. Derived from Latin (*discursus*) and French (*discours*) origins, discourse means to converse, particularly in the context of a speech, although such conversations need not simply be spoken. The intent is that of an argument, a to-ing and fro-ing (as in the Latin *discurrere*) of ideas, beliefs and values, even when opposing arguments appear absent or silent and, hence, the argument itself appears less than argumentative. At one level, such definition means that discourse is wide ranging and not restricted to obvious influences of ideology on text. Foucault (1972) expresses this similarly, with respect to the use of discourse in his own work:

> Instead of gradually reducing the rather fluctuating meaning of the word 'discourse', I believe I have in fact added to its meanings: treating it sometimes as the general domain of all statements, sometimes as an individualizable group of statements, and sometimes as a regulated practice that accounts for a number of statements.
>
> (Foucault 1972: 80)

Yet, in all of these usages, discourse is concerned with *how* or *the ways in which* meanings are portrayed through language. That is, with some modification to Halliday and Hasan's (1985: 46) theatrical analogy, discourse has more to do with relations among 'the players' (the tenor of the text) than with 'the play' (the field in which the text is located) or 'the parts' (the mode through which meanings are conveyed), even though a text's field and mode are influenced by discourse. Describing all discourses that occur in classrooms and schools as 'educational', for example, often says more about the field of a discourse than the discourse itself. Similarly, expressions such as 'conversational discourse' seem redundant, given that they describe discourse in general, or at best say more about the avenue through which meanings are conveyed.

These relational matters (among tenor, field and mode) allude to two central features of discourse, neatly encapsulated in Ball's (1994: 21) observation that discourse determines not only 'what can be said, and thought, but also . . . who can speak, when, where and with what authority'. The first of these observations draws attention to the place of discourse in the vertical relations between ideology and text, to utilize the imagery in Figure 1. Specifically, discourse is the domain within which textual meanings are interpreted and produced. Hence, as the examples above illustrate, the discourses of classrooms tend to interpret texts in particular ways and to produce particular kinds of texts. In this process of signification, discourse acts like a double-hinged door; it both reads the signifier as the signified (that is, it interprets or decodes texts from a particular ideological perspective) and it writes the signified as the signifier (that is, it produces or encodes texts with a particular ideological perspective). Similarly, we are *affected* by discourse as 'objects of which they speak' (Foucault 1972: 49) and we *effect* or execute discourse to speak our own subjects.

Second, as implied by this to-ing and fro-ing, discourse is a dialogue characterized by struggle, experienced both horizontally (discourse-to-discourse) as well as vertically (text-discourse-ideology), as Figure 1 represents it. In other words, 'discourse is not simply that which translates struggles or systems of domination, but is the thing for which and by which there is struggle' (Foucault 1981: 52–3). Discourse is the domain in which struggles between dominant and competing ideologies are waged. To make this point more clearly and forcefully:

> Discourses are not once and for all subservient to power or raised up against it, any more than silences are. We must make allowances for the complex and unstable process whereby discourse can be both an

instrument and an effect of power, but also a hindrance, a stumbling block, a point of resistance and a starting point for an opposing strategy.
(Foucault 1978: 100–1)

Evidence of the first of these two aspects of discourse can be (re)read in the discussions above, particularly in the section where we attempt to make sense of text. This is hardly surprising, given that 'one never really talks about features of a text without some reference to text production and/or interpretation' (Fairclough 1992b: 73). Yet, evidence of discursive struggle is often less readily apparent. This, too, is the work of discourse: to 'form the objects of which they speak . . . and in the practice of doing so [endeavour to] conceal their own invention' (Foucault 1972: 49). Genres – standardized forms of discourse – are the quintessential example of such concealment, interpreting and producing texts with particular meanings as if there is general agreement over these meanings. In this sense, genres are related to discourse as stereotypes are to text.

In later chapters (particularly Chapters 7 and 8) we elaborate on these discursive struggles over the meanings assigned to texts. Here we want to dwell for a moment on discourses as instruments of power, on how they are used strategically to establish and maintain powerful relations (particularly in classroom contexts), as a way of illustrating some of the language strategies we have highlighted in this chapter. To demonstrate these technical aspects of discourse, we draw on the work of Gore (1998a, 1998b) – informed by Foucault's analysis of relations in prisons – and the eight techniques of power that she identifies in the pedagogy of teachers across a range of educational contexts. In what follows, we illustrate these techniques of surveillance, normalization, exclusion, classification, distribution, individualization, totalization and regulation, utilizing a selection of 'speech-events' or critical incidents between teachers and students observed within our own research (outlined in Chapter 1). Throughout, notice the similarities with various strategies above concerning the ways in which sense is made of text. In particular, consider the ways in which many of these techniques conjure up binary relations to give them force and legitimacy.

Surveillance

Surveillance involves 'supervising, closely observing, watching, threatening to watch, [and] avoiding being watched' (Gore 1998b: 3). In the following example, the teacher singles out the student for attention, enabling specific comparisons to be made – particularly in relation to inconsistencies – between her behaviour and performance and the teacher's expectations. Illustrated here is that surveillance is a discursive technique that searches for inconsistencies in order to eradicate them. In this case, for example, the standards of comparison are the amount of work to be completed in a set period of time. In other circumstances, other students could be used as a basis for comparison.

Teacher: Have you completed your work yet, young lady?

Student: No not yet, but I've nearly finished.

Teacher: What question are you up to?

Student: Question 4, Miss.

Teacher: That's not good enough. You're as slow as a tortoise. Why is it that you're only up to Question 4?

Student: I don't know, Miss.

Teacher: Is it because you've been talking ever since you came in this morning?

Student: But I, I . . .

Teacher: There is no excuse, you've had plenty of time. You can come back in your own time to finish it.

Normalization

Normalization is a technique like surveillance in that it seeks consistency in behaviour and performance across students, although normalization tends to be proactive rather than reactive in its efforts to achieve these. It includes 'invoking, requiring, setting, or conforming to a standard, [and] defining the normal' (Gore 1998b: 3). The following extract is not a speech-event as such, but provides a young student's reflection (written during a classroom exercise) on these normalization processes. Notice the clear delineation between appropriate and inappropriate behaviour relative to age, particularly the way in which these are generalized across all girls, and the expectations on the student to conform to processes that will transform her from one state of maturity to another. Notice, too, that while the student experiences difficulty conforming to this standard, the legitimacy of the standard itself is not questioned.

> My daddy told me I have to go to sleep at night with the light off. He says I am growing up and if I want to be a big girl it is what I need to do. I try to sleep with the light off but I can only go to sleep looking at my books because I don't like the noises in the dark. I am growing up and Daddy says the noises can't hurt me because they are the same in the daytime, so I will try to sleep with the light off.

Exclusion

Gore (1998a: 238) regards exclusion as 'the negative side of normalization', defining it as the means of 'tracing the limits that will define difference, boundary, zone, [and] defining the pathological' (Gore 1998b: 3). While surveillance and normalization tend to emphasize what is appropriate, even though this is always in relation to what is inappropriate, exclusionary techniques are concerned more directly and primarily with naming the pathological: the conditions of inappropriate behaviour and performance. Along these lines, consider the naming of Colin's condition in the following conversation and his subsequent exclusion from certain activities.

Teacher: Did I just see what I thought I did in this classroom?
Student: Yes, Miss.
Teacher: You're a disgusting creature, Colin. Don't you know anything about germs?
Student: Yes, Miss.
Teacher: Well, we all know what you'll be doing at lunchtime, and it won't be playing.
Student: But Miss . . .
Teacher: I don't want to hear about it, Colin.

Classification

If techniques of exclusion determine the conditions under which students are excluded, by virtue of certain behaviours and performances, those of classification determine the conditions under which students are included. More specifically, they regulate the relations among included students and between teachers and students, 'differentiating individuals and/or groups from one another' (Gore 1998b: 3). The labelling of students with disabilities provides a good example of the effects of such classification, as we have indicated in this and other chapters. Whether they are classified as 'disabled', as students with 'special needs' or in need of 'learning support', 'the effect of these categorizations can be to divide and separate people into mutually antagonistic blocs, eroding solidarities which are crucial to the survival of individuals facing processes of atomization in the wider world' (Meekosha and Jakubowicz 1996: 80). The following example raises issues of students' gender relations and practices, what behaviours are considered acceptable and unacceptable, and highlights the 'sorting functions of schools' (Gore 1998a: 240) even when this is not explicitly recognized.

Teacher: What do you have for show and tell today?
Julie: I have my new sports Barbie doll.
Robbie: Where did you buy it from?
Julie: From 'Toys 'Я' Us'
Mark: You always ask that Robbie.
Teacher: Robbie just wants to know so he can go and buy one.
Class: (Laughter)
Robbie: I don't play with Barbie dolls!
Teacher: You don't have to be a girl to play with Barbie dolls. We talked about this last week.
Mark: Yeah, my cousin's a boy and he plays with Barbie dolls.

Distribution

Like classification, distribution is a technique of inclusion. Like techniques of classification, distributive techniques give the appearance of being primarily quantitative in character, given that they involve 'dividing [students] into parts, arranging, [and] ranking bodies in space' (Gore 1998b: 3). However, with similarities to our discussion concerning redistributive notions of social justice in Chapter 2, distributions also involve issues of quality, as indicated in the example above concerning the placement of 'these kids' and 'those kids' in classrooms. That is, techniques of distribution raise questions about the kind of education that students receive and the extent to which they are permitted to participate in classroom relations. We take up some of these issues in the next chapter but the following example also points to similar matters. It is worth noting, for example, the distributive references to fairness and how these are accepted as legitimate reasons for particular classroom practices.

Teacher: OK, who knows the answer to number six?
Student: I do! I do!
Teacher: No, you've already answered one question. Who else knows?
Student: I do! I do!
Teacher: I said no. You've answered one question. Now wait your turn.
Student: But I know the answer.
Teacher: It's very good that you know the answer, but I'm sure some-one else does too. If I asked the same person, it wouldn't be fair to the other boys and girls who know the answer too, OK?
Student: OK.

Individualization

Individualization involves 'giving individual character to, [and] specifying an individual' (Gore 1998b: 3). The following example provides a good illustration of this technique, where the problem is reduced to whether Brooke is able to take on particular characteristics of student behaviour, one set represented as desirable and the other as undesirable.

Teacher: Hello Brooke. Peta came to me saying that you had run away from her. What happened?
Student: You see, last Friday me and my friends were playing and . . . well . . . we didn't run away, we just pretended to tell things about her.
Teacher: Peta doesn't feel like it's pretend. She feels left out. Have you ever been left out, Brooke?
Student: Yes.
Teacher: Are you the type of person who can play with many friends or just one friend?

Student: No, I can make lots of friends.
Teacher: All right. It really upsets me when someone in my class is feeling unhappy. Can you at least try to be more friendly and make many friends?

Totalization

There is a clear relationship between techniques of individualization and techniques of totalization: both tend to essentialize the nature of student dispositions. Specifically, totalization involves 'giving collective character to, specifying a collectivity/total, [and a] will to conform' (Gore 1998b: 3). Such totalization is evident in the collective address given to students in the following example. What is particularly interesting is the way in which this collective naming is utilized when addressing individual students and then by the students themselves. Clearly, the intent of the teacher here is to secure conformity but notice how she is also able to step outside of this collective when the need arises.

Teacher: Now, Grade 3, remove everything from your desk except for your book and marking pencil.
Student: Do we need our rulers?
Teacher: Do we mark with our rulers?
Student: No.
Teacher: Then we don't need our rulers.
Student: *(puts ruler away)*
Teacher: What pencil did I ask you to use?
Student: Our marking pencil.
Teacher: Right. We don't mark with our lead pencil, so put it away.
Student: *(puts lead pencil away)*

Regulation

As Gore (1998a: 243) notes, all of the above techniques of power 'could be seen to have regulating effects'. However, techniques of regulation more explicitly involve the practices of 'controlling by rule, subject to restrictions; adapt[ing] to requirements; [and] act[s] of invoking a rule, including sanction, reward, [and] punishment' (Gore 1998b: 3). The explicit nature of such regulation often generates references to knowledge of a rule, as in the following example, while sanctions and rewards are present but often backgrounded or assumed.

Student: Miss, can I go to the toilet [bathroom] please?
Teacher: What did you just ask me?
Student: Can I go to the toilet please?
Teacher: You know you're not allowed to go to the toilet during class. Why didn't you go at lunch time?

Student: I don't know.
Teacher: That's not a good enough reason. If you don't know, then you've got problems, haven't you? Go and sit down.

Conclusion

In this chapter we have outlined a metalanguage for thinking and talking about language. It is an approach that regards discourse as centrally positioned in relation to ideology and text, not only as the instrument through which meanings are engaged but also within which there is struggle to establish and maintain such meanings. Throughout, we have represented these struggles as negotiated through strategies that we have sought to name as a way of revealing their intentions and the ways in which they advantage some and disadvantage others. We do not mean by this that all ideological and discursive strategies are intrinsically 'bad' and should be avoided at all costs. As noted above, they cannot be avoided – all teachers, for example, use classroom management techniques similar to those we illustrate above – but individuals and groups should be held accountable for their use, if not their allegiance. We think that one important way in which to do this is to identify and question their (strategic) practices and thereby create spaces for alternative ways of thinking, acting and being in the world, in line with socially just purposes.

For example, in Gore's (1998b) questioning of teacher's pedagogies, she found issues of class associated with techniques of individualization, issues of race/ethnicity associated with techniques of classification, and issues of gender associated with both. In the educational contexts she researched, Gore also noted differences in the (legitimate) ways that gender, class and race were essentialized, through techniques of individualization and/or totalization. But we want to be clear here. We are not claiming in any way that our illustrations of Gore's techniques of power provide similar evidence in relation to gender, race and class. We simply make the point that questioning teaching practice, like this, allows for hidden and potentially discriminatory practices to be addressed in a way that might not be otherwise possible.

Naming these associations and identifying the techniques through which they are established and maintained, for example, enables Gore and those who engage with her work to think differently about these issues in at least two ways: first, to recognize that the popular social dynamics of gender, race and class are not necessarily (re)produced in the same ways within classrooms; and second, that there are ways to think about power relations (apart from gender, race and class) that might prove to be more fruitful in redressing the injustices of schooling.

These are matters we engage to varying degrees in the chapters that follow. In particular, Chapter 6 provides an analysis of teaching practices in three (fictional) classrooms as a way of creating space for a more democratically informed pedagogical imagination. Chapter 7 follows and addresses discourses of inclusion (including classification and distribution) and exclusion evident in schooling, while Chapter 8 addresses discourses of essentialism (individualization and totalization) in relation to gender, race and class. Throughout this book, ideological analyses are also prominent, particularly in Chapters 2 and 3 where we considered the nature of social justice and language respectively, but also in Chapter 5, in which various ideologies of education are examined.

Questions for discussion/research

- What is the relationship between ideology, discourse, text and culture?
- How might a discursive analysis be sustained and conceived that employs both a bottom-up and a top-down approach?
- What are the most common techniques of power employed by teachers?

Suggested readings

Fairclough, N. (1992) *Discourse and Social Change*. Cambridge: Polity Press, Chapter 3.
Mills, S. (1997) *Discourse*. London: Routledge, Chapter 1.
Popkewitz, T. and Brennan, M. (eds) (1998) *Foucault's Challenge: Discourse, Knowledge and Power in Education*. New York: Teachers College Press, Chapter 9.
Seddon, T. (1994) *Context and Beyond: Reframing the Theory and Practice of Education*. London: Falmer Press, Chapter 4.
Tripp, D. (1993) *Critical Incidents in Teaching: Developing Professional Judgement*. London: Routledge, Chapter 4.

five

Getting a good education: from whose perspective?

Introduction

In Chapter 4 we noted that even those ideas and associated social practices that appear to be natural – the only logical and rational things to think and do – reflect certain values and beliefs that become hegemonic. Education is a concept that people tend to think of in this way, as if everyone knows what they mean when they talk of getting an education. As Raymond Williams (1961: 145) notes, 'we speak sometimes as if education were a fixed abstraction, a settled body of teaching and learning, and as if the only problem it presents to us is that of distribution: this amount, for this period of time, to this or that group'.

In this sense, education can be seen as a concept much like social justice, although (as argued in Chapter 2) these are matters that involve much more than issues of distribution. Like social justice, there is not one single use for the term 'education' and there have been several attempts within the academic literature to define the different ways in which it is understood. To illustrate, some definitions construct dichotomies or binaries between what are often referred to as 'traditional' and 'progressive' educational perspectives (see, for example, Barnes and Shemilt 1974), representations not too distant from the first two perspectives on language use we considered in Chapter 3. Other definitions recognize a greater variety of perspectives, although many are still seen as separate from each other. Raynor (1972), for example, names four educational perspectives: aristocratic, bourgeois, democratic and proletarian. Similarly, Cosin (1972) distinguishes between elitist/conservative, romantic/individualist, rationalizing/technocratic and egalitarian/democratic positions. Davies (1969) variously refers to education as conservative, romantic, revisionist and democratic. Again, these latter two categorizations could be regarded as having similarities with the four perspectives on language considered in Chapter 3.

In this chapter we are concerned not only to identify differences but also to recognize similarities among these kinds of educational perspectives and their politics. That is, we suggest that at particular times and in particular locations, particular educational perspectives are able to achieve dominance over others. Such propositions are not new. For example, from his examination of the history of British education, Williams (1961) identifies three broad and interrelated educational purposes pursued in educational systems, perspectives that we refer to below as academic, democratic and vocational. Demonstrating the interrelationships among these, Williams (1961: 147) notes that, 'schematically one can say that a child must be taught, first, the accepted behaviour and values of his [*sic*] society; second, the general knowledge and attitudes appropriate to an educated man; and third, a particular skill by which he will earn his living and contribute to the welfare of his society'.

Here, Williams (1961: 143) sees 'the training of social character shading into specialised training for particular kinds of work, and the definitions of general education taking their colour from both'. While these purposes can be closely interwoven, in practice they more often appear in tension, resolved to some degree by the tendency for one to claim dominance over the others.

To illustrate, in nineteenth century Britain, Williams (1961: 163) suggests that the public (government) school curriculum represented 'a compromise between all three purposes but with the industrial trainers predominant'; a victory for advocates of a skills orientation 'who, in the early decades, had been a minority' (1961: 161). Further, Williams (1961) claims that it was a victory made possible through the support of the 'public educators' (those who sought a democratic curriculum) over an 'old humanist' advocacy for a liberal education. In short, a skills orientation to education dominated at the expense of an academic approach and with the support of those who desired more democratic educational purposes and processes. Of course, this was played out in state schools where the majority of students were 'trained' and not in the elite schools where the future rulers were 'educated' in a liberal academic sense. Concerning recent public education in the UK, Ball (1990: 5) suggests that the balance between these three competing perspectives has changed such that 'the public educators [advocates of a democratic education] are in disarray and that the field of education . . . is overshadowed by the influence of the old humanists [advocates of an academic education] and industrial trainers [advocates of a vocational education]'. It is a view that is, on the whole, supported by Marginson (1993) with respect to the Australian educational context and which we suggest is also applicable to the US.

Acknowledging, then, both the historical and contemporary lack of consensus over what knowledge should be transmitted by teachers and how it should be taught, this chapter considers three positions on education: the academic, the vocational and the democratic. The point has been made, however, and is reiterated here, that these are difficult issues to identify and separate since it can be seen that education in any particular context involves a particular set of emphases and omissions, drawn from several and sometimes competing ideologies. Here, we endeavour to unpack what we have called academic, vocational and democratic perspectives on education in order to identify more clearly what people mean by this term and how it can change according to particular emphases and omissions. In the process, it should become clear that the formal curriculum for basic education has always been the result of conflicting ways of interpreting the goals of schooling (Kliebard 1986).

In this chapter we represent the third of these perspectives – a democratic view of education and schooling – as the approach most promising in terms of emphasizing the necessary skills and preparing an educated population to participate in an inclusive democracy. Taking this approach, schools should not function primarily to sort and select individuals for their place in an educational and occupational hierarchy, but instead enable individuals and groups to contribute to the development of democratic institutions (including schools) and to the possibilities for meaningful work.

Guiding questions

Throughout the chapter, the following questions guide our discussion of these issues:

- What changing needs does/has education respond/ed to?
- How do different people define the purpose of education?
- Are there any necessary connections between school and work?
- What makes for a democratic view of education?

We begin with an exploration of academic perspectives that tend to represent education as individualistic and valuable in its own right. This is followed by vocational accounts of education as preparation for work and then by democratic representations of education as a social good.

Education for its own sake

An enduring perspective on the legitimate nature of education is the classical liberal or academic model that values both the all-round development of the individual and knowledge for its own sake. For this reason it is sometimes referred to as a generalist curriculum, although the term is misleading since a general education also implies learning work-related skills and preparation for citizenry, issues that we return to below.

The origins of this first perspective on the purpose of education are patrician, that is, designed for the preparation of an exclusive ruling elite. 'Old humanists' (Williams 1961), who promote this academic view of education, trace their origins to classical Greece and its preoccupation with the training of the ruling elite, the traditions of 'Oxbridge' (the universities of Oxford and Cambridge) and the general education of the landed gentry. This academic curriculum organizes or fragments knowledge into subject areas and arranges these in hierarchical relationships, where typically the humanities (such as English literature and foreign languages) and the natural sciences (such as calculus and physics) are given status over others that are considered to be less mentally taxing (such as manual arts, home economics and typing). Hierarchies are also created within subjects through various forms of 'streaming' or 'tracking' – the practice of placing students into similar ability groups – and the creation of lower status alternatives.

From a classical conservative standpoint, Kirk (1989) explains that academic education is important because it preserves the intellectual and moral order of society through its transmission of the finest elements of Anglo traditions and practices. Accordingly, content-based subjects should be organized in a theoretical, abstract curriculum. For Kirk, liberal studies develop 'wisdom and virtue' for all and a 'philosophical habit of mind' for the intellectually capable. Within such thinking, elites are seen as necessary to a democracy and it is an academic curriculum that will best prepare select youth for their future leadership responsibilities. The perspective maintains that while academic knowledge may be forgotten, some residue remains. Further, the intellect is developed through the discipline of learning this content, irrespective of the specific uses to which it might later be put.

Significantly, contrary to its claim to be a pursuit in and of itself, the academic curriculum is strongly utilitarian (as is the vocational view we consider below) in that the intention is to gain access to particular forms of work, notably high status ones in medicine, law and management. Here, there are clear links between an academic curriculum and the preparation of professional elites. Bruce Smith (1991), for example, notes that Australian universities were established for this very purpose. As has been argued elsewhere, they have been influential in the determination of secondary/ high school curricula ever since:

> Almost from their inception, [Australian] secondary schools have maintained a goal of preparing their students for university [and academic] study. As students with different abilities and ambitions have entered secondary schooling, this goal has been challenged and other educational goals have been adopted. Although these have been, in some measure, in conflict with university determined curricula, the lure of university study continued to drive subject selection, development and assessment, particularly at the upper secondary [senior high school] level.
>
> (Gale 1994: 48)

Thus, while the academic curriculum is ostensibly open to all students, it remains class based (Connell *et al.* 1982). Indeed, it is used for sorting and selecting out those special students for higher education, status, work and the 'good life' in general (see, for example, Gale 1999a). The highly competitive nature and purpose of this kind of education is not lost on students. Indeed, the pressures that such education generates for students is well illustrated in the following extract of a suicide note authored by a 10-year-old boy from Hong Kong:

> Everyday, there are many homework. They are not only in large quantity, but also difficult to do. Each recess is only engaging in 10 minutes.

If getting one day more holiday, [I] will be given ten odd homework.
Especially in long vacation, the homework will be more. [I] can get no
rest in any day. Dictations, quizs and examinations will be more. Though
over 12 o'clock every night I still have to revise my homeworks. I can't
go to bed until 1 o'clock odd. At 6:50 hours in the morning, I have got
to get up. [I] am so hard, I do wish no studying.

(cited in Speak 1992: 73)

These pressures are not confined to students in Asia, as illustrated in the
following comment from a 12-year-old boy from New York. Looking around
nervously, Jacob reflected on his schooling, one with a strong academic
orientation: 'There are so many things to do right and so many people
watching to see if you do them right.' It is a response that speaks of the techniques of surveillance canvassed in Chapter 4 and which tend to accompany
this view of education.

An academic view of education also remains strong in the minds of teachers,
although there is evidence that this is coming under increasing challenge.
For example, David – a primary/elementary school teacher interviewed in
our research, described in Chapter 1 – holds to an academic perspective
even though he recognizes some of its shortcomings; particularly, what
Freire (1972) refers to as a banking concept of education. Freire uses these
terms to criticize how an academic educational approach 'extends only as far
as receiving, filing, and storing the deposits' (Freire 1972: 46) through its
often didactic pedagogies. While apparently placing the blame on students
rather than on teachers' pedagogies, David describes the not surprising effect
of a curriculum that views students as passive consumers rather than active
human beings, capable of thinking for themselves:

this whole issue of playing school. You'll get kids, in Grades 5 to 7 [ages
9 to 11], wanting to do a project on horses. OK, that's fine but what do
they do? 'What colour are horses? What do horses eat?' There's not a
damn kid in Grade 5 and 6 who does not know what colour horses are
or what they eat. They're playing school. They are not really learning
anything new. They are just doing something for the teacher. They are
just going to make it look pretty, and I'm not interested. Personally,
that's what I call playing school. That's not what we're here for and I
find that they switch onto that pretty quickly after I take them through
a process that exposes them to different levels of thinking. So, I set
conditions for those sorts of projects that it must be something that they
have a genuine interest in.

(David)

Education as preparation for work

One of the prominent themes in education, particularly since the Industrial
Revolution, has been the role of education in teaching the particular skills

demanded by the labour market. Indeed, with the introduction of new forms of work – the work of the factory rather than the farm – the need became apparent for educational institutions to prepare children with work-related skills; children who previously would have been prepared by their families to follow in their fathers' or mothers' footsteps. Williams (1961: 162) has argued that as the nineteenth century unfolded and industrialization began to have a significant impact in Britain, education became increasingly dominated by the views of the industrial trainers, which included the teaching of 'habits of regularity, self-discipline, obedience and trained effort'. As Henry *et al.* (1988: 67) explain, 'the introduction of mass schooling served specific class-based economic and political interests requiring a massive cultural onslaught on working class people in order to prepare them for the realities of life under capitalism'.

Commenting on this industrial heritage, Little (1985: 8–9) has described the vocational view of education as a 'factory tradition' and notes that 'no education system took up this essentially mechanistic model more than the Australian colonies'. So, for example, the 1852 Select Committee on Education in Victoria (an Australian colony at the time) required teachers, among other things, 'to observe themselves and to impress upon the minds of their pupils, the great rule of regularity and order – a time and a place for everything, and everything in its proper time and place' (cited in Bessant 1983: 9).

In the US, the early vocational education movement (1900–17) was informed by the assumption that traditional schooling was not appropriate to emerging social-economic demands. At the time, business interests played a powerful role in establishing a vocational component to school curricula. The argument was simple: American business could best deal with the problems of production by more aggressively entering the international market. For American business to compete successfully, however, schooling would have to become more efficient in the training of future workers. The pedagogical and psychological rationale for this view of education – that education should, above all, help the economy function efficiently – was provided by such figures as David Snedden, Charles Prosser and Edward Thorndike.

Complaints continue to be voiced at the present time by employers (and employees) in the UK, the US and Australia about the supposed irrelevance of school to the adult world of work. Underlying these complaints is the assumption that the main purpose of schooling is job preparation. Schools, the argument proceeds, are responsible for unemployment and low worker productivity because they have neglected to equip youth with the skills needed for employment. The solution for industry and the economy is to establish a closer relationship between work and education; a commitment reflected in contemporary vocational curricula that champion generic workplace competencies, predominantly defined in behaviourist terms and often expressed within schools as student performance standards. As Norris (1991: 331) suggests, 'the concept of competence has become associated with a drive towards more practicality in education and training, placing a greater emphasis on the assessment of performance rather than knowledge' (see also Floud and Halsey 1961; Bowles and Gintis 1976; Carnoy and Levin 1976; Grace 1985).

A performance or skills-orientated education draws heavily on the concept of human capital: the view that education and training increase the capacity of individuals to be more productive, which in turn leads to more earnings for both individuals and groups. Human capital theory views individuals as economic resources; that is, one's labouring ability is likened to forms of capital such as money or steel. Hence, young people's ability to work is viewed as a commodity in the labour market and schooling is the means of increasing their capacity to work, instilling in them the appropriate skills (Dale 1989; Bowe *et al.* 1992; Marginson 1993; Ball 1994). Contemporary partnerships between school and business are an example of this ideology where business invests in developing individuals' skills and abilities to work, just as it invests in all other forms of capital.

There are, however, a number of problems with this theory and the discourses it mobilizes, including the fact that the connections between education, work and earnings are neither as direct nor as certain as assumed (Snook 1991; Marginson 1993). Equally important, (vocational) education is reduced to simply meeting job requirements, drastically limiting the development of human creativity and potential. The implication is that life itself is essentially about selling your ability to work and allowing others to profit from your labour. Such reasoning encourages the ethics and values of market competition, which tend to undermine any sense of civic responsibility to others and enshrines consumerism as a supreme value.

Human capital theory and its apparent resurgence exemplifies the relevance of power, ideology, control and knowledge to debates, however limited, over what should be taught in schools, various conceptions of the purposes of education and competing notions about the relationships between schools and the economy. The lack of necessary connections between education and employee productivity suggests that human capital theory legitimizes the interests of social allocation and the control of people, serving important ideological and political functions. These are power relations reminiscent of deficit models of social justice outlined in Chapter 2. In brief, the rationale is that if the marketplace for labour power is freely competitive, then individuals are unemployed because they are deficient in some way. They are viewed, at best, as in need of skills and perhaps attitude training to make them more productive and disciplined workers and acceptable to employers. While at one level this argument is defensible, at another it obscures the relations of class, control and competition that underlie the buying and selling of labour (Korndorffer 1991). Hence, the institution of unemployment and underemployment in our economic system, and how this differentially affects different groups of people, remain unexamined.

The vocational view of education – equipping students with skills that enhance their employability – typically includes components such as work experience, career counselling or school-to-work transition schemes. But all too often, vocational education programmes aim at simply equipping those students for whom the school is most ineffective, with easily learned and barely relevant skills (in the narrowest sense of the term). In practice, 'older and more powerful meanings [of vocational education] . . . contribute to maintaining rather than ameliorating social divisions' (Henry and Taylor 1995: 99) In such programmes, social discipline appears to be the real intention (Korndorffer 1991), particularly when a division between the academic and the vocational is maintained through separate curricula for general knowledge and the skills that relate to employment, selection procedures that encourage certain types of students into certain types of courses and the general attribution of lesser status for vocational education. In our research, and particularly in our conversations with David, we found that these separate and hierarchical relations between academic and vocational ideologies of education are evident even in primary/elementary schools, where

> there is still that distinction there between different sorts of discipline areas. I very much see my role as instilling a feeling for, a love for mathematics, a love for language, a love for music, et cetera. I would focus and I do focus, in fact, on the relationships that exist between those things. I think I'm at an advantage in that regard in that I have a very genuine personal love of mathematics, love of language, love of music . . . I know I feel quite confident when kids leave me, that they are interested to pursue mathematics. They are interested to pursue language, et cetera. And they will choose their own focuses as they go through [school] themselves. But at the stage they leave primary school, all those avenues should be wide open, I think; . . . that each of those things will be of interest to them and they will refine those interests in later years.

> *Is that what education means: a collection of subjects offered at school?*

> Yes. We need those 'core' ones. There are a thousand other things that obviously go in, in terms of personal relations and all that side of things that are a part of education, for sure. But I think . . . it is the academic disciplines you tend to focus on when you are talking about what you set out to do in education.

> *What about students who don't measure up, academically? How do they get an education?*

> I think it's a real bind. I think it's definitely a problem that the focus [of schooling] is academic. I don't think there's any getting away from that. I mean, again, we use nice sort of rhetoric to talk about [schooling] – developing the whole child and that type of thing – but I think that that rhetoric is a bit loose. I think it is a genuine concern, but the scope for input, I think, is rather limited given the expected focus on academic subjects.

> *Is it possible to conceive of some other kind of education in primary schools? Is a vocational education possible, for example, at this level?*

Possibly. Personally I have difficulty with a vocational education in high school anyway.

Why is that?

It's a philosophical perspective of mine. I'm not particularly comfortable when it becomes sort of an either/or construction of education. You know, the alternatives where you either do an academic or you do a vocational education. I'm really uncomfortable with that idea. I really am.

Why?

Well, I think the academic line, the philosophy that drives the academic line, equips children to become informed citizens. And it does it in other than direct ways. By dealing, say, with literature and questioning literature and then reading between the lines . . . even at those levels I think it is terribly important to our society. And I think vocational training can come at any stage, whereas with regard to these other opportunities, if you've missed them, they are probably never addressed. That is my concern. I really do feel that.

Is the purpose of education, then, for individuals to benefit personally?

Absolutely. I have no qualms about that . . . Those core understandings should be there and if [students] have those understandings I have no difficulty with vocational education. I just don't feel that there is any appreciation of that in much current vocational education.

(David)

Other schools opt for integrating the academic and the vocational. They require academic subjects to address real-life issues and be partly practical (to develop general competencies) and require vocational subjects to be partly theoretical (to develop cognitive and critical skills). From this perspective, the notion of competencies bridges the academic–vocational divide, addressing the knowledge, skills and attitudes required to be a productive employee. Some theorists, for example, argue that to be job-ready in the current 'post-Fordist' work environment means being more flexible and multiskilled. The argument proceeds that the more narrowly occupationally specific the vocational courses provided by schools, the less likely it is that they will adequately prepare young people for their working lives. Hence, contemporary workers require generic skills; for example, communications skills, interpersonal skills and the skills to survive independently in periods of unemployment or of employment mobility. Appropriate generic vocational competencies, it seems, can be applied across industries and occupations. The new vocationalism, then, no longer means training in a particular occupation but aims instead for more general, less specialized learning, requiring workers to bring a set of generic competencies to any vocation.

If schooling is to serve these ends, it must be more relevant, it seems, to the demands of industry and business, imparting knowledge and equipping students with skills that enhance their employability. As noted above, schooling has been criticized for being irrelevant to the workplace, too abstract and too theoretical. Many teachers have responded positively to this criticism and the vocationalization of schooling, particularly in relation to a more integrated relationship between things academic and vocational. In our research, for example, Carl provided a clear articulation of these relations:

> there's no relevance in teaching the theory of a particular subject . . . if there's no direct application. A great criticism that's levelled at us as educators is, 'Why have I got to learn this stuff? How am I going to use it?' . . . what I attempt to do is to teach whatever theory is necessary within the context of how that person will actually use that theory. So you have got to give relevance to all you teach . . . [Also] We have to identify what is necessary to know . . . The criteria reference system enables you to actually identify what you want to learn in a particular time. So the students that I have here, because we operate in competency based terms, were able to establish a set of criteria for what's to be learnt. I can present them with that and then I can say, 'We will do it within the context of what your vocational outcome is going to be'. So if I teach them mathematics then I will teach them mathematics associated with horticulture or hospitality or hairdressing or whatever else.
>
> (Carl)

At other times, this same idea is structured as a core of general subjects supported by a range of specialized academic and vocational subjects. Michelle, a physical education teacher whose comments we referred to in Chapter 3, interpreted this integrated model of education as a 'whole body process':

What do you think the role of schooling is for these students?

> From my experience of different schools, it's not only just teaching them maths, science, English, whatever. In a lot of cases, especially the kids I teach now, it's also about teaching them general manners, respect and how to behave and to respect themselves, to have confidence in themselves, and trust. It's a whole body process. It's not just academic because so many kids can't pick it up anyway, no matter how much you try to drum it into them. Their learning curve is very low and their learning ability is very low.
>
> (Michelle)

Thus, for some teachers, an integrated notion of vocational education means a curriculum that emphasizes dominant social attitudes and values as well as basic skills. This is strikingly similar to education in the nineteenth century discussed above, where dominant social requirements for proper attitudes towards work and social relations in general were central to the curricula (Bowles and Gintis 1976; Dale and Esland 1977; O'Donnell 1984). Importantly, the attitudes and relationships emphasized were those that best lent themselves to social control, the needs of industry and the interests of dominant social groups (see, for example, Bernstein 1971). In brief, training for work and social discipline defined, and in some cases may still define, the purpose of education (see Henry and Taylor 1994, 1995; Taylor and Henry 1994).

In the early twentieth century, educator and philosopher John Dewey was an articulate advocate for a more complex kind of socially useful vocational education. Dewey argued for integrating the liberal arts with vocational, technological and scientific studies. He believed that such curricula could turn classrooms into communities where students could engage and inquire into creative occupational work while they simultaneously developed democratic values and dispositions. This, he reasoned, would contribute to wider social transformation, reducing class divisions and fostering democracy. Dewey's position on orientating education towards training students to be efficient workers and to take their place in society's occupational hierarchy, is reflected in his following comments:

> The kind of vocational education which I am interested in is not one which will 'adapt' workers to the existing industrial regime; I am not sufficiently in love with the regime for that. It seems to me that the business of all who would not be educational time-servers is to strive for a kind of vocational education which will first alter the existing industrial system, and ultimately transform it.
>
> (Dewey 1915: 42, in Wirth 1991: 60)

In our view, the challenge is to prepare students so that they receive a broad education, they are prepared to and for work, and they are disposed to critique and to transform our economic system so that it meets their and others' needs.

Education as a social good

In line with Dewey, a democratic perspective on the purpose of education accepts the need for schooling to prepare youth to enter the world of work while simultaneously being prepared to operate in an increasingly multicultural and technological society. Narrow thinking about what our economy requires or myopic job preparation has the tendency to stifle creative personal growth and socio-economic change. Education also needs to help young people understand the importance of democracy and to explore what this means for our lives individually and in relation to one another. In other words, economic productivity is important but only insofar as it is conceived as part of that which is necessary for improving the quality of social life. A democratic society also depends upon its population being concerned with and able to practice equity, social justice and cultural sensitivity (Connell 1993).

Marginson (1993) sees education as the right of all people and an important preparation for the equal participation of citizens in all aspects of social life, including political life: understood as the opportunity to make informed choices and decisions necessary to meet their needs. Within this perspective knowledge and power are intimately related, or as Marginson (1993: 19) describes it, 'the democratic objective implies a broad education through which understanding of the world, and the capacity to act within it, are constructed simultaneously.' Gramsci's (1971) critique of an education defined as skill development is very much along these emancipatory lines: 'democracy, by definition, cannot mean merely that an unskilled worker can become skilled. It must mean that every "citizen" can govern and that society places him, even if only abstractly, in a general condition to achieve this' (Gramsci 1971: 41).

Education, from this perspective, must be concerned with developing the understandings and skills necessary for individuals to participate in determining their actions and the conditions of their society. Educators should prepare students to be eager and able to take charge of their personal and public lives.[1] According to Lauder (1993), a democratic education requires

an open, non-selective system of education which promotes equality of results. A strong notion of equality of opportunity [applied in a plurality of sites] of this kind is required, because in a society differentiated by ethnicity, gender and class in which those who conceive policy are nearly always highly educated, a voice needs to be given to those groups who traditionally do not succeed in education.

(Lauder 1993: 19)

Thus, the groups who are the targets of social justice strategies must be allowed and prepared to participate in determining both what their needs and interests are, which institutional conditions would enable them to meet their needs, and what equitable outcomes from our school system would look like. Individuals and groups could then contribute both intellectually and actively to creating a just and democratic society, one in which we would witness a restructuring of control over all forms of capital. The end result of being educated in such a society would be 'that people can take their place in the workforce on terms roughly of their own choosing and in a society that offers dignity to all its citizens' (Henry *et al.* 1988: 286).

It is possible to distinguish between 'meaningful work' on the one hand and 'constrained labour' on the other (Corson 1991: 14–18). Similar to Karl Marx's distinction, meaningful work is part of a worthwhile desirable life and contributes to self-respect; it is creative, productive activity. Constrained labour, in which many are engaged, is primarily a means to an end (a wage or salary, for example) where work has little intrinsic value. Vocational education programmes can thus be scrutinized for the extent they prepare students for meaningful work or whether they assume that youth are destined for constrained labour. In a similar vein, Hamilton (1989), in his analysis of the universalization of education, notes the emergence of a democratic curriculum in nineteenth century Britain:

In 1814, for instance, Robert Owen had claimed – following an upsurge of industrial unrest – that the 'inconsistencies and follies' of adults were traceable to two features of popular schooling: the practice of teaching children to 'believe without reasoning' and the fact that children were 'never taught to understand what they read'. In turn, Owen argued that the school system should be reconstructed. All children – including those from the 'poor and labouring classes' – should be equipped to make 'rational judgement[s]'. To this end, their reasoning faculties were to be exercised, and their minds were to be furnished with 'all the facts'.

(Hamilton 1989: 99)

In Australia, the US and the UK, the 'public educators', as Williams (1961) calls them, have been influential in promoting opportunities for all citizens to access institutions of education. More children than ever before progress through pre-school/kindergarten, primary/elementary schools and secondary/high schools with many students remaining to complete the post-compulsory years of schooling. From there, students often continue their education at either a technical institution or at a college/university. However, for some educators the democratic project seems to end with issues of access. That is, the legitimate concern to provide all children with an equal opportunity to acquire an education, seems to overshadow more than a cursory interest in the *equality* of what is being offered, a point made by Connell (1993) through his reference to 'curricular justice'.

Like Connell (1993), we know that what is being offered by schooling is differentially appropriated by different groups. Further, we know that school curricula largely represent the interests of dominant social groups. If the involvement of individuals and groups in making decisions that affect their actions or the conditions of their actions are important areas of concern in a democracy (Young 1990), such involvement must also be important in public education. As John Dewey so eloquently argued, while democracy is a prerequisite for an adequate educational system at one level, at another the education system itself must teach and embody democratic social relations and practices. For example, individuals who regulate and occupy our schools must treat one another in some fundamental sense as equals. Also, making decisions, both as an individual and as a member of a group, over matters of importance, fosters the development of capacities of thinking about one's own situation with respect to that of others and the development of interest concerning the relations of various peoples to existing social institutions (see Chapter 9). The point here is that the skills and dispositions of citizenship are best developed through their free exercise.

If students are to develop these skills and dispositions, the content of education must be challenged and changed to make social justice issues central to the curricula that all students receive (Connell 1993). Students will need to learn about the histories of the oppressed. For example, throughout a school's academic curricula and within vocational education in particular, questions should be raised about why some jobs command higher pay and status than others and how this influences how different groups of people are treated in society. Teachers would explore with students the subtle and hidden ways in which class bias is present in curricula, why poverty persists, and other issues directly affecting the lives of low-income students. The many forms expressing the power differential between men and women would also be examined. Feminist theory and the study of gender would be used not only to add information about women to the curriculum but also to learn different ways of seeing the world and engaging in life. Studying institutionalized racism can also serve as a framework within which students can learn how well-intentioned, everyday practices, norms and symbols oppress people of colour.

Shor's (1993) development of Freire's problem-solving method represents one concrete teaching strategy for taking this approach to education. Guided by the teacher, students focus on and investigate real-life objects and situations. The focus of investigation is problematized by considering ever widening contexts, starting from the immediate and progressively moving out to more global contexts, always considering historical aspects of those contexts. Students are encouraged to question what it is they think they know about these objects and experiences, including how their knowledge might be influenced by dominant ideology and interests. As an intellectual method, this approach offers a depth to students' experiences and their understandings of these experiences as they learn to identify problems, pose and weigh alternative solutions and act to create more just social structures and relations.

Adopting an approach with similarities to Shor's, Carl, a post-secondary technical college teacher, provides an interesting critique of academic and vocational views of education. He notes what the schooling system requires (this he refers to as the formal aspects of education) and the ways in which his Black students 'really' learn (which he refers to as the informal aspects of education). In Carl's terms, what students really learn has mostly to do with their personal interests (what he calls 'personal education') and how these interact with their particular circumstances (a process he refers to as the 'random acquisition of knowledge'). Here, and in the comments above regarding the involvement of Carl's students in identifying the competencies and criteria for measuring their learning, the involvement of students in their own education is highlighted. Elsewhere in our discussions with Carl, he relates an example of a student who regards himself as incompetent in mathematics and yet can place a bet on a horse and calculate his anticipated winnings, given the pay out for a win and a place. Carl's point in providing such illustration is to draw attention to the interrelationships between who his students are and what schooling requires of them, not simply for our benefit as interviewers but primarily for the benefit of his students. In his own words:

> The . . . [students'] community has had, for a long time now, high periods of unemployment and a lot of them will spend a third to two-thirds of their working life unemployed. In those circumstances, they're not as driven by the desire to get educational qualifications that would drive them towards work . . . these are the formal aspects of education that

tend to preoccupy people like you and me; it is the informal aspects of
education that we tend to overlook. And I describe these in terms of
two levels. One is 'personal education' and the other one is what I call
the 'random acquisition of knowledge', which is just randomly learned
things: things that we don't know at the time we're learning . . . I find
quite often with [this] . . . community that because they are not so linked
to this work orientation of education they are a lot stronger on personal
levels of education and particularly on this random level of education
. . . That's what interests me, I guess, with this group and with a lot of
work that I do here: that the focus is more on that personal and random acquisition of knowledge. Therefore, I consider it to be an integral
part of their education process. But they place a lot less emphasis on
these formal aspects of education that lead towards work. You can
understand it for groups that haven't been favoured in the work stakes
or the economic stakes throughout the whole of their lives and for
probably several generations.

(Carl)

These comments reflect Carl's awareness of the specific experiences of his
students and how his classroom can serve as a central site for both challenging and legitimizing those experiences.

Conclusion

In this chapter we have attempted to provide an overview of three different
perspectives on the purpose of education. We want to end by suggesting
that the tensions between the different approaches can be instructive and
creative. In our own view, a democratic approach to education encompasses
both the end objective associated with the academic perspective – the expansion of the mind through the exposure to such things as great historical
literary and scientific works – as well as the preparation for remunerative
work. It is an approach that embraces what UNESCO's *International Commission on Education for the Twenty-First Century* proposes as the four 'pillars' of
schooling: the first pillar, 'learning to live together', given greater emphasis
than the other three, 'learning to know', 'learning to do', and 'learning to
be' (Delors 1996: 20–1).

We have argued that work skills curricula typically aim at low-income
students while academic curricula aim at an elite. Historically, the academic
or liberal perspective has elevated abstract knowledge above practical knowledge while vocational education has had a tendency to elevate technical
skills over abstract or theoretical content. Critical thinking within an academic perspective is practised after the digestion of the intended content and
is, therefore, practised within parameters set by the powerful, as Freire's
(1972) banking concept of education illustrates. In order to acquire this
knowledge, the student enters social relations based on dependency and
deference. Vocational education, while equipping students for (skilled) jobs,

does not emphasize critical thinking as a key ingredient for improving the quality of democracy in our society but as a way of improving services and goods production. Clearly, this is not the critical thinking that informs a critical approach to language use that we discuss in Chapter 3.

In contrast, a democratic approach to education assumes an interactive relationship between abstract knowledge and practical experience. Bodies of knowledge – the canon *and* popular culture – are resources to be used and transformed by inquiring people as they critically reflect on and address real problems in their lives. Given the importance of work, especially for the life chances and lifestyles of low-income youth, curricula should include and use as a starting point the experiences of youth, examining how these are connected to broader social issues and histories. Rather than competing with one another to show mastery of the academic curriculum, students would learn out of their interdependencies with one another and in dialogue with themselves and their teachers. Drawing from Freire, such dialogue would involve exploring why we think what we do and which interests are being served by our knowledge, including the 'practical reason' (Bourdieu 1998) of our individual and collective common sense and experiences. Critical analysis and explanations would, when feasible, lead to action towards transforming untenable conditions and relations. This kind of dialogue stands in distinction to the more common discussion held in academic curricula, devoid of significant practical applications and teacher led. In short, democratic education is ongoing, preparing us for life in the widest sense and enabling us to deal with the latest challenges from our changing world.

Questions for discussion/research

- How does your view of the nature and purpose of education compare with those presented here?
- What do you think is the dominant view within your educational setting?
- What should be the connection between school and work?
- What does a democracy require of its education system?

Suggested readings

Apple, M. and Beane, J. (eds) (1999) *Democratic Schools: Lessons from the Chalkface.* Buckingham: Open University Press. Chapter 3.

Connell, R., Ashendon, D., Kessler, S. and Dowsett, G. (1982) *Making the Difference: Schools, Families and Social Division.* Sydney: Allen & Unwin. Chapter 3.

Cornford, I. (1998) Schooling and vocational preparation: is a revolution *really* taking place? *Australian Journal of Education,* 42(2): 169–82.

Marginson, S. (1993) *Education and Public Policy in Australia.* Cambridge: Cambridge University Press. Chapter 1.

Preston, N. and Symes, C. (1992) *Schools and Classrooms: A Cultural Analysis of Education.* Melbourne, Vic.: Longman Cheshire. Chapter 3.

(Re)structuring teacher–student relations: what's missing?

Introduction

This chapter provides a critical reading of 'the figure of the Teacher, as a central term' (Green 1998: 177), as a way of revealing whose interests are served within classrooms of popular and normative pedagogical relations and curricula designs that narrowly order interactions from teacher to student. In addressing these popular accounts, we consider the teacher–student relations within three Hollywood movies: *Dangerous Minds* (1995), *Kindergarten Cop* (1990) and *Dead Poets Society* (1989). According to Henry Giroux (1997: 300–1), films of this kind have become 'powerful pedagogical forces, veritable teaching machines in shaping the social imaginations of students [and teachers] in terms of how they view themselves, others, and the larger society'. It is this viewing that is questioned here, creating space for a review of classroom practices and for the possibility for these practices to be re-(in)formed by a radical democratic politics.

Guiding questions

In undertaking this second screening – and adapting Connell's (1995: 71–6) 'three-fold model of the structure of gender, distinguishing relations of (a) power, (b) production and (c) cathexis (emotional attachment)' – we take the (epistemological) standpoint of students to reflect on how these films depict

- who they are and who teachers tell them they are
- who does what and who decides what to do
- how they feel about it and how they are told to feel about it.

These three levels of interest are related to the discourses mobilized by three onscreen teachers (LouAnne Johnson,[1] John Kimble and John Keating), discourses that are variously employed to control the minds, bodies and emotions of their students. Preceding this analysis, we also outline several of Bourdieu's tools of analysis utilized within the chapter and which provide a language with which to narrate a different reading of these films. The chapter concludes by considering what is missing from these celluloid classrooms – that is, what they forget about authentic classrooms – and, therefore, what needs to be reinserted into discussions about how classrooms should be characterized.

Tools of analysis

In pursuing such an evaluation of classrooms, we employ what Bourdieu and Wacquant (1992: 104) refer to as a 'field analysis' that 'involves three neces- sary and internally connected moments'. The first of these analytical moments draws attention to relations between a particular field and broader 'fields of power' (Bourdieu and Wacquant 1992: 104–5). In this chapter, we particularly explore how classrooms, as fields, are related to and connected with powerful discourses that discriminate between individuals on the basis of their race, class and gender. A second level of analysis maps the 'field of positions'. Positions legitimized in classrooms are commonly referred to as teacher and student but their mapping also involves identifying what interrelations are legitimized by these positions. Bourdieu's third level of analysis involves the 'field of stances'. Here we examine individual teachers' and students' practices and expressions or the stances they take within classrooms, in Bourdieu's terms, their 'habitus' and 'dispositions'.

There are at least two methodological issues here that we want to draw to the reader's attention, before returning to Bourdieu's analytic tools of capital, habitus and dispositions. First, like Bourdieu, we do not see his three aspects of field analysis – of power, positions and stances – as inseparable in the analysis of any one general field. They are better understood as different facets of what constitutes a field. One discursive moment might provide evidence of power, positions *and* stances or, as Bourdieu (1992: 105) ex- plains, different 'translations of the same sentence' even though 'the space of positions tends to command the space of position-takings'. Second, 'to think in terms of field is to *think relationally*' (Bourdieu and Wacquant 1992: 96, emphasis in original). There is more to this way of thinking than simply focusing on individuals' intersubjective actions (including their discursive practices), which limits analysis to what is detectable through the senses and 'reduce[s] the effect of the environment to the effect of direct action as actualised during an interaction' (Bourdieu 1990: 42). To think in terms of field is to identify the objective relations that the interactions between indi- viduals imply and to contemplate the determinations field relations impose on individual position holders (Bourdieu and Wacquant 1992: 97).

Bourdieu pursues such thinking about fields by conceiving of three forms of economic, cultural and social capital and relating these to one's habitus and disposition. According to Bourdieu (1997), cultural capital represents an individual's stored or accumulated 'wealth of knowledge' that can be drawn upon to produce more of this wealth; that is, knowledge of the world and how to engage with it, or what Lankshear *et al.* (1997: 72) refer to as 'knowledge about . . . [and] knowing how'. Under certain conditions, cultural capital can be exchanged for economic capital (and then for money and goods) – hence its value – as can social capital, which is no less effective but often less visible to the observer. This is because social capital is related to and constituted by an individual's accumulated networks of mutual acquaintances (individuals who possess cultural capital of often similar quality and quantity). Thus, the value of one's social capital is related to the aggregate value of the cultural capital of one's networks, which in turn can have a 'multiplier effect on the capital he [*sic*] possesses' (Bourdieu 1997: 51).

Not all cultural capital is highly valued, however. In particular, the knowledge of dominant groups, the ways in which they see and experience the world, tends to be exclusively and positively valued in society's institutions, such as schools, while that of marginalized groups is often allocated a negative value, even though such capital might be regarded as important in relationships internal to those groups (Bourdieu 1997: 56). What makes these social arrangements even more discriminatory is that the cultural capital of the dominant is acquired through labouring within its midst and over extended periods of time, yet neither of these modes of acquisition are readily available to marginalized groups. Their access is frequently limited to time at schools of suspect quality and constrained by comparatively lower quantities of economic capital that cannot sustain individuals over long periods of time away from pressing economic necessities (Bourdieu 1997: 49). It is in these senses that Bourdieu (1997: 47) refers to 'capital (or power, which amounts to the same thing)'.

When a particular cultural capital becomes an integral part of a person's identity, to the extent that the person takes on its character, Bourdieu refers to an individual's habitus. Social and cultural capital both contribute to the character of this habitus, which itself can become metonymic (see Chapter 4). That is, individuals become representative of a particular cultural or social capital – teachers can be representative of schooling systems, for example – to the extent that they are seen to speak on behalf of particular capitals. Individuals also hold dispositions or long-lasting inclinations, tendencies and propensities to act in certain ways. In effect, one's disposition is an 'arrangement' (from the Latin *dispositio*) of one's self; an internal control mechanism over mind, body and emotions that comes into effect at the point of action. Thus, in employing a Bourdieuian analysis of the following films, we seek to identify the dispositions that teachers and students exhibit, the habitus that informs these dispositions, and the capitals they represent.

These tools of analysis suggest that the objective structure of relations within each of the onscreen classrooms below – 'the cumulative product of its particular history' (Bourdieu and Wacquant 1992: 105) – is concerned with instructional pedagogies; specifically, teachers instruct and students heed their instruction. Green (1998: 177) has described these relations in terms of activity and passivity, in which 'the teacher's active, directive role in the classroom economy . . . [is] contrasted with the student's role, which is characteristically passive and reactive'. When the logic of these relations is sustained teachers are seen to be 'in control' but when they are challenged or abandoned students are regarded as 'out of control'. The struggle over the legitimacy of these relations informs the narratives of the films in question in at least three significant ways. Each teacher, new to the school, is presented with a classroom which is out of control in one sense or another. At one level this is less true of *Dead Poets Society* (hereafter DPS) although, as we explain below, it is the emotional dispositions students have learned in other classes (socio-economic and educational) that resist the logic of John Keating's poetry classroom and render it in need of instruction. Each teacher is also monitored by the school's administration, which seeks to maintain established teacher–student relations of instruction. Teachers seek resolution of the 'problem' through innovative means, often because of their limited socialization into shared understandings of conventional teacher practices. In the case of DPS, however, they are practices that are understood but not always shared. Yet, as we illustrate below, the underlying and traditional structure of relations in these classrooms remain largely unchallenged.

What follows is an analysis of this pedagogical politics of classrooms as it is expressed in three sub-fields within the US: the academy within Parkmont High School, located in an inner city area of California; the kindergarten class of Astoria Elementary School, near Portland, Oregon; and Welton Academy, a private college in Vermont. While these are fictional classrooms – the inventions of Hollywood – we think that they represent the normative view of teacher–student relations in western societies, particularly those views espoused by a contemporary and dominant restoration politics that exerts considerable influence among teachers, students, administrators and parents. In particular, these films convey the assumption that individual teachers can overcome nearly all obstacles to learning, even those originating outside the classroom. For these reasons and others we highlight below, this perspective merits analysis and challenge. We begin by focusing on how one onscreen classroom teacher instructs her students to think about themselves and their world. This is followed by analyses of two Hollywood classrooms that respectively inform student bodies and emotions.

Who students are and who teachers tell them they are

The emancipatory narrative in *Dangerous Minds* (hereafter DM) is familiar enough in Hollywood films of 'troubled' classrooms in which the teacher-hero embarks on a project of 'connecting' with the students, notwithstanding a few teething problems. Such teachers appear intent on generating greater freedoms in (or acceptance of) classroom relations and, potentially, freedoms in relations experienced outside schooling. If its box-office success is any guide, many of us are attracted to this seemingly emancipatory discourse. Superficially, it is reminiscent of the work of teacher-activists like Paulo Freire whose pedagogy was directed at empowering the poor, illiterate, socially and politically disenfranchised peoples of Brazil and Chile. There is even the hint of Latin America in DM – several students are Latino – and Michelle Pfeiffer, as beginning teacher LouAnne Johnson, employs a curriculum not strictly of the school establishment's making or liking.

But the resemblance is, at best, shallow. Freire's work was part of a broader agenda for counter-hegemonic social movements, whereas Johnson's agenda is promotion and advancement of individuals to escape poverty through the system as it currently exists. Ownership of the curriculum in Johnson's classroom may have shifted away from the traditions and author-ity of the school's Board of Education, but her new parameters of curric-ulum development have not embraced her students as co-designers, able to contribute to understandings of what is worth knowing. The culture to which this new curriculum appeals – the 1960s/1970s poetry of Bob Dylan – is clearly Johnson's, not her students'. In this apparent renegotiation of the curriculum, Johnson's dominance in relation to her students is retained; it is *her* knowledge that is legitimized and *her* authoritative position that is reinforced.

There are at least two aspects of this curriculum 'take-over' worth dwell-ing on for a moment and which can be fruitfully explored through Bourdieu's notion of cultural capital. First, there is the issue about whose cultural capital – whose knowledge of the world and how to engage with it – that is valued. What is represented as a radical move by Johnson, in reworking the 'official knowledge' (Apple 1993) of the Board of Education, in fact repres-ents a retention of that knowledge and experiential base. Even if Johnson is not in full agreement with members of this board, her cultural capital is accumulated through the same processes and from the same sources. The curriculum to be learnt in Johnson's classroom remains that valued by dominant social groups. Second, there is the issue of how this assigns value to the habitus and dispositions of Johnson's students. In this respect, the new curriculum is like the old, regarding other knowledges as irrelevant. Johnson's students are required to study the poetry of Bob Dylan not the lyrics of hip-hop music that informs and reflects their lives, despite the fact that the latter plays in the background to the opening scenes.

The 'game' – as Bourdieu (1997: 46) refers to the regularities of social arrangements – may have changed but the rules remain much the same, despite the discourse that suggests otherwise. This is well appreciated by one student who challenges the legitimacy of Johnson's discursive logic, given its ignorance with respect to broader fields of power. Incredulously, he inquires: 'Lady, why are you playing this game? We don't have a choice'. Granted, these are the lines of an actor playing the part of a student or, more accurately, an actor voicing a screen writer's reading of how students from non-dominant groups see their social and economic positions and how they challenge dominant ideologies. It is, perhaps, difficult to imagine such an exchange in many classrooms, but the script provides opportunities for this counter-discourse to be answered; albeit narrowly, given the simplistic individualism of Johnson's response and its failure to consider the structural arrangements that constrain students. To the extent that the film does consider broader contexts, it relies on metonymy: the run-down housing and neighbourhood crime become embodied in Johnson's students.

Many of these issues find expression around one pivotal scene in which Johnson declares 'there are no victims in this classroom'. Others might use these words to inspire oppressed students to be proud of their culture, to understand their situations as informed by existing social structures such as social class, race and gender, and to work collectively towards making civil society more responsive to their needs. But for Johnson, it seems that there are no structural arrangements in society – at least not in nice western societies – designed to ensure that groups of individuals have differential access to social and material goods on the basis of their social and physical differences. It is ironic, then, that Johnson's classroom is characterized by students of particular racial and socio-economic backgrounds who have access to limited resources; ironic because such concentrations and restrictions suggest the very arrangements that Johnson's comments deny. Johnson prefers to explain these positional arrangements in terms of choice rather than oppression. As she puts it:

> There are a lot of people who live in your neighbourhood who choose not to get on that bus [which would bring them to this school]. What do they choose to do? They choose to go out and sell drugs. They choose to go out and kill people. They choose to do a lot of other things but they choose not to get on that bus. The people who choose to get on that bus – which are you – are people who are saying [in Bob Dylan's words], 'I will not carry myself down to die. When I go to my grave my head will be high'.

But the choices for individuals are clearly limited. Johnson's students, for the most part, do not have a choice concerning whether to apply for law school or medical school. They have been assigned to the academy, a sub-school of 'problem' classes within Parkmont High School, not a college preparatory programme. Unlike Johnson, who is able to pass up the invitation by one of her students to 'come and live in my neighbourhood for a week', most of her students are limited in their choices over where to live or, as illustrated below, whether or not to attend school. It is because of these constraints on their lives that they have difficulty relating to the logic of Johnson's neo-liberal challenge: 'Do you have a choice to get on that bus?'

Choice does not necessarily or universally empower individuals as neo-liberals claim, particularly those (such as in DM) whose resources are inadequate to meet the costs of society's benefits. Effectively, you cannot choose what is not available nor what you do not have the (cultural) capital to secure. A market model for the economy and society, in which choice is a central plank, is empowering primarily for those (such as in DPS) with sufficient (cultural, social and economic) capital to purchase its most desirable goods. By imploring her students to accept this flawed logic of choice as freedom, Johnson reinforces their subordinate positions. Left unchallenged are hierarchical societal arrangements that restrict access to certain highly valued goods and undervalue or discount the resources that her students do possess. For these students, Jameson's (1991) description of economic markets could equally apply to the logic of their classroom:

> as a concept [it] rarely has anything to do with choice or freedom, since those are all determined for us in advance, whether we are talking about new model cars, toys or television programs: we select among those, no doubt, but we can scarcely be said to have a say in actually choosing any of them.
>
> (Jameson 1991: 266)

This analogy of the market is also useful in highlighting significant aspects of Johnson's pedagogy that rely on rewards such as chocolate bars, excursions to amusement parks and dinners at expensive restaurants. This is juxtaposed beside her claim that 'learning is the prize. Knowing how to read something and understand it is the prize. Knowing how to think is the prize'. The reality is, only certain kinds of readings and knowledge are prized, rewarded or even recognized. That is, schools are by no means equal and play a significant role in maintaining a highly stratified society. There are two central and interrelated myths of dominant neo-liberal ideology that deflect interest away from such realities: a belief in an equality of opportunity and in just rewards for hard work (see Chapter 2). The shortcomings of such ideology and Johnson's pedagogy are clearly evident when they confront the structural realities of lived experiences. As noted, Johnson's students do not have access to opportunities afforded their peers in other classrooms and schools, and nor are they likely to experience similar rewards for their labour. These structural realities are clearly acknowledged by one parent in her rejection of Johnson's version of empowerment:

> *My boys don't go to your school no more and that's going to be it.*

You took them out of school?

> *You're damn right I did. I saw what they were bringing home: poetry and shit; a waste of time. They got more important things to worry about.*

Don't you think that finishing high school would be valuable for their future?

> *That's not in their future. I ain't raising no doctors and lawyers here. They got bills to pay. Why don't you just get out of here. Go find yourself some other poor boys to save.*

Having bills to pay is not an invention; it is real. Preparing students for work, while viewed by many progressive and liberal educators as a betrayal of the true purpose of education (see Chapter 5), is necessary for low-income families. The neo-liberal discourse of choice has its defence against such views: failure, like success, is framed as a matter of choice. This is a marketized version of the classic 'blame the victim' rhetoric with which critical theorists are familiar. For Johnson, if individuals are disempowered it is because they choose to be, but for those who buy into the 'poor boy makes good' ideology:

> Each new fact gives you another choice. Each new idea builds another muscle. It's those muscles that are going to make you really strong. Those are your weapons and in this unsafe world I want to arm you.

And that's what these poems are supposed to do?

> Yeah. Hey try it. You're just sitting here anyway. Look, if at the end of the term you're not faster, stronger and smarter, you will have lost nothing. But if you are, you'll be that much tougher to knock down.

Nothing for poor, ethnic minorities to lose in a market economy of the classroom? On the contrary, Johnson's students have little to gain from accepting the legitimacy of her cultural capital as an organizing logic for their classroom. In such circumstances, Parkmont High Academy students, because of their limited accumulation of this capital, are necessarily assigned 'dispositions that are given a negative value in the educational market' (Bourdieu 1997: 56). This is starkly evident when consideration is given to the position that Johnson herself inhabits and which she secures through cultural-economic exchanges – such as, trading her qualifications for employment – that serve to reinforce its positive value. Indeed, within the academy and its neighbourhood, Johnson's cultural capital enjoys a heightened value because of its scarcity. This is because 'the structure of the field, i.e., the unequal distribution of capital, is the source of the specific effects of capital, i.e., the appropriation of profits and the power to impose the laws of functioning of the field most favourable to capital and its reproduction' (Bourdieu 1997: 49).

But it is Bourdieu's notion of 'the logic of transmission' of cultural capital that makes Johnson's invitation so unattractive. Accumulating cultural capital takes time: 'external wealth converted into an integral part of the person, into a habitus, cannot be transmitted instantaneously' (Bourdieu 1997: 48); hence the imperative to start early and to pursue its accumulation for as long as possible. Not only are Johnson's students invited to begin this process from a negative disposition, but also they are further handicapped by having wasted time and, being so positioned, are now required to make up for this while also forging ahead. Again, their material conditions frustrate attempts to achieve such a remarkable comeback, given that 'the length of time for which a given individual can prolong his [*sic*] acquisition process depends on the length of time for which his family can provide him with the free time, i.e., time free from economic necessity' (Bourdieu 1997: 49–50).

Time in school is a luxury for many poor ethnic minority students. Moreover, their accumulation of dominant forms of cultural capital is made all the more difficult because of their limited access to sources other than schools and, hence, to its 'educative effect' (Bourdieu 1997: 56). While Johnson portrays the accumulation process in terms of choice – similar to roulette or other 'simple games of chance offering at every moment the possibility of a miracle' (Bourdieu 1997: 46) – the reality is of a highly structured process that favours those who begin early and who are more exposed to the educative effects of the cultural capital of dominant groups.

Who decides what and who decides what to do

The problems of classroom control displayed in *Kindergarten Cop* (hereafter KC) are for many beginning teachers their worst nightmare. In the school psyche, to 'lose control' is often interpreted (even by students) as failure, with the physical behaviour of students an obvious manifestation of a teacher's skills in classroom management. But a classroom 'out of control' is not simply a matter of student disobedience, even when teachers' explicit instructions for the movement and management of student bodies are flagrantly ignored. Institutional imperatives for physical behaviour in classrooms are not always highly valued by students who possess physical dispositions – bodily functions and behaviours – that are commensurate with their level of maturation. As substitute teacher John Kimble (Arnold Schwarzenegger) discovers, it is difficult for teachers to deny young students leave from the classroom to attend to their toiletry needs when the adverse consequences of doing so, for student and teacher, are likely to outweigh the benefits. Crying is another supposed involuntary behavioural response for which young students often find sympathy, even when this is recognized as the child's intention. And play, generally regarded positively and necessary for child development, can be noisy and disruptive and can raise the ire of adults.

While these expressions of the young body have a degree of legitimacy in some fields, the work of the school and its teachers is often directed at their renegotiation and/or at constraining their legitimacy to more 'appropriate' times and places – during recesses and in playgrounds, for example. That is, schools and teachers are actively involved in the socialization of the young body into a particular institutional way of life. Clearly,

> schools are not just places which educate the minds of children, they are also implicated in monitoring and shaping the bodies of young people ...one has only to think of the attempts of teachers to get young children to dress themselves 'properly', ask to go to the toilet in time for accidents to be avoided, sit still and be quiet during lessons ... to realize that the *moving, managed* and *disciplined* body, and not just the speaking and listening body, is central to the daily business of schooling.
>
> (Shilling 1993: 21–2, emphasis in original)

'Shaping' the student body – always an unfinished entity – is a feature of all levels of schooling but can seem most transparent in the early years when students are new to school, its values and its dictates of when, where and how to stand, sit, arrive, leave, walk, run, ask, answer, eat and generally perform. Nevertheless, social exchange of this kind 'presupposes a much more subtle economy of time' than the 'economical transparency of economic exchange, in which equivalents change hands in the same instant' (Bourdieu 1997: 54). This is because 'a social capital of relationships (or social obligations) . . . cannot act instantaneously, at the appropriate moment, unless they have been established and maintained for a long time' (Bourdieu 1997: 54). Not only are the institutional norms of schooling unfamiliar to beginning students, so are the requirements of individual teachers.

Acts of labour are required to turn bodies into social entities (Bourdieu 1978) and the kindergarten class of Astoria Elementary School is illustrative of such a construction site. As its makeshift teacher, Kimble is unschooled in how to gain control over his students' bodily dispositions and is cautioned about underestimating their strength by one of his colleagues: 'Kindergarten is like the ocean. You don't want to turn your back on it'. In a similar vein, Bourdieu (1997: 55) describes succession as 'a critical moment for all power'; its appropriation appearing arbitrary when strategies aimed at securing it are elusive. These control problems are later addressed by emphasizing Kimble's 'physical capital' (Bourdieu 1978) – accumulated through muscle-building and strenuous physical activity – and its transformation into teacher authority. Throughout KC, particularly in its initial scenes, much is made of Kimble's physique. Single-handed, he dispenses with the strongest of criminals and aggressively relates to his fellow police officers. His entry into the classroom is similarly physical. Juxtaposed with the school's principal, a woman small in stature, his superior strength and size is also accentuated by the camera angles and the reaction of his students at his introduction. It is this physical capital that he draws on to reconstruct teacher-student relations in his new environment:

> it's [now] called 'Police School'. I'm going to be your Sheriff, you're going to be my Deputy Trainees. *(Groan.)* Come on, stop whining. You kids are soft, you lack discipline. Well, I've got news for you. You are mine now. You belong to me. *(Oh.)* You're not going to have your mommies run behind you any more and wipe your little tushes. Oh no. It's time now to turn this mush into muscles. No more complaining, 'Mr Kimble, I have to go to the bathroom'. Nothing. There is no bathroom!

The strategy is not unlike that employed by LouAnne Johnson in DM who adopts a stance associated with a previous military occupation to gain physical ascendancy in classroom relations: 'You'd make good marines. In fact, from this moment each one of you is like an inductee'. Bourdieu (1997: 55) suggests that this 'reproduction strategy is at the same time a legitimation strategy'; that is, the reproduction of control is legitimized by 'exploiting the convertibility of the types of capital', in this case, the conversion of physical capital into social capital. At the same time, the arbitrariness of the transmission of entitlements associated with this reproduction is disguised by these legitimation strategies.

For example, Kimble's appeal to his physical prowess repositions him as a 'body expert . . . involved in educating bodies and labelling as legitimate or deviant particular ways of managing and experiencing our bodies' (Shilling 1993: 145). Mobilizing this discourse enables Kimble's physical capital to be exchanged for more regimented teacher–student relations and student bodies; there is no place for the bodily distractions discussed above, embodied in the bathroom, which are now banished from the classroom. Moreover, student bodies are no longer their own. Under this new regime, Kimble's students navigate a barrage of physical activity: marching, jogging, squats, obstacle courses, star jumps, neck rolls, see-saws, rope climbing, hula hoops, fire drills, sprints and sit-ups – at which 'Zac is [declared] the winner'. The latter is revealing of the subtly gendered nature of Kimble's classroom activity; not exclusively so but nevertheless indicative of

> the greater encouragement boys usually receive in comparison with girls to engage in strenuous physical exercise and 'cults of physicality', such as football and weight training, which focus on the disciplined management of the body and the occupation of space.
>
> (Shilling 1993: 110–11)

It is significant, then, that the major challenge to Kimble's 'Police School', and its physical consequences for his 'trainees', comes from Emma. Emma's bodily disposition is informed by a different discourse; one that is (potentially) more empowering for her and often associated with young girls. The challenge unfolds in response to Emma's disregard for Kimble's instruction to his new trainees:

Emma! Emma! Bring your toy back to the carpet.

I'm not a policeman. I'm a princess.

Take your toy back to the carpet.

I'm not a policeman. I'm a princess.

Take it back!

All right.

The discipline of Kimble's classroom – his 'Police School' – does not allow for and cannot accommodate the freedoms associated with being a princess. Emma eventually succumbs to the insistence of Kimble's instruction but not because it offers an attractive alternative. In this case, control is underwritten by both gender and physical strength and its resistance has consequences for the body. It draws on a 'capital of obligations'; not 'economism' in which power is reducible to things economic, nor 'semiologism' in which power is reducible to matters of communication (Bourdieu 1997: 54).

How students feel about it and how they are told to feel

Like the training of their physical bodies, males are often lauded for their control over their emotions, as are whites and the upper classes of western societies. It is not surprising, then, that this particular interaction of gender, race and social class in the private boys' school of Welton Academy – the onscreen classroom in *Dead Poets Society* (DPS) – should address the construction of young men as 'civilised bodies' (Shilling 1993) adept at emotional control. Schooling itself is central to the production of this defensive style of 'hegemonic masculinity' (Connell 1995) with its tight control over emotions. As Seidler (1989) explains, current constructions of masculinity are informed by the elevation of abstract thought in western academic traditions. In tracing the greater demands placed on these matters from the period of the Renaissance, Shilling notes that:

> there has been a shift in emotional and physical expression as a result of long-term civilizing processes in the individual and society. To simplify, the civilized body characteristic of modern western societies . . . has the ability to rationalize and exert a high degree of control over emotions, to monitor its own actions and those of others, and to internalize a finely demarcated set of rules about what constitutes appropriate behaviour in various situations.
>
> (Shilling 1993: 150–1)

Such 'civility' in DPS is unmistakable. For example, teachers and students are explicitly addressed in courteous terms, their surnames prefaced with the title 'Mr', a vain attempt at times to mask emotions that are often betrayed by associated actions and/or tone of voice. But for Robin Williams, as Welton alumnus and incoming teacher John Keating, these and other controls placed on his students by the academy are indicative of emotional restrictions that are, in a sense, 'out of control'. In his view, the school's collective pedagogy has effectively deadened its students' emotions, much like the physical bodies of the poets which they are required to study. This is the issue for Keating: that the study of poetry has been divorced from the emotions that produced it; a disengagement reinforced by Pritchard's clinical rating scale that prefaces students' poetry reading and acts to keep their emotions in check.

Bourdieu's (1997) distinction between two forms of social capital delegation – namely, diffuse and institutionalized delegation – aptly describes the respective positions held by Keating and Pritchard. Both are members of a 'subgroup [of delegates] . . . who may speak on behalf of the whole group, represent the whole group, and exercise authority in the name of the whole group' (Bourdieu 1997: 53), albeit delimited by its purpose of schooling students from and in the ways of the dominant. Institutionalized as its official delegates and bearing the titles of academic and teacher, Pritchard and Keating enjoy the concentration of the group's social capital. However, such concentration also allows the possibility for its 'embezzlement', which,

in the case of Welton Academy, eventually leads to 'expelling or excommun-
icating the embarrassing individuals' (Bourdieu 1997: 53), namely, Keating.

In Bourdieu's (1997: 53) terms, Keating's misappropriation of the school's
social capital can be understood as 'the internal competition for monopoly
of legitimate representation' or, more specifically, as the internal competition between institutionalized and diffuse delegations. Bourdieu (1997:
53) suggests that 'diffuse delegation requires the great to step forward and
defend the collective honour when the honour of the weakest members is
threatened'. This is how Keating is positioned in relation to his students
and the school. In the imagery of the film, he defends his students against
the emotional detachment of the academy. In addressing this denial of self,
Keating intentionally stages his pedagogy to provoke an emotional response.
Breaking out of the school's traditional mould of poetry pedagogy, Keating
declares war against the prevailing academic wisdom:

> Excrement. That's what I think of Mr J. Evans Pritchard. We're not
> laying pipe, we're talking about poetry . . . Rip it out. Rip. Be gone J.
> Evans Pritchard, PhD . . . this is a battle, a war, and the casualties could
> be your hearts and souls . . . Armies of academics going forward, meas-
> uring poetry. No, we'll not have that here . . . In my class you will learn
> to think for yourselves again. You will learn to savour words and lan-
> guage. No matter what anybody tells you, words and ideas can change
> the world . . . We don't read and write poetry because it's cute. We read
> and write poetry because we are members of the human race and the
> human race is filled with passion. Medicine, law, business, engineering,
> these are noble pursuits and necessary to sustain life, but poetry, beauty,
> romance, love, these are what we stay alive for. To quote from Whitman,
> '. . . you are here . . . life exists . . . the powerful play goes on and you
> may contribute a verse'. What will your verse be?

What is important to note here is Keating's realignment of the school's
curricula. Studies that lead to prestigious professions – those to which his
students might fully expect to be destined – are repositioned as peripheral,
no longer the central subjects that students would expect to dominate elite
educational institutions. These are to be displaced by and take their meaning
from poetry, which is represented as the bearer of the very elements of life
itself, experienced through the savouring of words and language. There is
also an internal rearrangement of the poetry curriculum. Ownership is now
to reside in the hearts of students, not in the measured minds of remote
authorities whose practice, if not intent, is to suppress emotion and independent thought. This is the distinction that Kenway *et al.* (1996) make
between teachers' therapeutic and authoritarian orientations to students'
emotional worlds. For Keating, adopting this therapeutic stance means that
it is emotion that is to form the rationale for studying poetry, not its utility.
As he explains, 'Language is developed for one endeavour and that is . . .
Mr Perry? *To communicate?* No. To woo women!'

But such explanation reveals a second and more subtle theme in Keating's language treatise that is far less radical and which reinforces rather than challenges the utility of poetry that he attempts so passionately to discredit. Fashioning language as an instrument for men to seduce women not only constitutes a particular gendering of poetry – informed by a 'hegemonic masculinity' (Connell 1995) that legitimizes some emotions and not others – but also reduces the value of language and emotion to the purposes they can advance. In the process, women are objectified; they too become utilities or things to be tricked into serving the interests of (young) men.

Keating continues his attack on what he portrays as the battle against the establishment for his students' hearts and minds:

> Just when you think you know something, you have to look at it in another way. Even though it may seem silly or wrong, you must try. When you read don't just consider what the author thinks, consider what you think. Boys, you must strive to find your own voices but the longer you wait to begin the less likely you are to find it at all . . . most men lead lives of quiet desperation. Don't be resigned to that. Break out . . . Dare to strike out and find new ground.

The emotional revolution in DPS induced by Keating's pedagogy is perhaps not surprising, given its 1959 setting on the verge of 1960s social experimentations. But as Wouters (1986, 1987, cited in Shilling 1993: 169) explains, the period is better understood as ushering in a 'highly controlled decontrolling of emotions'. In a similar vein, it is also difficult to ignore the dilemmas inherent in reconciling Keating's *imposed* pedagogy and emotionally liberating curriculum. Emotional freedom, it seems, does not come without its own constraints. Moreover, if his students are to take him at his word – to beware the uncritical acceptance of authority – they are faced with the choice of rejecting Keating's own voice and authorship of their dispositions. Bourdieu (1997: 53) refers to aspects of this dilemma as 'one of the paradoxes of delegation . . . that the mandated agent can exert on (and, up to a point, against) the group the power which the group enables him to concentrate'. At another level, the embezzlement of the social capital entrusted to Keating is represented in the metonymy that links him to the group. Keating's students take on his passion for poetry and revive Welton's Dead Poets Society of which he himself was a member as a Welton student. In a sense, he gives his personality to the group and its revival; he is the group personified, 'it is by him, his name . . . that the members of his group . . . are known and recognized' (Bourdieu 1997: 53).[2]

Still, it is important to acknowledge the role of the group and the film in ascribing Keating with this symbolic power. This is probably the crucial issue in DPS: Keating's students *do* have a choice; their particular gender, race and class relations are at work to ensure their disproportionate accumulation of social, cultural and economic capital. The realities of these social arrangements are not lost on students in DM, whose voices echo in the distance, 'why are you playing this game? We don't have a choice'. Indeed, these insights of

Parkmont High School Academy students belie Keating's 'critical' under-standing of the function of poetry in Welton Academy and like institutions. Poetry, too, can lead to prestigious professions. Centralizing it within elite institutions and sharing the ownership of its interpretation with elite students do nothing to address the structural inequalities of society.

Elsewhere, Ball (1994: 26) describes such arrangements as 'first order (practice) effects' as a way of comparing them with 'second order [structural] effects' that bring real change. In this 'first order' sense, it is not hard for Welton students to 'break out' when the dangers of doing so are minimized by the safety nets of wealth and position and when 'breaking out' simply means the generational exchange of control from white-haired masters to their younger counterparts. In Bourdieu's (1997) terms, Keating may have provided an internal challenge to the 'monopoly of exchanges' that constitute the social capital of dominant groups, but this hardly threatened 'the limits of the group'. Nothing in this challenge to Welton Academy addresses the social processes 'which bring together, in a seemingly fortuit-ous way, individuals as homogeneous as possible in all the pertinent respects in terms of the existence and persistence of the [dominant] group' (Bourdieu 1997: 52).

Refocusing on authentic classrooms

What is missing from these accounts of classrooms? More pertinently, what does their analysis have to offer a re-evaluation of pedagogy and curricula for authentic classrooms? Drawing on Farber and Holm (1994) and on the above discussion, we suggest that these films forget at least four matters related to teacher–student relations and that attention to these issues is a necessary first step in a radical democratic reorganization of classrooms and their normative representations. The omissions we highlight in these films and which have relevance for radical democratic schooling include the insti-tutional realities of students' lives; opportunities to challenge the familiar and embrace the foreign; ambiguity and complexity; and the 'ordinary' of teacher–student relations. While these have points of potential overlap, for analytical purposes we consider each of them in turn.

First, acting as a distraction from what is missing, the camera work of these three films tends to focus audience attention on individuals. The audi-ences of these films are confronted by the personal experiences of Johnson, Kimble and Keating rather than the varying experiences of teachers within schools. They are also introduced to particular students not students in particular; it is the lives of individuals that are represented as important more than the life of being a student and/or how these student lives differ from one group to another. This is particularly so in KC and DPS but it is also evident in the discourses of DM that emphasize individual choices. Certainly, individuals are important in any reorganization of classrooms but to focus exclusively and narrowly on them is to miss the point of their connectedness with other individuals and within particular material and social contexts.

Hence, in DM, for example, it is easier to blame individual students for their 'bad' choices than to recognize the institutional constraints on individuals that make some choices unavailable (for example, whether to attend school) and which rework the value placed on other choices (for example, whether studying poetry will lead to a suitable career). In DPS, too, the out-of-frame realities are glossed over in a way that entices us to forget that the deadening of emotions to which Keating's students are subjected, are mediated by their access to considerable amounts of the 'right' sort of social, cultural and economic capital. This wider angle, missing from the audience's frame of reference, helps us to understand that while these students appear under an authoritarian rule, they are themselves being groomed to inherit this authority. Whereas, a radical democratic view of pedagogy and curricula in authentic classrooms seeks to foreground this institutional backdrop to teacher-student relations by proposing the conditions described in Chapter 2. Each of these conditions – self-identity, self-respect, self-development, self-expression, self-determination and so on (see Young 1990) – reinserts institutional realities back onto the agenda, creating spaces for individuals but also relating them to others and to specific contexts.

The first of these conditions in particular, draws attention to a second absence within the onscreen classrooms we examine above; that is, the treatment of the familiar and the foreign. Representations of teacher–student relations have the potential to 'deepen or transform our sense of that which we might otherwise take for granted as part of the familiar, or challenge us to come to grips with domains and perspectives that are foreign to us' (Farber and Holm 1994: 168). The three films we consider above fail to do either of these things. For example, early in KC audiences might initially wonder where Kimble falls on the good–bad continuum constructed by simplistic binary narratives, but they are soon assured of his positive positioning and of the eventual fate of his opponents. Similarly in DM, while its scenes provide the potential for a fruitful exploration of difference (see Chapter 7) – 'the possibility of genuinely conflicting views among reasonable and sympathetically presented characters' (Farber and Holm 1994: 169) – a far more black and white characterization is forthcoming. In short, what is familiar is presented as good and relevant, and what is unknown, what is foreign to us, is presented as either bad, irrelevant or unknowable (see the discussion in Chapter 4 concerning the construction of binaries). There is no space here to identify oneself as reasonable *and* different, and there is no space to tell different stories in a context of respect. By contrast, authentic classrooms informed by a radical democratic politics require opportunities for students to challenge the familiar and embrace the foreign, that is, to develop respect for 'the other'.

Third, these three films leave little room for the audience to stray from the director's interpretation of events; for different meanings to be ascribed to activities and exchanges, and for dialogue over what might be meant by what is screened. On the surface of this screening – its framing, music, script and so on – audiences are led to believe, first, that Kimble's students are happier and more content when they succumb to his authority, second, that Keating's teaching methods are not only more engaging than his counterparts but also 'better', and third, that even though Johnson lacks teaching experience, this is adequately compensated by her 'heart' being in the right place. This is no space to wonder, for example, whether there is merit in the apparent chaos of Kimble's initial encounters with his kindergarten class; whether Keating's poetic exorcism of Todd, one of his students, is ethical; or what Johnson stands to gain from fashioning her students in particular ways. Ambiguity and complexity are unwelcome visitors to these classrooms; there is little 'to work out a view on, mull over, or argue about' (Farber and Holm 1994: 169). Radical democratic classrooms, however, welcome dialogue, indeed they construct opportunities for it to occur as a central organizer of teacher–student relations. In such organizations, difference is recognized and welcomed.

Fourth, it is the exceptional that is screened in these films, not the ordinary. It is telling, for example, that all three onscreen teachers enter these classrooms from outside the schooling system and even in KC it is this distance from the system that is portrayed as critical in transforming students. Ordinary teachers, it seems, are unable to approach the heights of these exceptional individuals who are not teachers in the standard sense. Kimble, for example, excels in training his kindergarten students in ways that elude others teaching higher grades. Johnson, too, succeeds with her students where her predecessors had failed and/or had abandoned them. The final scene of DPS bears testament to the dramatic influence Keating wrought on his protégés, voiced in their declaration of allegiance – 'Captain, my captain' – and their associated actions. In short, these films feed off incidents rarely observed in authentic classrooms and provide little guidance for everyday teaching practice. By contrast:

> The vast majority of critical incidents, however, are not at all dramatic or obvious: they are mostly straightforward accounts of very commonplace events that occur in routine professional practice which are critical in the rather different sense that they are indicative of underlying trends, motives and structures.
>
> (Tripp 1993: 24–5)

The point here and throughout this chapter is that seemingly ordinary events can be more critical in (re)organizing classrooms for radical democratic purposes when they are seen as 'an example of a category in a wider, usually social, context' (Tripp 1993: 25) rather than as isolated and, therefore, unimportant incidents. Young (1990: 150) writes in this vein about the response that marginalized people can receive when they highlight the discriminatory behaviour embedded in the seemingly ordinary actions of others. The phrase, 'Oh, he didn't mean anything by it', becomes a way of backgrounding and dismissing the institutional realities of social interactions. These are the very matters, as ordinary as they might seem, that require our attention in (re)organizing classrooms towards radical democratic ends.[3] In this (re)organization, we are mindful of Young's (1990: 151) distinction between allocating blame and claiming responsibility for classroom relations: 'blame is backward-looking . . . responsibility . . . is forward-looking; it asks the person "from here on out" to submit such unconscious behaviour to reflection, to work to change habits and attitudes'. Teachers bear such responsibilities towards their students; they and interested others are obligated to think again about the classroom relations they establish and how these might be reworked to better serve their students' interests.

Questions for discussion/research

- How might films portray teachers and students in more socially just ways?
- Whose knowledge of the world (and how to engage with it) is privileged in your educational setting?
- To what extent is metonymy relied on to explain the broader social context of your educational setting?

Suggested readings

Dalton, M. (1995) The Hollywood curriculum: who is the 'good' teacher? *Curriculum Studies*, 3(1): 23–44.

Farber, P., Provenzo Jr, E. and Holm, G. (eds) (1994) *Schooling in the Light of Popular Culture*. Albany, NY: State University of New York Press, pp. 153–72.

Giroux, H. (1997) Rewriting the discourse of racial identity: towards a pedagogy and politics of whiteness, *Harvard Educational Review*, 67(2): 285–320.

Griffiths, M. and Troyna, B. (eds) (1995) *Antiracism, Culture and Social Justice in Education*. Stoke-on-Trent: Trentham Books, pp. 115–32.

Representing (self and) others: discourses of inclusion and exclusion

Introduction

This chapter introduces and analyses three broad discourses of academic achievement and failure, specifically those that speak of students' *deficits*, *disadvantages* and *differences*. In our view, these represent discourses of considerable influence in determining how teachers, students and parents define what constitutes success or failure in schools, which respective approach educators employ, and the beliefs they hold about students who fail and those who succeed. In this respect, the chapter explores several issues raised in Chapter 2 in discussions concerning social justice. Our intention here is to expand on those concepts and to offer a different slant from which to view them. In particular, we seek to tease out the stories that discourses of deficit, disadvantage and difference tell about student diversity, as a way of unmasking how students are differently represented and how these representations serve to include some and exclude others from the benefits of schooling and society. In introducing these matters, we begin with two brief but very different descriptions of schooling and its prospects for students from marginalized groups; these accounts provide a context within which to explore the discourses of deficit, disadvantage and difference as they interpret and produce dispositions for these students.

The first of these proceeds as follows. For many poor students and students from non-dominant groups, school and the media are their main chances to acquire a grasp of the public culture. In particular, education is often viewed as the primary means through which individuals can improve their life chances and become upwardly mobile. Perhaps because of this special importance, public schooling is commonly believed to be a positive social force, providing everyone with equal opportunity in a democratic society. Schools are open to everyone and apparently provide all students with basically the same curricula as well as equal access to school resources. Despite biting reports of 'savage inequalities' (see, for example,

Kozol 1991) among public schools in terms of the financial resources they have at their disposal, many people still believe that once their children are in school, they receive approximately the same instruction and experiences as their classmates. Academic performance is, therefore, considered to depend upon individual students, that is, on their individual ability and effort.

There is another account, however, with strikingly different explanations of these matters. As noted in Chapter 2, there have been numerous studies over many years that demonstrate that the above assumptions are not supported by the facts. Such studies conclude that public education in western capitalist societies does not equally foster the academic achievement of poor students, of most students of colour, nor of many females. Even though more students are staying in school longer, this has done little to decrease the dependence of their educational outcomes on race, class and gender. While exceptions can be found, and although there have been improvements in recent years, particularly in relation to the education of white middle-class girls, still, students' academic performances are typically related to their social descriptors. One argument is that schools engage in particular social practices that tend to favour certain attributes over others (see, for example, Delgado-Gaitan 1990; Apple 1996; Lankshear *et al.* 1997). The problem, as several theorists have noted – many utilizing variations of Bourdieu's (1984, 1997; Bourdieu and Passeron 1977) notions of cultural, social and economic capital – is that the attributes that schools favour are not equally available to all students. The corollary of this is that schools promote students who bring to the school those attributes that schools reward. That is, schooling empowers certain groups of students by making what they already possess that which is necessary for success; for example, the specific language-related habits and forms of questioning (Heath 1983) evidenced in dominant forms of 'linguistic capital' (Bourdieu and Passeron 1977; Bourdieu 1984). 'Indeed, a close examination of social experience leads to the conclusion that schooling is not an instrument of social advancement; on the contrary, it actually promotes social stratification and inequality' (Preston and Symes 1992: 100).

Such are the accounts of schooling and the performances of students from marginalized groups that are variously constructed by discourses of deficit, disadvantage and difference and which we explore in this chapter. Because they are frequently used, these discourses have become familiar and have slipped into our collective 'common sense', despite their detrimental consequences in many instances. Well-known stories, it seems, develop a way of hiding their hegemonic functions and effects. For these reasons, we seek ways of rethinking 'the evidence and the postulates, of shaking up habits, ways of acting and thinking, of dispelling commonplace beliefs, of taking a new measure of rules and institutions' (Foucault 1991: 11–12). Our purpose is to find plausible and useful accounts of diverse student populations that also recognize and promote the value of this diversity.

Guiding questions

Guiding this exercise are three questions:

- How can we best explain differential academic achievement by groups of students?
- What do explanations of school failure have in common with our understandings of *diversity*?
- What would an understanding of *difference* look like if it enabled us to critique the relations of power within which our knowledge of ourselves and others and our pedagogical practices are created, and if it furthered social equality?

While the first of these questions has been researched and debated for a long time, it matters today as much as it ever has. Indeed, as we begin the twenty-first century, all three questions are of critical importance. To begin with, since the discourses of deficit and disadvantage especially, tend to address only surface or individual features of students' failures and successes, they provide an incomplete and distorted understanding of the 'geography of the problem' (Connell 1993). On these grounds alone they are worth questioning. Second, there are significant changes taking place in our school communities. With the growing cultural mix of students in many urban areas of the UK, the US and Australia, for example, fed by an ongoing influx of immigrants, discourses of exclusion have increasing potential for wide-spread and deleterious effects on student groups, depending on the extent to which they are respectively taken up. This is occurring at the same moment as the emergence of a widening gap between the rich and the poor, not only in income and wealth distribution but also in such areas as public and private schooling and in health care. Third, the questions we ask of these discourses and the stories they construct about schooling are ones directed at what can be done about the problems that students face. This is important given that two of these discourses – those that speak of student deficits and disadvantage – tend to remove significant responsibility for students' academic failure from those things over which interested people could exercise some influence, namely, school practices and relations of power in society. Finally, these questions matter a great deal today because they raise the question of who really benefits from schooling, anyway?

Of course, questions of this kind and our justifications of them reveal something of our own theoretical and political dispositions. It is our contention, for example, that to understand what is going on inside schools, scholars and practitioners alike must take both local and global contexts into account. This means that the validity of discursive explanations for diversity and differential academic achievement that we examine, can be found, in large measure, by looking at their effects within the cultural context and relations of power in which they operate. More generally, we examine where these discourses diverge in locating 'the problem' and the different 'solutions' they offer. We pay special attention to the differences in the degree to which schools are believed to be a force for change. Finally, we look at some of the beliefs and practices that inform and are informed by these discourses and we consider how they are expressed in the debates and dialogue around notions of diversity.

Discourses of deficit

The first discourse of exclusion we consider in this chapter, which speaks of *deficits*, represents schools as unable to do much about differential academic achievements since they essentially reflect individual differences in innate intelligence and talent. Ability is said to be a discrete, quantifiable, indi- vidual characteristic that has little, if anything, to do with social context. In other words, one's genetic make-up predominates over environmental fac- tors in determining intelligence. Much educational psychology has reinforced the idea that each person is born with a largely determined mental capacity despite differences in history, culture and environment. It is not surprising then, the story proceeds, that only a relatively small number of students benefit from higher-level outcomes of schooling. While we can work to pro- vide more equal educational opportunities, differential academic achievement, as well as subsequent employment, should be expected, given individuals' innate intellectual inequalities. Genetic deficits thus ensure and justify dif- ferential educational and social rewards. More generally, statistically measured intelligence explains social inequalities as well as privileges.

The idea that individuals are rewarded on the basis of their innate talent and effort has wide appeal in modern societies and often has been used to explain or justify social inequalities.[1] Even though objective impediments to socio-economic justice and equality exist, many people are convinced that capitalist societies, in particular, offer equal opportunities (that is, equal access to education and, hence, to 'advancement') to the vast majority, placing the responsibility for educational and economic success (and failure) on indi- vidual's talents and effort. By focusing on individuals' merits in this way, deficit discourses usher in formal equality as well as popular agreement that individuals should not be legally discriminated against because of their race, ethnicity, sex or socio-economic class. In short, racism, sexism and other forms of social discrimination are technically eradicated and any vestiges of these oppressive relations will, in time, disappear. The parallel story that this discourse tells, then, is that if you remain poor or disadvantaged in some way, either you are not trying hard enough to succeed or you simply do not have the talent to warrant better circumstances. Sharp (1980) explains that it is not uncommon to find low-income students across cultures internaliz- ing this discourse, explaining their academic failure in terms of their own individual deficiencies.

Teachers who also believe these stories tend to hold lower expectations for those students whom they perceive to have limited ability. While this is often done with good intentions, for example, to avoid the fear of embarrassing or frustrating a student by giving him or her unreasonably difficult work, these fears reflect a patronizing stance, one that can do more to reinforce the student's perceived deficits than anything else. The solution, to give these children less difficult tasks, ostensibly to preserve their self-esteem, can in reality add to the difficulties these students already face. By never being held to high expectations, these students can end up being prepared for positions in society that are the least rewarding and respected. This is one way in which educational tracking or streaming reinforces social stratification. Reliance on IQ and other forms of testing to decide where students should be placed and the acceptance of different kinds of education for students with different abilities, guide students towards various graded types of employment. In short, differential preparation in school destines students for different niches in the occupational hierarchy (see Bowles and Gintis 1976; Anyon 1981).

A good illustration of this exclusive discourse is evident in the following interview extract. In our conversations, Michelle described her secondary/high school as having a few 'fairly low ability students'. We were interested to know what discourses were at work within the school to produce these assessments and what practices they implied for teachers and schooling:

> *How do teachers identify students who are not as able to meet the academic requirements of the school? How does that happen and what does the school do about it?*

They work a lot with the primary [elementary] school in terms of identifying incoming students with difficulties. Perhaps it is easier in a smaller town to do that and for the [secondary] high school to be able to ascertain students at certain levels. I think being in a small country town they are luckier in terms of having that knowledge filter through to them from the primary [elementary] school and just from the local area and knowing people and knowing the community. We have a programme at school that caters for students with learning disabilities. I have three of these students, actually, in my HPE class . . . They have been integrated into my class because I only have six other students enrolled in that class and we have adapted the programme for them. The Grade 9 HPE curriculum does not include an aquatics unit, but I'm taking an aquatics unit because I know that for these students that is an interest for them. So the programme is adjusted for them and the main purpose is to integrate them in with the rest of the school and to allow them to be involved in what is going on; to integrate them in with other people and allow them to socialize with other students. But at the same time, they are not allowed to go into certain classes that are just too far over their heads. It would be pointless for them to sit there and for them to think, 'What am I doing here? I am too stupid for this'. I think the whole purpose is they don't want the students to feel that they are at any disadvantage or that they are worse off than anybody else. The whole emphasis is to get them in and get them involved.

(Michelle)

Illustrated clearly in Michelle's comments is the deficit discourse at work: identifying students through formal and informal assessments; tracking students and their deficits through the system; 'watering down' the curriculum; keeping expectations low and, therefore, achievable; avoiding embarrassments and frustrations; closing some doors and opening others; and maintaining that this is all in the best interests of students. What is more revealing, however, is to consider what these arrangements mean for teachers and schools, particularly in relation to issues of change. Certainly, there is work involved in identifying students who are experiencing learning difficulties and in making adjustments to the school's administration, pedagogy and curricula to accommodate them. But there are also considerable benefits in this form of accommodation since schools and schooling, on the whole, are not required to change very much. That is, the special programme designed to cater for these students seems also designed to do so with minimal disruption to institutional arrangements.

We see this when Michelle comments on the school's rationale for selecting her class as the site for the students' placement: 'they have been integrated into my class because I only have six other students enrolled in that class'. Only a few 'mainstream' students, then, are affected by adjustments to the curriculum, an adjustment made not on the basis of its difficulty, although this is implied, but on the basis of student interest. It is revealing how 'interest' becomes an issue for students deemed to have learning difficulties, more so than other students. Revealing, too, is who determines what these interests are (see the discussion in Chapter 6 regarding LouAnne Johnson's adjustment of the curriculum). These students are also denied access into other presumably higher populated classes that apparently would require adjustment to their curriculum to accommodate them and, therefore, disruption to greater numbers of students. In this context, and despite the rhetoric of accommodating student interests, what is taught and learnt appears secondary to maintaining current administrative arrangements. As Michelle explains, 'the main purpose is to integrate them in with the rest of the school', not to change the school. In this, the school even anticipates the assistance of other students to socialize diverse students into the system. Standing outside of the system, then, constitutes disadvantage, not students' deficits *per se*. Deficit discourse has a place for everybody!

Such discourse does recognize diversity among students but anticipates a very narrow range for it. Essentially, most students are the same and only a few differ from the norm. Informed by western experiences, the analogy it draws on is a medical and/or physiological one, which suggests that few children are deformed at birth and most are able to function normally in the physical world. Similarly, as teachers, we can try to help students with academic deficits but some do not want to be helped – that is, they do not want to help themselves – or their deficits are so extreme that they cannot be helped very much. We just have to make things as comfortable as we can for them. Different views about a person's 'essence', or about whether or not individuals even have an essence, have played an important role in understanding diversity and its relation to school performance. By suggesting that an individual student either has or does not have ability, deficit discourses have a ready-made explanation for politicians, prospective employers and parents who want to know, 'Why can't my child read?' Neither teachers nor the school can do much with students who lack ability, it is argued. By locating the problem in one's nature, a particular notion of the individual is implied: that because there is something innate and inevitable about a student's poor performance in school, it cannot be remedied.

Discourses of disadvantage

A second discourse of exclusion shares with the first the assumption that there is something natural or inevitable about disproportionate academic failure among students from marginalized groups. Discourses of disadvantage respond to the question, 'Why can't my child read?', by pointing to individuals' cultural and/or economic disadvantages. This view suggests that when we look at the home backgrounds of students from non-dominant groups we see that they are deprived, lacking in motivation, stimulation, proper values and discipline for success in school and later, the job market. The origins of inequality are thus located at the early stages in one's life. White, middle-class homes are seen as the norm for all students, regardless of their race, ethnicity or social class. Similar to students with less innate intelligence, these students are considered to have accidentally inherited a lower intellectual aptitude given their lack of a proper upbringing.

Again, Michelle provides evidence of how this discourse of disadvantage influences teachers' thinking and practices. We began this section of the interview by asking Michelle about the demographics of her school community:

> it's a very low socio-economic area and a lot of the students come from pretty horrific backgrounds; parents running off all over the countryside and students living with girlfriends, single mothers or single fathers. The students are living with whomever they can actually live with. And there are aunties taking care of kids because their parents are unfit or their single parent families aren't fit to take care of them. There's a high percentage of that but I'm not quite sure of the figures . . . my experience, so far, although it's limited, is that they are [Black] students who come from those fairly broken, unstable backgrounds . . .

What do you think the role of schooling is for these students?

From my experience of different schools, it's not only just teaching them maths, science, English, whatever. In a lot of cases, especially the kids I teach now, it's also about teaching them general manners, respect and how to behave and to respect themselves, to have confidence in themselves, and trust. It's a whole body process. It's not just academic because so many kids can't pick it up anyway, no matter how much you try to drum it into them. Their learning curve is very low and their learning ability is very low.

In learning what?

In learning the things like maths or science or English, grasping concepts and having to solve problems. [So] I am really one for teaching them, 'Well, hang on, you have just entered the room incorrectly. What should you say to me if you come in late? What would you expect me to say to you?' Just that sort of thing. I know a lot of teachers do that. They really concentrate on that aspect as far as proper behavioural and social skills are concerned . . .

Why wouldn't they learn those behavioural and social skills at home?

A lot of their parents have other priorities, to put it nicely. Their children don't mean a lot to them. For instance, poker machines have just been introduced into this area and one of the teachers has told me that one particular mother is too busy with the poker machines to worry about her children; whether they get home from school, if they have done their homework, if they have clean clothes for the next day, or if they have lunch packed. She is just down there at the poker machines all the time. That is her distraction. I think there are quite a few students whose parents really don't care. To get them to go to school is to get them away for the day. And, whether their children are down the back or wherever, they might be at a friend's place smoking Marijuana or whatever they might be doing, the parents wouldn't know . . .

You don't think there are worthwhile things these students can learn outside of school?

They can learn certain things without schools, certainly. I mean, you look at our parents. My parents, my father especially, had to leave school at a very young age, and he's one of the brightest men I know. But he was very lucky in that he had a home environment that enabled him to learn, and continuously learn, and he is secure enough in himself and in his background that he will take information in. Whereas I think there is a need for schools – maybe not so much for education as students see it – for somebody who has a very bad home life. That's an escape for them when they get to school. They're around their friends. They're around, possibly, other cousins or family members and they are around familiar things that are going to stay constant all the time. And they learn the rules, even if they're not soaking up any academic information, like maths or English or science. They do learn something. They learn something from school: be it how to behave properly, how to sit properly in a class, how to concentrate for two minutes, how to play sport, or how to ask nicely at the school shop, 'Can I have this please?' It's a continuous learning thing.

(Michelle)

Notice the similarities between deficit discourses and those of disadvantage, between students whose 'learning ability is very low' and those who come from 'pretty horrific backgrounds'. In both cases students are deemed to be without some quality important for academic achievement at school. That these two discourses are mobilized by the one teacher – although, we could have provided similar comments from other teachers in our research – is another indication of their close relationship, that they are different ways of making similar claims. Another important similarity is their emphasis on individuals; even though discourses of disadvantage tend to focus more on groups of individuals, they still identify these as particular groups whose individuals have similar characteristics. That is, the group is seen as little more than describing similar individual traits. Where discourses of disadvantage differ, however, is they suggest that social context has an impact on students' school performances. This is clear in Michelle's comparison of her father's 'home environment that enabled him to learn' with the 'very bad home life' of many of her students, which presumably explains why 'they can't pick [the academic] up anyway'.

What is absent from Michelle's analysis, however, is a broader account of the relationships between what these homes value and what is valued by schools. Without fully realizing the significance of her comments in this regard, Michelle puts it aptly: 'their parents have other priorities'. For Michelle, this is a criticism even if a polite one; the norms of schools are those which are 'right' and 'good'. They also happen to be her own. Stories of the immorality of parents – who are 'running off all over the countryside' and are 'too busy with the poker machines' to adequately prepare their children for school – are contrasted with the virtues of the school itself; the site of 'familiar things that are going to stay constant all the time'. Inevitably, there are stereotypes in Michelle's account – typical in disadvantage discourses – that associate poor, Black students and others who live in family arrangements different from those of white middle-class families, with habits and dispositions that are detrimental to students' academic achievement and their general well-being. In one respect, Michelle is right. Having priorities different to schooling does make a difference to how well students fare.

Nonetheless, Michelle is optimistic for the future of these students, given the right conditions at school. From this perspective, programmes to expand opportunities for the disadvantaged, termed 'cultural enrichment', can make an important difference. The solution to cultural deprivation or disadvantage is to target these individuals, and sometimes their families, to make up for what they lack; to compensate them with what they are not likely to get at home. Notice the similarities here with the practices associated with deficit discourses, that the curriculum is designed, albeit more overtly, to include the social norms of dominant groups (not unlike Johnson's curriculum planning outlined in Chapter 6). So, what are the outcomes of this new curriculum? As Michelle puts it, 'they learn the rules, even if they're not soaking up any academic information, like maths or English or science. They do learn something'. One suspects that this social curriculum becomes almost more important than the academic, although it is important to understand that the latter is itself imbued with social rules (as noted in Chapter 3). This gives a much richer understanding of Michelle's description of schooling as constituting 'a whole body process', which has similarities with the 'whole language' approach we described in Chapter 3.

Educational and social policies informed by a discourse of disadvantage thus typically aim to modify diverse cultural practices. Compensatory and remedial programmes, particularly popular in many western societies in the 1960s and 1970s, aim to make poor students of colour behave and perform more like white middle-class students (Fordham and Ogbu 1986). Given that schools are structured around white, middle-class norms, this is logical: if students could be changed to fit into these norms they would have the same opportunities for both educational and economic success. This perspective is not new. Historically, schools have been charged with socializing the young into the dominant culture and norms of appropriate behaviour (see, for example, Tyack 1974; Lazerson 1977). In the US, for example, the 'founding fathers' rejected the idea of a multicultural society and instead advocated a unified American culture, one formed from Protestant Anglo-Saxon traditions (Takaki 1993; Spring 1997). Both the strategy of assimilation and the socializing function of schools take the Anglo-Saxon, Protestant, male, middle-class culture as the benchmark, assume we live in a meritocracy, and consider students who do not succeed in school as having special needs, with extra problems, and as forming a subset of the majority of students. Pedagogically, these students are typically excluded from powerful forms of knowledge and cognitively challenging curricula. Yet when these students fail, teachers often remark, 'This child isn't reading because of the home s/he comes from.'

Discourses of difference

Discourses of *difference* provide alternatives to the two exclusive discourses discussed above and are represented by various strands. In this section, we discuss two of these before we turn to a third strand that we believe has the greatest potential for explaining school failure and for furthering social equality. Collectively, discourses of difference distance themselves from deficit and disadvantage accounts that represent student diversity as problematic and something to be remedied. Nevertheless, the two versions of difference discourse we initially consider still tend to be exclusionary, the first attempting to do away with notions of *group* diversity and the second attempting to do away with *critique* of diverse groups. In this they continue the debates concerning individuals and groups, interestingly, both drawing on essential-ist rhetoric associated with the nature side of nature–nurture debates. The third strand of difference discourse we consider is more inclusionary and is identifiable by its points of departure from these posturings. In brief, it asserts the importance and value of groups in explaining diversity, but also goes beyond this to argue for different forms of interaction between groups and different forms for their representation among others.

In our own way, we are all different

Diversity is often used to account for the array of different students who attend a particular school and for their different student collections. But are these differences meaningful? Some people think not. Some of the people who think not generally deny or are oblivious to the existence or signific-ance of group differences. Still others may agree that social groups exist but consider them undesirable, viewing them as necessarily divisive and, there-fore, to be avoided. The implicit notion (and the importance) of the individual in these views has its philosophical roots in the European Enlightenment of the late seventeenth century. During that period, a person's identity was believed to be constituted by an essential inner core, existing from birth. Any influence of culture or society on a person's sense of self was independ-ent of, and came after, this essential core. From this individualist conception of the person, groups impose limits on the individual. Therefore, eliminating obstacles to one's development requires treating people as individuals with universal needs, not as members of groups with special needs because of that membership.

Many teachers, for example, aware of the dangers of stereotyping, strive to deal with their students as individuals in order to best meet their indi-vidual needs. Diversity for these educators might be conceived in terms of learning styles or personalities. Further, well-meaning teachers may ignore group differences because they consider it impolite or insensitive to recognize students' colour, gender or poverty. Many of these teachers regard their task as one of working towards the eventual demise of group differences, or at least the socially ascribed 'evils' associated with diverse groups. Young (1990) summarizes the perspective as follows:

> A truly nonracist, nonsexist society . . . would be one in which the race or sex of an individual would be the functional equivalent of eye color in our society. While physiological differences in skin color or genitals would remain, they would have no significance for a person's sense of identity or how others regard him or her . . . People would see no reason to consider race or gender in policy or everyday interactions. In such a society, social group differences would cease to exist.
>
> (Young 1990: 158)

In our research we found several examples of this discourse at work, few more explicit than the one that follows. Among a number of questions concerning inclusive teaching practices, we asked David for illustrations of how he sought to address diversity in his primary school teaching:

> Well, I guess the ones that spring to mind are more the ones which are purposely constructed. You know, it would be interesting for me to look at my language when I'm not guarded and just see how it is constructed. There are sort of two levels here. I mean they are not levels but two approaches. At times I know that through the materials I bring to the class I deliberately address, say sexism. So, I'll go out of my way to talk about women mathematicians. I won't bring it in as women mathematicians, I don't like doing that, but I will bring in the work of a mathematician who happens to be a woman. In this way I try to make it very clear to the kids – even though I'm not doing it explicitly – to make the case that it's really incidental to it. You know, make it explicit, but incidental . . .

So, you have two agendas?

> Well, I definitely have another agenda in that there may be two mathematicians that I could bring into the same area and I may purposefully select the female because it gives the opportunity to reinforce the point that mathematics should not be gendered. For primary school kids and for secondary school students, I think that's important, I really do. So yes, it's deliberate. What I'm saying is that the actual process by which I introduce it to the class involves making it sound completely incidental. I won't tell them I had a choice of two and I chose this one.

> (David)

Although David's intentions are to challenge the stereotypes associated with mathematicians and women, and thereby instil in his students a 'natural' acceptance for this combination, it is difficult to see how this approach addresses the gendering of social interactions in mathematics classrooms and in mathematical contexts more broadly, simply through the (virtual and silent) 'absent presence' (Apple 1996: xiv) of female mathematicians. 'Mathematics should not be gendered', but it is and why should we think it to be otherwise? We wonder what a classroom might look like that explicitly took this on board: that mathematics is gendered and that it silences particular ways of thinking about the world (see Orenstein 1994). More generally, it is striking how this strand of difference discourse actually works to negate differences from the norm through their assimilation under a seemingly universal umbrella.

Difference is to be celebrated, not questioned

By contrast, a second strand of difference discourse places great emphasis on *group* diversity. Some (but not all) of the people who adhere to this discourse also assume that not only individuals but also groups as well have a pre-existing essential core to their identity, that there is some inherent quality that characterizes the essence of a particular socio-cultural group. From this position and even that of a more social constructivist orientation, diversity is seen as related to the cultural traditions of groups and as intrinsically positive. Hence, cultural differences should be not only maintained but also (uncritically) recognized and affirmed, particularly since such maintenance, recognition and affirmation is believed to enhance a group's self-esteem. This is also important in a context where culturally defined groups are assumed to be struggling for the (moral) right to maintain their culture and for recognition against common oppression: cultural domination by the Anglo middle-class male norm.

While critics argue that the minority-group politics that mobilizes this discourse is narrowly self-interested, in fact, these movements arose in the first place to protest the fictions of a society that boasted it offers a 'level playing field' for all its members (Fraser 1997: 5). Other critics argue that this form of discursive difference does away with the need to specifically address racial inequalities and other wider structures of exploitation and oppression, given their preoccupation with issues of group identification. There appears some support for such criticism in the way difference discourse plays out in (teachers') actions. Representing, in some ways, the flip-side to the view that groups are deprived if they fail to match up to the norm, this strand of multiculturalism romanticizes cultural variations or differences and endorses the cultivation and maintenance of distinct cultural identities. By reflecting the cultures, experiences and perspectives of diverse groups in school curricula, it is posited, teachers can provide the means to improve the academic performances of students from non-dominant groups (see Banks 1988). Many contemporary multicultural programmes are based on these assumptions, celebrating cultural differences in the belief that if people learn about cultures different from their own, this in itself will promote tolerance and social harmony.

A number of these issues presented themselves in an interview one of us conducted with a secondary/high schoolteacher (T10) in Australia. The discussion ranged across the teacher's experiences with indigenous (Aboriginal and Torres Strait Islander) students, at one point focusing on issues relating to their identities:

I notice that you seem to use the phrase 'Aboriginal and Torres Strait Islander' very deliberately.

Yes, yes.

Why is that?

Well, I lived in the Torres Strait and I've lived with Aboriginal people as well and I know that they are different groups. They identify very strongly as separate groups. I also never use the term 'ATSI' [Aboriginal and Torres Strait Islander]. The reason for that is that ATSI to me is a derogatory term, because it's a shortening.

I have had Aboriginal people tell me that too.

Yes. I won't use it for that particular reason. Aboriginal people around here call themselves 'Murries'. I consider the word 'Murri' to be something that that group would use but I don't feel that I have the closeness or that it's up to me to use it. It's not appropriate for me to use that term because I'm not part of that group. It's something they would use more among themselves. I am part of the formal community of Aboriginal and Torres Strait Islanders here because I am part of this teaching unit, but I am not really part of that group. No matter what I do or attempt to do to be included in that group, I'm not. And so, therefore, I refuse to use that term and I think that, to a lot of people, that is considered as the right approach. I don't immediately assume that I am going to be that close and that well liked or well accepted to be able to use that particular term. Also, Torres Strait Islanders don't like the term 'Murri' at all because it tends to be a Queensland term. And then in Victoria, Aboriginal people call themselves 'Koories', but Queensland Aborigines would never use that word to refer to themselves because they think it implies someone who is neither white nor black but something in-between.

(T10)

There is a great deal of intended respect for indigenous Australians in this teacher's comments, evidenced in his deliberate use of what he regards as positive language in keeping with his knowledge of how his students see themselves. There is also a degree of separateness, a lack of closeness and a feeling of inappropriateness in using terms which 'belong' to other groups. Indeed, the label 'Aboriginal and Torres Strait Islander' is not one claimed by indigenous Australians for themselves but assigned by others. In this sense, it too could be regarded as derogatory as its shortened version. Our purpose in highlighting these matters, though, is not so much to raise the issue of how groups are identified – whether they are involved in their own identification or not, even though that is an important issue – but as a way of looking beyond issues of identification, to where they fall short of a positive positioning for all groups in society. To be fair to this teacher, he may well have been willing and able to provide further evidence in this regard, had we asked. And had we asked, we would have wanted to know what space this particular discourse of difference creates for groups, particularly non-dominant groups, to foster their own development and expression and to participate in decision-making processes that directly affect them. In other words, how does the celebration of difference – and its attendant rejection of criticism – contribute to differences in the circumstances of marginalized groups?

We create our social differences, and distances

Through these critiques of discourses of deficit, disadvantage and difference we have attempted to signal points of departure for a third and more inclusive strand of difference discourse. Here we address this project more directly, although not without revisiting some of the more persistent themes that prevail in current accounts of schooling. In this new accounting of 'the problem', we identify potential 'solutions' in not only seeing differences as variations rather than deviations from a dominant norm (Fraser 1997), but also in recognizing the intersections among groups and in school curricula (including its assessment procedures) that represents the interests of groups, taking account of their differential capacities to assert these. We begin by making the case that inclusion requires a concern for social processes that produce the standards by which we make judgements about social groups' relative worth.

Inclusive discourses of difference do not assume that assimilation into the dominant culture is the preferred avenue through which diverse groups can be accepted and contribute to the larger society. Rather, assimilation is viewed as a process through which dominant, privileged groups define the standards according to which everyone else will be judged. Social and cultural differences between marginalized groups and the dominant group become institutionalized in social practice or in legal, labour and educational codes, placing oppressed peoples at a disadvantage in measuring up to dominant norms. In this way, policies of assimilation perpetuate disadvantage in a diverse society (Young 1990: 164). For example, by believing that our common culture is 'colour-blind', privileged white people construct ideologies that allow them to deny the existence of racial inequality while simultaneously benefiting from it (McLaren 1997: 262). Further, assimilation can perpetuate disadvantage by assuming we have a common democratic culture, so that people avoid recognizing practices that have excluded and continue to exclude oppressed peoples from full participation, especially the poor and immigrants.

Inclusive discursive practices, therefore, should be about the *inclusion* into public life of diverse groups – not their assimilation into a mainstream norm – so that all people are able to express their interests and experiences on an equal basis with everyone else (see Young 1990). This is significant at a time when Corson (1998: 3) argues that today's 'capitalist social relations are the most assimilatory cultural forces that the world has ever seen'. Such observations are germane for schools that are increasingly viewed as businesses and which are necessarily reworking the kinds of relationships that exist between students, teachers, parents and administrators, as well as the quality and kinds of outcomes for which we strive. Even though diverse groups are being recognized more than before, often as potential markets for products, at the same time, capitalist social relations create pressures towards sameness of values and behaviours that do not challenge the system of exploitation. Administrators, teachers and students are having to perform according to prescribed criteria in a market environment over which they appear to have less and less control.[2]

Conventional pedagogical wisdom in the 1990s posited that rather than understanding how social class, gender and race contribute to school failure, educators should focus on how teaching itself can contribute to academic success for all students. In schools throughout the western world, new performance standards with prescribed skills and learning outcomes have been adopted, which all students must meet by a specified date. While this approach does not necessarily deny the existence of social difference, it consciously ignores it. In part, this may be a response to the frequent misuse of 'diversity', for example, when teachers use knowledge of different cultures to stereotype students or when students themselves internalize these stereotypes. Nevertheless, as Johnston (1990: 29) argues, to say 'this is the knowledge, here is the exam and everything else is a matter of will' is a deceptively simple, impoverished notion of teaching and learning.

The proposal that adopting uniform standards for teaching and learning will automatically result in academic success is challenged by an inclusive discourse of difference that views formal education as perpetuating pedagogical practices and which impede academic growth of certain groups of students in ways that most people do not seem to recognize. Indeed, research suggests that poor students and students of colour – groups that typically have to contend with stereotypes of low ability and poor motivation – will be among the first to suffer from the push to establish a narrow range of performance indicators (Gillborn 1995). Racial, gender and class oppression persist in capitalist societies generally and in education in particular. A large and growing body of scholarship demonstrates that inequalities among racial groups are reproduced through systematic school practices (see, for example, Giroux 1983). The most powerful explanation for school failure, from this perspective, is that the needs of students from poor and disadvantaged backgrounds are neither well served nor are their interests adequately represented by the public school system. We find, therefore, a disproportionate academic failure rate among these students.

Thus, in order to understand differential academic achievement, we must look at the structures and processes of schooling, including the kind of relationships schools have with the broader society outside their gates. Arguably, the solutions in the discourses discussed above are focused on individuals' attributes and their family backgrounds instead of what are ultimately problems generated by structural inequities in society. These solutions ignore the unequal distribution of economic resources and the extreme difficulties certain groups of people have in accessing them. They also fail to critically interrogate multicultural diversity, its implications for both identity formation and larger social issues. While inclusive discourses of difference are concerned with *recognition* of cultural particularities, they do not simply adopt an oppositional stance towards the 'mainstream', uncritically affirming all aspects of all cultures and identities. Critical post-structuralists and critical multiculturalists, for example, argue that much of the scholarship around diversity has made cultural difference *an end in itself,* either by focusing on the vast heterogeneity of new cultural and political formations or by only looking at similarities based on race, for example, and omitting interactions with class or gender. Indeed, Gillborn (1995: 83) cautions against a form of racial difference that recognizes culture not only as an important factor in the structuring of social experience but also as *the essential* category.

Rather than this single-factor approach, by focusing on the fluid nature of cultures, including their intersections with race, class and gender, we can better understand the multiple forces at work on and through individuals and groups. Thus, contrary to essentialist perspectives, anti-racist theorists view race, culture, identity and gender as complex relations that are contradictory and dynamic in character (McCarthy 1990). Some who hold this perspective emphasize the social construction of identity and culture rather than assuming some objective inherent character. Gender relations, then, for example, are constructed in interaction. Individuals thus create and choose for themselves the identity they wish, to some extent, and modify them accordingly, depending upon one's situation, experiences, associations, and so on. Differences and identities, in this view, are created; they are not given as a matter of fact.

Conclusion

It is our position, along with hooks (1989), that while it is true that identities are being shaped and reshaped as we interact with different people and acquire experiences, and although different identities overlap, alternative identities are not equally available to everyone. Class, race and gender stratification, their intersections, and objective constraints and historical circumstances, create a different range of choices and options for any individual's identity, status and circumstance. Consequently, we need to understand issues of culture and identity in ways that reveal their relation to social and material inequalities. We also need to discern which forms of human diversity embody the potential to create and sustain genuine democracy with equal justice for all.

Drawing on McLaren (1997) and Fraser (1997), we believe that recognizing diversity alone – emphasizing only the need for diverse groups to be given more respect – cannot eliminate differential academic achievement nor can it eradicate social injustices in the present-day world. By itself, cultural recognition does not necessarily critique or alter class divisions, for example, nor the role that schools and other institutions play in reproducing these divisions. The task before us, therefore, is to examine all of the structural arrangements that variously position different groups of people as unequal with one another. We need to understand how culture and the economy work together to produce injustices (Fraser 1997), both inside and outside of schools. We need ways of talking about the interaction of gendered and racial relations in the economic functions that schools perform. We need to analyse how power relations work within different contexts and how they influence our perceptions of other people, as well as of ourselves.

From this standpoint, we would no longer assume that it is only natural, fair and efficient for schools and society to differentially reward the most talented students, according to the norms of the dominant culture. Rather, we would challenge their inherent bias. Teachers' pedagogy would be informed not only by knowledge of students' background experiences and understandings but also by a radical critique of power relations inside and outside of school. We tend to assume that the group interests of students who come from marginalized backgrounds deserve differential treatment in educational policies and practices to bring out their potential, instead of conforming to what are for them alien norms and practices (Corson 1998: 11). Instead of implying deficits or disadvantage, our reading of inclusive discourses is that socio-cultural differences are mediated by social relations in modern societies largely based upon economic exploitation. This particular understanding can help us construct more emancipatory pedagogical practices; important work as our social institutions become increasingly imbued with the values of the market.

Questions for discussion/research

- Why is an understanding of difference so important for effective teaching and learning?
- How can teachers recognize individuals and groups in ways that account for both student differences and similarities?
- What does inclusive teaching practice look like?

Suggested readings

Comber, B. (1998) Problematising 'background': (re)constructing categories in educational research, *Australian Educational Researcher*, 25(3): 1–21.

Gibson, M.A. and Bhachu, P.K. (1988) Ethnicity and school performance: a comparative study of South Asian pupils in Britain and America, *Ethnic and Racial Studies*, 11(3): 239–62.

Gillborn, D. (1995) *Racism and Antiracism in Real Schools: Theory, Policy, Practice.* Buckingham: Open University Press, Chapter 7.

Orenstein, P. (1994) *Schoolgirls, Young Women, Self-Esteem and the Confidence Gap.* New York: Anchor, Chapter 12.

_____ *eight* _____

Thinking differently about gender, race and social class

Introduction

For many years educators and interested others have been working to improve the educational experiences and outcomes for students unfairly discriminated against on the basis of their gender, race and/or social class. While it is comforting to believe that sexism, racism and discriminatory practices associated with class are no longer serious problems, either in society generally or in classrooms in particular, this is demonstrably not yet the case. Whether practised intentionally or not, these particular forms of oppression are deeply rooted. In this chapter we consider the distinctive discourses associated with these three popular categories and particularly examine their expression within the context of schooling. Given that the literature on gender, race and class is extensive, we confine our discussions to dominant tendencies within each of them – particularly those informed by notions of essentialism – and the extent to which they contribute to understandings of student success and failure.

Our discussion of these matters is informed by what some (for example, Young 1990; Jenkins 1994; Banton 1998) in the literature refer to as a distinction between a category and a group:

> A category is defined by the categoriser, as when persons earning incomes of more than *x* and less than *y* are made a category for the purposes of taxation. They are not necessarily a social group, because a group is constituted by the relations between its members; they are conscious of belonging to it, and identify themselves with it in varying degrees.
>
> (Banton 1998: 196–7)

This is to say that we suspect too much work by academics and practitioners in the areas of gender, race and class is attributable to a top-down approach to analysis (see Chapter 4), which can result in the categorization of students without sufficient account of their lived experiences. In the course of this review, then, we tend to highlight difficulties with these categories while also seeking to explore bottom-up approaches to understanding the social and political differences and similarities between and within groups.

Our purposes are to add to, rather than to substitute one approach for another. That is, we think that gender, race and class remain useful concepts for explaining injustices experienced by students in schools but that they also inhibit understanding in certain instances. We are also aware that despite the significant mobilization in western democracies of appropriate discourses in relation to these issues, we still witness inappropriate outcomes for students who are so categorized. Hence, our efforts to (re)insert the complexities of students' experiences into the following discussions are motivated by both theoretical and political concerns with practice. Banton (1998: 235) would have us also consider the changed empirical conditions of contemporary life that have softened the boundaries between groups, as further justification for these efforts.

Guiding questions

Guiding this discussion are four broad questions:

- Why are gender, race and class significant educational issues?
- Which social practices are operating and legitimized when we think and act in terms of gender, race and class?
- What kinds of relationships exist between social inequalities and gender, racial and class differences?
- What do discourses associated with gender, race and class have in common? Why do they, by themselves, offer limited solutions to problems?

We begin by (re)examining contemporary approaches to the question of cultural difference as understood within these three discourses, including the extent to which they universalize and individualize differences in ways that render them invisible or 'other-ed'. Discussion of these matters includes specific accounts of discrimination based on categories of gender, race and class, although, as we argue, these are never completely separate issues. Finally, we consider how these matters might be conceived within a general understanding of oppression, as a way of outlining a starting point for addressing barriers to students' development within schools.

Cultural difference

A recurring concept that informs discourses of difference is essentialism. This is an issue discussed at some length in Chapter 7 but is revisited here specifically in relation to gender, race and class, now well-recognized categories of difference. In Chapter 7 we noted that recent and celebrative notions of difference developed out of attempts to acknowledge and understand the social positions, conditions and experiences of oppressed groups. Since the late 1950s, members of these groups have increasingly voiced their frustrations with being excluded or stereotyped, if they are included at all. The civil rights movement and civil rights legislation in the US, for example, brought much of this frustration to the attention of the American public. Similar movements in other western democracies, such as Australia and the UK, also raised concerns about the oppression experienced by marginalized groups. These movements were often mobilized around discourses of 'community', as a way of highlighting perceived commonalities of interest and experience and to legitimize members' claims through the weight of their numbers. One result has been that the citizens of many western nations are generally more aware now than they were previously of the idea that everyone speaks from a particular standpoint, from their particular experiences, out of their particular histories.

While this might seem only a matter of common sense, many westerners still find it difficult to relate to people different from themselves. The difficulty largely arises from their greater familiarity with alternative meanings of difference informed by notions of 'the other'. Although there is evidence of their continued persistence, if not dominance, past discourses of otherness suggested that anyone other than white, middle-class, able-bodied, middle-aged males were different in a way that connoted less status, less value, less knowledge, less authority and often, less trustworthiness. It is against this view that feminists, anti-racists and other critical theorists and activists have been struggling. Yet, although we can identify concrete victories (for example, legislation against discrimination, more inclusive curricula, and so on), the more we understand what we are struggling both for and against, the more we realize how complex is this social context within which we are operating and how intransigent are problems of racism, sexism and class discriminations.

At the heart of these 'problems' and their complexity is the notion of essentialism. As discussed in Chapter 7, this is the belief that individuals have a unique essence that transcends historical and cultural boundaries and/or that there are intrinsic characteristics particular to groups that reinforce these boundaries. One example of how historical and cultural boundaries are transcended can be seen in the persistent belief that women, unlike men, inherently possess the capacity for nurturing; a stereotyping upheld by the fact that in practice, women do more of the actual caring and feeding of children than men do. A second example, which reinforces boundaries between groups, can be found in the self-identification of indigenous peoples as intrinsically different and through which they 'unintentionally reinforc[e] culturalist explanations of Aboriginal poverty and damage' (Pettman 1992: 112). In this account of difference, 'while Aboriginality is here given positive valuing, it is essentialised and deterministically associated with "blood" in ways similar to racist discourse' (Pettman 1992: 112).

As already noted, positive or celebrative accounts of essentialist thinking mobilized in these examples grew out of a particular understanding of culture and particular experiences of communities and movements of oppressed peoples (for example, Blacks, women, indigenous peoples and so forth), struggling *for* equality and social justice and *against* the idea of assimilation.

These social movements celebrate notions of difference and identity and seek to affirm and preserve differences rather than view these as a kind of deviance. Even though this involves a reworking of previous essentialist thinking, which posited that ' "culture" is something that people "have", and some of us have a better kind than others' (Pettman 1992: 121–2), in its own way it reproduces the power relations of dominant ideology that perpetuates racism, sexism and classism. In short, essentialism of whatever kind reinforces stereotypes and assumptions about inherent differences between groups of people. From this essentialist position, the underlying assumption about culture is that it is something fixed and homogeneous, differentiating communities in terms of distinct values, language, mores and customs. We witness this in classrooms when teachers call upon Black students, for example, and ask those students to speak as representatives of their people.

In this chapter, we argue against these essentialist notions of difference and static versions of culture that imply antagonistic divisions among groups of people or the exclusion of some groups from rights enjoyed by others. We view culture as something that is continually shaped and reshaped (Gilroy 1990) although within relatively stable relations of power and oppression (Gillborn 1995). It is from this position that we explore the question: what kinds of differences foster and hinder the development of a fully democratic society? We begin with a consideration of differences often associated with gender, particularly those conceived as matters of self-esteem.

Feeling good about gender

Gender-based inequalities have the potential to pervade all spheres of life. Accordingly, feminists strive to eradicate the unequal power relations embedded within interactions between men and women. Feminist theory and practice has challenged ideologies and discourses that construct and represent women's subordination as resulting from their innate biological differences and which dictate particular gendered roles. From a feminist perspective, the quality of the experiences and outcomes of schooling for girls continues to be of great concern. Even though many victories have been won for female students (for example, higher rates of retention and achievement, increased enrolment in science, mathematics and so on), sexism persists, though to varying degrees, in specific areas and in different parts of the world. The differential treatment generally of males and females, with respect to school structures, curricula, instructional strategies and interactions, is well documented. As Sadker and Sadker (1994) report, well-intentioned and otherwise effective teachers (many of whom are female) frequently interact less often with female students, require females to answer fewer questions and give them less feedback than they give male students (see also Spender 1982). Girls, as a group, are often expected to be quieter, more passive and attentive than boys. Differential academic and occupational outcomes based on gender are also well documented (see, for example, Wyn 1990; Nieto 1992).

Educational disparities between the sexes, including attempts to explain these disparities, have been addressed by a number of different feminist discourses. The promotion of self-concept and self-esteem figures prominently in much of the literature in the field. Inspired by a sense of unease about the uncritical and simplistic ways in which these concepts are used to explain girls' academic performance and occupational aspirations, Kenway and Willis (1990) have brought together a valuable collection of essays to explore how self-esteem initially became a 'problem'. In brief, the contributors argue that there is a problem with how the problem is conceived, in how sex role stereotypes are assumed to lower girls' self-esteem and expectations for themselves, impeding their academic and occupational achievements. Girls, therefore, are perceived as lacking certain necessary characteristics, primarily self-confidence.

We saw evidence in our own research of this perceived need for encouragement, based on female students' supposed lack of self-confidence. A good example of this way of thinking was provided in our research by David, who related the following experience of coaching a team in a sport that traditionally had been the sole domain of males:

> There are two girls in the team. One has been there for two years now and she recently – last week – was presented with an award for the most improved player in the team. Now, as the coach, I made that selection and it was a toss-up between this girl and one of the boys on the team and it came down to her. I thought I would be invited to make the presentation and say why the recognition was being given to this particular student, but it didn't work out that way. As it happened, the person who had donated the award was called on to make the presentation, which is fine. But I never had an opportunity to have input and I remember being really quite distressed about that, in that I was most afraid that the award would be interpreted as somehow related to the fact that she was a girl. I was afraid that it would come across as, 'Oh, look, here's a girl on the team. Who gets the award? The girl!'

As tokenism? Let's encourage these girls?

> Exactly, and it was not the case. It really wasn't. In fact, when I thought I was going to make the presentation, I had made some preparations. I was going to talk about what this student had done and make no mention of her gender at all. Simply, when it came to announcing the name, it would just turn out to be a female name, but I would have explained all the things that had led to this person receiving the award . . . I deliberately thought about exactly what I would say, so that there would be no mention of gender at all at any stage, not even in the announcement. It would just simply be a statement of her ability . . . It wouldn't sound like I was trying to cover whether it was a boy or a girl.

It just wouldn't occur to them to consider gender in what I was talking about. That was my idea.

As it turned out, you didn't present the award, someone else did. I assume you listened very closely?

Yes. There was the anticipated 'Ooh' from the presenter and then he said something like, 'This is something that we haven't seen before. It's good to see'. But the tone in his voice spoke of complete surprise and amazement: 'Oh, look at this. This is a freaky situation'. Exactly what I didn't want. Then the principal [head teacher] said, 'Did I hear right? Did I hear that . . . ?' It was everything that I had worked against.

(David)

Similar to the literature on disadvantaged students, these discourses portray girls as deficient or, at best, different in some reduced way and in need of encouragement and/or remedial programmes to make them feel better about themselves. Invoking discourses that 'blame the victim', this self-esteem rationale suggests that the problem is best located within girls themselves. Rather than analysing which precise factors in our educational and occupational systems militate against the development and maintenance of positive identities for girls and instead of devising strategies for social change, educators who are informed by this discourse tend to see their role as helping girls fit into these systems. That is, the problem is viewed as an individual's maladjustment rather than caused by flawed social systems or institutions. In the language of such discourse:

the problem is these individuals who belong to oppressed groups in society. They lack key attributes; if these attributes can be compensated for, the problem will take care of itself . . . [Yet] seeking to raise self-esteem within the terms of the educational and social status quo may well have the effect of underscoring the dominant sex, class and ethnic groups in society.

(Kenway and Willis 1990: 11–12)

Ironically, the self-esteem literature reinforces sex stereotypes by its assumption that girls passively and uncritically absorb these messages. Females tend to be treated as all alike when the specific cultural and class backgrounds of schoolgirls and gender-biased, educational and occupational rewards are ignored. Discourse promoting the homogeneous female has been challenged by scholarship that has focused on the complexities of socialization, in particular by looking at female subcultures (see Deem 1978, 1981; Fuller 1981). For example, Anglo perceptions of sex roles, conditioned by the emphasis that western societies place on individualism, can effectively undermine the self-esteem that Indo-Chinese females in Australia derive from their family roles and traditional networks of support. Western perceptions of oppressive sex roles also tend to devalue other cultures (Wenner 1990). Findings that show that some females place priority on relationships, friendships, and on establishing themselves as adults – in roles that western feminists criticize as patriarchal – make sense when we see that they are derived from collective experiences (Connell *et al.* 1982; Wyn 1990).

Understanding how this socialization occurs may provide us with a better vantage point for recommending strategies to challenge occupational segregation and improve the quality of girls' schooling, rather than accepting ethnocentric ideas about sex role stereotypes and about what it means to possess high self-esteem. In her study on privileged females in one of Australia's most elite private (non-government) schools for girls, Kenway (1990) suggests that the dominant group's conception of self-worth is sometimes used to devalue others and to reinforce class distinctions. For some girls in these schools, a context of high self-esteem is developed through an orientation towards competitive self-interest rather than collective action or a sense of 'sisterhood'.

Clearly, whatever means schools and teachers use to support female students' academic progress and personal development, such support must respond to and respect the cultural and social class attributes that shape their social position and experience. In other words, while it is important to acknowledge women's subordination as women, it is equally important to understand the heterogeneity of women's experiences and social conditions (Brah 1992). The everyday of real life is forged out of a complicated fusion of specific histories, material circumstances and cultural experiences. For example, a Black working-class woman in Alabama in the US occupies a different position in society than a white working-class woman in Sydney, Australia. The racism that a Latinna woman experiences in southern California at the beginning of the twenty-first century is likely to be different from the racism a Jewish woman experienced in western Europe in the 1930s. As Brah (1992) acknowledges, an appeal to essentialism – unique bonds of common cultural experiences among all women – is understandable when different oppressed groups begin to mobilize their constituency. Yet, this can result in one group (for example, white women) ignoring the distinct plight of other women (for example, Blacks) and can lead to pitting group against group.

Instead, in order to understand and effectively challenge any one group's oppression, we need to understand all types of oppressions and how they interact with one another in specific historical and material circumstances. Encouraging females to look inward in order to build their self-esteem does not encourage them to analyse relations of domination and subordination that really exist outside of themselves. Individual change, by itself, cannot result in general societal change. As Wenner (1990) argues, when teachers' answers to the challenges of cultural diversity in their classroom consist of mostly individualizing instruction, it is likely that failure will be perceived to be located within individual students, rather than in the educational and social system that confers advantages on some groups of students over others. In this way, unjust social structures and ideologies of special privileges that underpin our educational and social systems, remain unchallenged.

Celebrating racial and cultural differences

Since the mid-twentieth century, biological scientists and social scientists alike have demonstrated that both physical and intellectual/psychological differences between races are insignificant, discrediting the idea that any human race is innately superior to another. Since the end of the Second World War, United Nations conventions against genocide and civil rights legislation throughout many western democracies have outlawed race-based discrimination. As we begin the twenty-first century, apartheid in South Africa, one of the last bastions of state-sanctioned and overt racism, is slowly crumbling. Now, many people suggest that thinking and acting towards others in terms of race can prevent us from recognizing what we have in common. Many of these attitudes have been taken up by teachers so that, at the very least, they are more willing to (re)interpret disciplinary problems as issues of racial and cultural difference. While not necessarily an example of exemplary practice, Michelle's comments to us in our research, on her dealings with secondary/high school students from minority groups, do reflect an appreciation for this shift:

> Initially, when I first started teaching, before I learned or became accustomed to their [Black] culture, I said, 'Just look at me when I am speaking to you. I am speaking to you. Look at me.' Then I realized, and I think someone told me, that's not part of their culture. They find it very difficult to look at somebody in the eyes. So, now I accept it. Sometimes I will say, 'Just stand still for a minute and listen to me.' Rather than saying, 'Look at me,' I say, 'Stand still and listen to what I have to say, and then I will listen to you.'
>
> (Michelle)

Despite these changes in attitude, race remains one of the most volatile issues in western societies. Indeed, racism appears to be on the increase in many countries throughout the world. Racial abuse on the streets, 'colour barriers' to employment and housing, poor treatment by service providers, over-representation in prison populations, and constant threats of crime, drugs and violence are daily realities in many marginalized communities, despite their resilience and strength. School lunch programmes for children from low-income families and government loans and scholarships for university/ college students from disadvantaged backgrounds have been either eliminated or reduced. Recent Supreme Court decisions in the US, for example, have abolished or weakened policies and programmes that were designed to encourage the participation of students of colour in universities and racist procedures stubbornly persist in many civic and governmental institutions.

Further, Lomotey's (1990) review of studies of secondary/high school drop-out rates, standardized test scores and the placement of students in special education and vocational programmes, substantiates the persistent, pervasive and disproportionate underachievement of African American students. In just one example, a survey of the Oakland district near San

Francisco revealed that 71 per cent of its 28,000 Black student population was located in special education programmes (Stewart 1997). Labov's (1987) work can be taken to indicate that such figures reveal the extent to which institutional racism is a primary cause of academic failure for students of colour. In short, despite the view that western societies are becoming more enlightened and that racism is not seen as a crucial factor in structuring social relations, and while many Anglos claim that they are not racist, issues of disadvantage and structural inequalities both inside and outside of schools still appear to be crucial issues to be addressed in the context of working towards social justice.

The issue of racism is a highly complex one. To illustrate, the relatively poor academic performance of Black students in many western democracies is widely accepted as fact. For instance, the Education Trust, a Washington-based non-profit organization, estimated that in 1996, 33 per cent of white eighth-graders in the US were proficient in mathematics compared to only 3 per cent of Black eighth-graders (Stewart 1997). Yet we also know that the social class and educational level of parents influence all students' school performances (see, for example, Connell 1993; T. Williams *et al.* 1993). Hence, research on racial inequality in education must be careful to distinguish, to the extent possible, which variables are specifically *racial*. Troyna's (1993) assessment in this area is that the existence of the differential *treatment* accorded Black and white students in school (evidenced in teacher expectations, assessment procedures and so on) is more easily detected than those factors that cause differential educational *outcomes*.

Moreover, while racism is a historical problem and, therefore, needs to be understood from a historical perspective, reviews of the literature suggest that in the English-speaking world, race-related problems are different *and* similar, with many of the same structural constraints. The US, for example, has a distinctive history in racial terms, but one that has similarities with other countries (see, for example, Pettman's (1992: 106–28) account of Australia's dealings with racial differences).

To elaborate, during the nineteenth century there were sharp conflicts in some communities within the US between what parents from marginalized (racial, economic and so forth) groups wanted for their children from public (government) schools and what the northern European school system offered. Schools were used by the powerful Anglo-majority to integrate, enculturate and socialize students, replacing Native American, Mediterranean, Slavic, Mexican and African American cultures and languages with that of the dominant. Similar experiences awaited migrants to the UK and to Australia, and were also felt by indigenous groups in both the US and Australia. In brief, a multicultural society was believed to be at odds with a stable unified culture. While attempts were made in the US to distinguish Americans from the dominant culture of England, the 'superior' Anglo-Saxon world view and traditions still provided the benchmark for comparison. Many immigrant parents both resisted this forced Americanization while at the same time acknowledged that public (government) schooling was the key to their economic security and success. However, such assimilation mostly benefited English-speaking white Americans, leaving untouched the pattern of poor academic performance among students of colour (McCarthy 1990). Demeaning and excluding diverse cultures and languages are believed by many to have contributed to this outcome (May 1994).

The failure of these assimilation policies, in the face of large immigration from Asia and Latin America, led many in the 1960s and early 1970s – a period of great social unrest, especially in minority-group communities – to embrace a multicultural approach to education and society and to cease other approaches such as Australia's 'White Australia' policy. Multiculturalism responded both to diverse communities' demands for recognition and to larger socio-economic demands for stable social conditions necessary for the accumulation of capital. While multiculturalism is not a homogeneous discourse, it is often defined in terms of racial minorities, although increasingly other marginalized groups (for example, women and the disabled) have also been included. Contrary to monoculturalism or assimilatory policies – in which the cultures and languages of subordinated peoples were viewed as impediments to an individual's and a nation's success – multiculturalists brought cultural differences to the fore. Teaching about and celebrating diverse cultures would, it was believed, help maintain and strengthen cultural identities, thereby enhancing self-esteem and, correspondingly, academic achievement and increase tolerance of diverse peoples by dominant groups. The hope of multicultural education was the possibility of reduced racial conflict and tension by affirming a culturally pluralist society (see, for example, Banks 1988).

Recent celebrations of racial and cultural differences reflect the essentialist nature of this multiculturalism that has spawned a renaissance in such cultural texts as the writing, art and performance of marginalized groups, particularly indigenous peoples, and spoken from the standpoint of their 'authors'. Legitimacy of authorship and, hence, ownership are as important as what is authored, and scandals of white artists imitating Australian Aboriginal 'blak' art, for example, have served to highlight what is being celebrated.[1] Essentialism is also evident, however, in the recent rejection by politicians, educational bureaucrats and language experts of African American 'ebonics' (a combination of 'ebony' and 'phonics' meaning 'black sound') as an official language in US school curricula (see Perry and Delpit 1997; Stewart 1997). Multiculturalism, it seems, can go only so far and the celebration has already begun to wane. For instance, indigenous languages previously legitimized by the state have in more recent times been removed from several bilingual programmes in Australian Aboriginal community schools.

Shortcomings with multiculturalism were taken up in the 1970s and 1980s by anti-racists, most notably in the UK, who critiqued multiculturalists for explaining racism predominantly in terms of individual prejudice. In their view, such explanations pay insufficient attention to other power relations, such as those defined by class and gender, or to institutions that produce and legitimize racial oppression (Sarup 1986; Troyna 1993). Anti-racists argue that economic structures and relations influence people's perspectives at least as much as cultural traditions and that these relations and structures merit attention, not simply individual attitudes.

Further, anti-racists claim that the definition of culture upon which a multicultural celebration of diversity is based, contributes to division and feelings of separateness between groups of people. Indeed, when an understanding of culture is reduced to distinct, exotic groups of people with a shared descent and fixed customs, it is understandable for people in one group to feel apart from others. Pedagogically, a stress on the celebration of lifestyles overestimates the capacity of schools to transform society. From an anti-racist perspective, racial inequalities cannot be reduced until the broader social and economic factors that help to produce it are also addressed.

Critics of this account claim that anti-racists, too, share beliefs about the essentialist nature of racial categories and imply rigid divisions among groups of people. They claim that anti-racists assume culture to be separate from class and gender relations, and from politics and history. Such conceptions of culture, it is argued, make it difficult to deal with the changing faces of racism over time and in different geographical areas. This, in turn, reinforces the (false) notion that racism is simply an 'unwanted blemish' on an otherwise just and democratic society (Gilroy 1990). Thus, hate crimes, immigration laws and the absence of equal opportunities are not systemically considered and can be dealt with separately. Gilroy (1990) further criticizes anti-racist education in as much as it implies that opposition to racism is the ultimate answer to the emancipation of Black people; that is, that the lives of people of colour are fully explained by an understanding of racial subordination. Finally, anti-racists have been criticized for reducing the problem of prejudice to the capitalist system.

Troyna, however, defends anti-racist theory, thus:

> I do argue that antiracist education should be geared towards an understanding of the social and racial formation of the state and how it might be possible to challenge and, ultimately, transform it . . . But to give primacy to certain sociopolitical structures in explaining the development and reproduction of racial inequalities is not the same as reductionism. To suggest otherwise is to oversimplify, distort and ignore the variants within Marxist thought.
>
> (Troyna 1993: 119–20)

Troyna also argues that recent work by anti-racists has made sophisticated advances in defining institutionalized racism and what an anti-racist pedagogy looks like. For example, McCarthy (1990), in his work on how race operates in schools, rejects the idea that racism can be understood only by looking at the influence of macro-factors on race relations. He equally rejects the notion that racism is best explained by analysing relations among individuals. Instead, McCarthy focuses on the intersecting and relational impact of race, class, and gender in the production and reproduction of educational and socio-economic inequalities. Drawing on the work of Hicks (1981), McCarthy uses the concept of 'nonsynchrony' to explain the contradictory and contingent character of the interactions between class, gender and race. Consequently, a more student-centred democratic pedagogy figures prominently in antiracist education as does collaborative dialogue and recognition and respect of difference. Drawing on Giroux's (1989) work, this pedagogy asks of students that which antiracist researchers ask of themselves: how do we link personal and social issues around the project of becoming more critical, more active and more effective in creating a truly democratic society?

Revitalizing social class

Schools in urban ghettos have long been poor, populated by relatively large numbers of students of colour and language minorities, and stigmatized by poor academic performance (see, for example, Tyack 1974). In recent years, this condition has become worse but the processes that concentrate poverty and underachievement within certain geographical areas have also become more widespread and intense. Many of the problems confronting schools in these locations are related to the deteriorating conditions within particular areas of our cities and are occurring at the same time as other inner city areas are being revitalized and populated by predominantly young high-income workers. While considerable amounts of money are being expended by governments on these selective revitalization programmes, declining urban infrastructures in the 'unattended' precincts have increased the numbers of students disadvantaged by their socio-economic backgrounds and have highlighted clear relationships among racial isolation, poverty, low academic performance and school drop-out rates (Rury and Mirel 1997).

At the same time, Kozol's (1991) important study dramatically documents the 'savage inequalities' and extreme disparities in educational resources between many suburban and city schools, reflecting the racial and economic make-up of respective school populations. Similar problems are appearing for students located in rural and remote areas who are often consigned to inadequate facilities, inexperienced teachers, and the odd classroom computer but with limited and expensive access to the internet. One result of this competition for resources is a middle-class 'white flight' to the suburbs and to select inner city areas, moves that have dramatically increased the predominance of poor students of colour attending rundown city schools or under-resourced remote schools. In short, the social and material circumstances of many low-income students suggests that the problems they are facing are not purely educational. Moreover, the geography of their circumstances also delivers disadvantages in areas of health, housing, transport, and economic prospects.

Recognizing that the conditions of schooling are not equal for poor and rich students, some parents are opting for private (non-government) schools, demanding vouchers (mobile subsidies) for their children to attend these 'superior' alternatives. At the same time there are increasing moves in many western democracies towards restructuring and deregulating public (government) schools. While these efforts emphasize parental choice in relation to which school parents send their children, the extent to which the market dimensions of these initiatives will function fairly is dubious. In fact, there are reasons to fear that the best prepared students will end up in select and selective schools (public and private), while low-income students, especially students of colour, will remain in relatively neglected public (government) schools (Bastian *et al.* 1986; Gewirtz *et al.* 1995; Whitty *et al.* 1998).

The dominant (neo-liberal) ideology of many teachers continues to suggest that schools function as a mechanism for social and economic mobility, and for developing a democratic society. Critical theorists, however, have argued over some length of time that the social and economic benefits from schooling are far greater for the rich than for the poor (see, for example, Spring 1972; Bowles and Gintis 1976; Willis 1977; Giroux 1983; Aronowitz and Giroux 1985; Apple 1986). In many western societies this appears to be increasingly true; poverty remains a strong predictor of academic success, undermining claims that academic failure is primarily rooted in factors unrelated to the social class of individual students (see, for example, Connell 1993; Apple 1996). While some school compensatory programmes have provided sorely lacking material resources, their curricula are typically lacking in challenging or creative presentations of academic knowledge or problems to solve, effectively reinforcing poor academic performance. Even when such curricula is available to students from low-income families and is supported by good teaching, this does not necessarily guarantee educational and/or economic advantages (Yates 1997).

Frequently, these connections between poverty and underachievement are interpreted as problems located not in schooling systems but in individual students or groups of students with parents 'who not only lack financial security but often also intelligence, knowledge, propriety and responsibility' (Freebody and Ludwig 1995: x). In Chapter 7 we noted the connections that Michelle made between her students' 'low socio-economic backgrounds' and their 'horrific' living conditions. Freebody and Ludwig's (1995) study of student literacy practices in low socio-economic communities in Australia is also illustrative of this kind of (unfounded) connection that some teachers make between students' poverty and their academic achievement:

> A heavily-weighted baggage of moral, intellectual, social, physical, cultural, and motivational dispositions is readily attached to poor people. Educators, like all of us, are members of a classed society, and whether or not such attachments are finally justified, the urgent question must be asked: 'Why would an institution teach those clients whom it takes to be heavily weighed down in ways so similar to the ways it teaches those who travel more lightly?'
>
> (Freebody and Ludwig 1995: xxxi)

Generally, students from wealthy backgrounds receive a qualitatively different kind of education than poor students or, at the very least, they receive an education with qualitatively different outcomes. Persell (1997), for example, found in her research that students are more different from one another when they *leave* school than when they *enter* it. That is, both the explicit and the implicit messages that students receive in school curricula replicate the stratification of social classes (see Bourdieu and Passeron 1977; Anyon 1980; Carnoy and Levin 1985; Oakes 1985). The underlying tendency for schools to generate unequal outcomes is likely to intensify in the future given the demands of the burgeoning global economy, its fierce competition, unprecedented scientific and technological advances, increased migration, and the sharp declines in remunerative employment for the majority, forcing more people into poverty (Gee *et al.* 1996). As teachers, we need to be sceptical about the extent to which sophisticated, analytical skills or a capacity for imagination are really required by the present or future shrinking job market (Carnoy *et al.* 1993).

Such challenges underscore the urgency for educators to include analyses of social and economic change in their proposals for educational reform. Yet, 'the tendency of much qualitative work of the past decade has been . . . to take gender or ethnicity as central concerns and to show class differences within these, rather than the reverse' (Yates 1997: 1). Similarly, there would seem to be few teachers who begin from the perspective of class as a way of understanding their students' difficulties with schooling. Carl, whom we introduced in earlier chapters and whose Black students are often categorized as belonging to the same social group, provides something of an exception among teachers:

> I would prefer to see the students as a homogeneous socio-economic group, that there is a socio-economic disadvantage that has caused various problems. Now, those problems are obviously linked to the race of the people . . . [but] they are at the lower end of the socio-economic scale, so, therefore, they suffer 'disadvantage' or bias in the educational system. . . . a homogeneous group, I guess they're not, but they are a community. I guess that gels [with them] a lot quicker.

> (Carl)

Clearly, broad social, economic and technological changes require major adjustments in our analysis and construction of educational systems. One change we are currently witnessing is an especially 'tight coupling' of capitalism within all aspects of social life (Corson 1998). We see this in the repeated exhortations to manage both public (government) schools and universities from a business perspective and on business terms. Neo-liberal ideology and its attendant market discourse have gained prominence in recent years, as has the monetary valuing of human relationships in the same way as inanimate products. That is, *human capital*, the market term for these relationships, is increasingly evaluated in terms of the standards of economic transactions rather than by social or cultural ties. Paradoxically, in the midst of much fanfare around freedom, diversity and multiculturalism, contemporary capitalist social relations exert pressures towards assimilation into a business culture that primarily rewards the hierarchy of individual wealth.

In schools, this means that the communal interests of students from marginalized groups, which tend to stress cooperative values, are not being served. This is in stark contrast, for example, to the (literacy) work of Freire (1972; Freire and Macedo 1987) that was aimed at encouraging oppressed peoples to recognize, articulate and act according to their communal interests and to take control over their own lives. Though Freire worked primarily in the 'developing' world, his methods still challenge teachers in the 'developed' world who believe that the teaching of reading and writing is a value free exercise, imparting technical skills that enable young people to do their own thinking. According to Freire, when these skills are perceived in this way, teachers perpetuate the very myths that maintain a highly stratified class structure.

Central to Freire's approach to education and literacy is the concept of conscientization: political, social awareness. Freire argued that because the dominant culture encourages most people to accept society as they know it, education and literacy can and must enable people to question society as it is currently organized and to transform that which inhibits individual and social well-being. His goals for literacy are based on the principles of recognitive social justice for which we argued in Chapter 2: to develop and exercise one's full capabilities, to become aware of the impact of existing socio-economic conditions on the lives of different groups of people, and to participate in making decisions that affect one's life.

As indicated in Chapter 3, Freire's work distinguishes between being genuinely or critically literate and being functionally literate. The former entails critical reflection on one's social milieu, including recognition and utilization of a student's first language and personal context. Functional literacy, on the other hand, encourages passivity by promoting a superficial approach to reading; one that does not emphasize the importance of students' analysis of their own lives nor their creative input into the world. For Freire, functional literacy primarily serves the interests of the dominant class by not challenging its social control. In contrast, genuine literacy enables people to transform existing institutions and traditions so that the interests of the members of oppressed groups are served (Mackie 1981; hooks 1989; Shor 1993; Gee *et al.* 1996; Lankshear *et al.* 1997; Roberts 1998). In our view, this is the kind of revitalization required to address the oppression of the poor and marginalized in our societies and schools.

Conclusion

Scholars, educators and activists have made significant contributions to our understanding of gender, racial and class relations. More recent scholarship has begun to appreciate that these relations are not isolated from each other, but combine in our lives, in different ways, at different times, and in different settings. Conceiving of these interrelations, however, can be difficult work: how can we 'get around' the separations between concepts of gender, race and class, to think differently about them but in a way that also retains the validity and potency of their analysis? In our view, efforts to understand why these discourses play the particular role they do in specific circumstances must be part of an effort to understand the particular settlement, matrix or framework within which these relations interact.

When educators or researchers think that their ideas or concepts are neutral or that they work in a context that is not significantly influenced by wider social relations and economic systems, they cannot properly define problems or generate effective, long-lasting solutions. Explaining academic failure, for example, in terms of the deficits of one group of people or another, avoids addressing the overall, often dismal, circumstances facing many young people today, narrowing both our understanding of the problem as well as the kinds of solutions that are generated (Altbach and Lomotey 1991). Similarly, by isolating a single aspect of the problem, such as low self-esteem, poverty, racist attitudes or lack of cultural pride, we end up with solutions that address these aspects, not the source of problems.

We believe that a better approach to the issues that we have raised in this chapter is one that recognizes and analyses the dominant influences of capitalist social relations on schooling, on occupational structures and on our personal relations with one another. These relations, as they currently stand, ensure that everyone *cannot* be educated, even though there is some 'effective schooling' research that suggests otherwise. Historically, educational systems in western democracies have been organized on the premise that only a few students are capable of significant academic achievement. The dominant ideology maintains, for example, that only a talented fraction of the population in any one country is really capable of benefiting from college or university education. Rather than the rhetoric of natural endowment, however, we can look to social hierarchies and the world views associated with them for the constraints that people experience in their attempts to learn and develop (Sabel 1984).

Moreover, we suggest that these social relations are established and maintained through a number of discursive strategies, similar to what Young (1990) describes as the 'five faces of oppression', which include:

Exploitation: 'the transfer of the results of the labor of one social group to benefit another'.

Marginalization: 'a whole category of people is expelled from useful participation in social life and thus potentially subjected to severe material deprivation and even extermination'.

Powerlessness: 'inhibition in the development of one's capacities, lack of decisionmaking power in one's life, and exposure to disrespectful treatment because of the status one occupies'.

Cultural imperialism: 'the universalization of a dominant group's experience and culture, and its establishment as the norm'.

Violence: 'random, unprovoked attacks on . . . persons or property, which have no motive but to damage, humiliate, or destroy the person' and which are 'directed at members of a group simply because they are members of that group'.

(Young 1990: 49, 53, 58, 59, 61, 62)

We have already outlined in Chapter 4 one mapping of how these strategies are played out in the context of classrooms and the pedagogy of teachers (see also Gore 1998a, 1998b). In Chapter 9 we outline a framework for democratizing classroom and school relations, as a way of more positively addressing these issues.

Questions for discussion/research

- How do teachers' pedagogies serve to perpetuate gendered, raced and classed relations in classrooms?
- How might Young's 'five faces of oppression' provide ways of understanding the extent to which gender, race and social class are similarly *and* differently experienced?
- What would a less essentialist understanding of culture look like? What implications for teaching might it entail?

Suggested readings

Agger, B. (1998) *Critical Social Theories: An Introduction*. Boulder, CO: Westview Press, Chapter 5.

Gillborn, D. (1995) *Racism and Antiracism in Real Schools: Theory, Policy, Practice*. Buckingham: Open University Press, Chapter 8.

Kenway, J., Willis, S., with Blackmore, J. and Rennie, L. (1997) *Answering Back: Girls, Boys and Feminism in Schools*. St Leonards, NSW: Allen & Unwin, Chapter 2.

Pettman, J. (1992) *Living in the Margins: Racism, Sexism and Feminism in Austialia*. Sydney: Allen & Unwin, Chapter 6.

Young, I.M. (1990) *Justice and the Politics of Difference*. Princeton, NJ: Princeton University Press, Chapter 2.

_____ *nine* _____

(Re)constructing practice: where to from here?

Introduction

What can teachers and schools do, if they are to take seriously the issues raised in this book? How can they work to improve the quality of their students' experiences of schooling? These are questions that we have been careful to address throughout earlier chapters, even though it might have seemed to some readers that our critique has been unduly harsh at times. In this final chapter, then, we want to focus more positively and exclusively on the character of relations within schooling that are informed by a recognitive view of justice and a radical democratic politics. Our intention is to outline a framework for principled action rather than to detail specific actions themselves, which inevitably would be appropriate for some contexts and not others. Some of what we outline we have already proposed, albeit expressed somewhat differently to what is reviewed here. What this chapter attempts is to bring these ideas together into a framework for (re)constructing teaching practice.

A central emphasis in this discussion are democratic social relations within and outside the classroom. There are several reasons for this. First and foremost, the relationships between social justice and schooling centre around the question of the quality of social life that exists for students outside of school. Second, as noted in previous chapters, democracy is a precondition for social justice, just as it is a precondition for schools if they are to fulfil their educative, social and cultural functions. Third, efforts to further the quality of democracy in society will be hollow without individuals who have the necessary skills and dispositions, making them capable of participating in a democratic society. In brief, effective teaching, from a perspective of just schooling, requires a continual striving towards extending and enhancing democracy in society, just as it demands the teaching and practice of democratic skills and the adoption of democratic dispositions inside schools.

In addressing these concerns, this final chapter draws on the work of Anthony Giddens (1994: 117–24) and particularly his advocacy of 'dialogic democracies'. Specifically, we adapt Giddens' four connected areas of 'life politics', which we apply to schooling and express as arenas of personal life, group life, institutional life and community life. We understand these as ever widening contexts, beginning with the immediate relations between students and teachers and spiralling out to relations among school members and their communities. In this respect, the approach is reminiscent of Shor's (1993) development of Freire's problem-solving method (outlined in Chapter 5). Within each arena we also identify those dispositions – or what Giddens refers to as democratic tendencies – necessary for the democratization of schooling. We see these as principles to guide socially just practices in schools, as ideals to struggle towards, and expressed through relations rather than experienced as (static) end points or outcomes. To reiterate, ours is not 'an approach to social justice that gives primacy to *having* [but] one that gives primacy to *doing*' (Young 1990: 8, emphasis added).

Guiding questions

Guiding this discussion of arenas and dispositions for just schooling are the following questions:

- How can we achieve greater democracy and social justice in the personal, group, institutional, and community lives of students, their schools and communities?
- Which principles for action and/or dispositions can guide us in each of these four areas?
- What is the role of dialogue in democratizing classroom and school relations?

We preface this exploration of arenas and dispositions with a brief discussion of points of agreement and disagreement with Giddens' (1994) account of radical democracy. This is important given that some of his views stand in contrast to those we have expressed in earlier chapters. Still, there are aspects of his account that we find useful in helping us to identify areas and ideas for action and think through how these might be applied within educational contexts. Such review also provides us with an opportunity to revisit, albeit briefly and in a general way, our own commitments to social justice and democracy in relation to schooling.

Democracy and dialogue

According to Giddens (1994), the shortcomings of liberal visions of democracy – those that currently dominate western societies – suggest the need for more radical forms. As a way forward, Giddens stresses 'dialogic democracy', viewing dialogue and discursive justification as the means, in principle, to resolve controversial issues arising from competing interests. Where conflicts cannot be resolved, he suggests that people can learn to trust others by taking into account the integrity of those with whom they differ. Given the reality of global interdependence and the common risks (for example, environmental hazards, economic crises, war, illness and the like) faced by everyone, Giddens believes that there is now a compelling basis for the emergence of universal ethical principles, shared values and common interests that can overcome social divisions.

By his own admission, Giddens does not deal with the formal political sphere. Similarly, while talking about capitalism, he avoids the language of power and exploitation and, unproblematically, identifies capitalism with democracy. His message is that radical (or full) democracy can be achieved within our present economic system; where production is for sales and profit, before social needs, and where citizens must sell their ability to work for their wages without opportunity to be involved in decisions controlling their own destinies. A study of history, however, teaches us otherwise. In our view, full democracy cannot be achieved without the elimination of exploitation and without addressing the contest for political power by antagonistic factions in society.

In short, we do not all share universal common interests as Giddens asserts. Some interests are exploitative; the power relations of gender, race and social class, and their influence over the access to resources, for instance, represent antagonistic interests. Giddens' particular emphasis on dialogue makes it function ideologically; that is, dialogue can ultimately reproduce relations of domination and exploitation. To mediate the problems facing modern society through the efficacy of dialogue, avoids confronting real solutions that are not purely solvable by discussion. In these respects, we find Giddens' analysis seriously flawed.

While we disagree with Giddens about the major problems currently facing western societies and, hence, their causes and solutions, we nevertheless recognize the importance of dialogue for democratic decision-making generally and for work within schools, in particular. Dialogue has the potential to allow for the social knowledge and perspectives of a wide range of people to contribute to public deliberations on matters of direct importance to their lives, including their personal, group, institutional and community lives. This is one way in which democratic decision-making tends to promote just outcomes (Young 1990). For example, focused and coordinated public deliberations among all levels of government, employee unions and grassroots organizations, are one way to encourage collaboratively developed policies on budgeting for social programmes and adequate resources for education at all levels in all communities. Such dialogue has the potential to militate against the current situation where several governments in western democracies resort (sometimes indirectly) to lotteries and gambling to fund schooling, in a context where their citizens have drastically reduced their relative support of public education generated through their taxes.

Clearly, social justice requires wider practices of democracy than are currently found in western societies. In particular, recognitive justice is concerned with the extent to which a society creates the necessary conditions for individuals with different capabilities, needs, and interests, to develop their potential and to fully participate in determining their actions and the conditions of those actions (see our discussion of these conditions in

Chapter 2). As Young (1990) argues, this form of justice also requires mechanisms that ensure oppressed or disadvantaged groups are represented in decision-making forums. To assist these representations, our societies need to take steps to ensure that poor and non-white youth, for example, complete secondary/high school, graduate from college and pursue university studies. Stimulating and relevant multicultural curricula, combined with remedial attention and counselling at primary/elementary, secondary/high and university/college levels, can help these young people complete their education. Attracting more teachers of colour at all levels of the educational system in the US, for example, is another way to improve the educational experiences of its students of colour, notably African American students and Latinos (Meier *et al.* 1989). Similar suggestions could also be offered concerning the improvement of school experiences for marginalized groups in the UK and Australia.

We live in societies sharply differentiated along gendered, racial and classed lines and, not surprisingly, social institutions such as schools are similarly characterized by various forms of these divisions and their corresponding discourses and ideologies. The kind of democracy that has the greatest potential to achieve social justice is one that implies ongoing action to promote personal and social development and to eliminate the strong tendency of localities to adhere to long-rationalized traditions of privilege for the few and indifference towards the many. Therefore, if teachers make the pursuit of recognitive social justice their priority, what steps can they take towards the democratization of their students' and their own personal, group, institutional and community lives?

Getting to know and getting along: democratizing personal life

Drawing on Giddens (1994: 117–20), there are at least three dispositions that characterize the personal lives of democratic classrooms and which inform *a democracy of emotions*. These democratic dispositions or personal arrangements of the 'intimate life' of classrooms are most often expressed in the arena of teacher–student relations, through dialogue. We identify these dispositions here as

- active trust
- mutuality
- negotiated authority.

Each is grounded in 'getting to know and getting along with *the other*' (Giddens 1994: 117, emphasis added). But 'getting to know' and 'getting along' do not depend solely on 'who does what' (as our discussion of bodily dispositions in Chapter 6 demonstrates). Rather, knowing, in this expanded sense, involves an appreciation for 'the other' on the basis of who they are. This is the point we made in Chapter 2 concerning the school's identification of Cindy as having a Level Six disability, a label that describes what she can and cannot do, instead of who she is. As Giddens (1994: 117) expresses it, 'the relationship [between persons] depends on who the other "is" as a person, rather than on a specified social role, or what the individual "does" in life', even if this is coded by particular social positions or group memberships, irrespective of whether or not these are privileged.

This concerns not only how we see students such as Cindy, but also how we view teachers. That is, in democratic classrooms teachers are respected not simply because they are teachers and hold the authority of their position(s) within the schooling system, or even that they possess some expert knowledge, but because of their willingness to 'open up' to their students and to related others. By this we do not mean a naive vulnerability or a 'giving over' of teaching responsibilities – there remain certain social and material constraints on teachers from which they cannot escape, even if they are able to retain some degree of manoeuvre – but it does entail a giving of self. Indeed, 'giving is . . . the very means of mobilizing active trust' (Giddens 1994: 118) and attributing integrity.

Giving of self, sharing one's identity, necessarily requires some familiarity with that identity. Teachers need to know who they are and what they believe. In this book we have been careful not to take teachers or their beliefs for granted and neither should they. What it means to get an education (Chapter 5), for example, is not as simple as some teachers' comments and practices would seem to suggest. Teachers also need to create opportunities to get to know their students and for their students to get to know them and themselves.[1] The chance to give and receive in this way is generally advanced through open discussions that give respect to others' traditions and histories. Through these kinds of supportive relations with their teachers, students can be encouraged to develop their interests and abilities. In short, students need to feel that their own culture is respected in school and they need to be encouraged and assisted to draw on these cultural experiences in order to succeed academically. For this to occur, teachers must learn to connect the discourses of classrooms and schools to those of their students' homes and communities.

This requires a certain amount of negotiation, not only of the curricula and how this might be engaged by students and teachers but also in relation to the mechanisms that give these arrangements their authority. Some teachers, for example, might view their own authority as natural, given their greater knowledge of what they teach and the position from which they teach it (see our discussion of these cultural and social capitals in relation to Pritchard and Keating in Chapter 6). But continual dialogue and interchange with students and parents enables teachers to earn trust and respect as others come to understand their work. This is what should legitimize the exercise of their authority more than what title teachers hold or what they know. Within ongoing negotiations such as these, an individual's authority is continually (re)invested or (re)delegated by the group; a delegation more 'diffuse' than 'institutionalized' (Bourdieu 1997: 53).

Further, negotiated authority invites student decisions concerning the learning that needs to be done. Teachers need to seek opportunities to dialogue with students in order to take their ideas and concerns into account, particularly, but not exclusively, in relation to classroom organization, curriculum, instruction and evaluation. In other words, self-expression and self-development should be encouraged in conscious relationship to and with the knowledge of others. It is everyone's responsibility within these parameters to refrain from asserting themselves when it is potentially to others' detriment. Kimble's dealings with Emma (in *Kindergarten Cop*) is illustrative of such assertiveness, although Johnson's discourse on choice (in *Dangerous Minds*) is more insidious and, therefore, more detrimental, even though it appears less physically aggressive. (See Chapter 6 for a fuller discussion of these issues.)

In socially just classrooms, teachers are responsible for modelling democratic dialogue and interchange with students, and for building supportive relationships based on mutual trust and respect. They should view their role as bringing out the best in each student. In Chapter 3, we critiqued David's comments in relation to these responsibilities when he declared: 'I think this business of the teacher being a focus and setting the agenda for the children is very real and I think they respond the way you respond'. Our critique is not of modelling itself or of its potential for effect, but in relation to what is modelled. Here, we have in mind the best and most appropriate qualities of 'governmentality' of the personal life, which includes an appreciation that 'to govern in this sense, is to structure the possible field of action of others' (Foucault 1983: 221).[2]

Letting others be themselves: democratizing group life

A second, although not unrelated, 'life world' involves what could be described as *a democracy of social space*, in which public dialogue is valued and groups are accorded authoritative voices and opportunities to find and be themselves. But, as Giddens (1994) notes, groups that help themselves are not necessarily democratic. 'Self-help' groups also need to be committed to others as well as to themselves and to democratic interactions, as implied in the discussions above. In addition to these, we envisage at least three dispositions that could advance the democratization of group life in classrooms and schools. We list them here as

- self-organization
- self-expression
- self-development.

In classrooms, both cooperative learning groups and informal groups that students establish among themselves can provide students with a sense of belonging and connectedness to one another. This is especially important for uprooted immigrant students and students learning English as a second language, for example, since small groups often make it easier for marginalized students to express themselves to their peers, to learn the subject matter at hand, and to develop their individual abilities to listen to and learn from others. This is one way in which students are able to 'retrieve' the learning agenda (Giddens 1994: 121), as it were. It is more than just a pedagogical trick because the very nature of what is learnt is mediated by the group; the content becomes entwined in who these students are as people. Moreover, it reworks the test of isolation that students face in classrooms that are organized to (re)produce their disconnectedness. (With respect to this, see the example of the student with learning difficulties discussed in Chapter 2.)

These are the experiences that teachers need to foster in classrooms and schools more generally. Rather than perceiving their primary role as simply exposing students to traditional bodies of knowledge or to the skills required to secure a skilled job, teachers need to help students acquire concrete understandings of how exploited groups can resist oppression and discrimination and to prepare them to defend themselves against such exploitation (Giddens 1994: 121). Curricula would include content matter on working people's struggles and cultural achievements, coupled with activities enabling students to take the perspectives of oppressed groups in problem-solving projects; 'curricular justice', as Connell (1993) refers to it.

Members of oppressed groups especially stand to benefit from self-organization, which can help them affirm who they are and determine their specific needs and interests much more clearly than when, for example, individuals from the dominant culture or 'management' are present. Students of colour, those who have a first language other than English, and women, in particular, may experience linguistic and cultural freedom and support, enabling them to reflect on who they have become in relation to who they want to be. These are issues that we first raised in Chapter 3 in relation to the 'identity work' (Green 1995) of functional language. Yet (as argued in Chapter 7) self-organized groups, influenced by discourses of 'difference politics', clearly run the risk of pressuring members not to integrate with others outside the group or of defining their identity in a narrow or essentialist way. This 'self-centred' reading of self is not what is intended here. Rather, emphasizing the self within group life draws attention to 'democratizing the numerous areas of . . . "subpolitics"' (Giddens 1994: 121) that traditionally represent group differences as silenced or 'settled'.

To illustrate, in some schools in California, Latino parents have organized bilingual advisory committees to operate *alongside* and *within* school councils, to ensure a voice for the group of parents who numerically comprise the majority of the population of the school but, in practice, wield the least power over school matters. Not only has their group solidarity created space for their self-expression, but also these parents have organized themselves in ways that allow them to contribute to their schools' agenda and 'force into the discursive domain aspects of social conduct that previously went undiscussed, or were "settled" by traditional practices' (Giddens 1994: 120).

Similarly, teachers, as a group, share a common interest in maintaining the gains that their unions and associations have achieved and in refusing to let themselves be divided against one another. But by expanding their definition of 'mutual interests', teacher-groups can also provide opportunities to reflect and act on classroom issues as well as broader social issues. They can, for example, establish programmes on gender discrimination and racism within their schools and communities, as well as within their own particular collectives. That is, in addition to teacher unions becoming more internally democratic, they are also obliged to gain popular support among the public at large. The democratization of group life necessarily requires dialogue within and between groups, including employee groups, so that their respective concerns, conditions and objectives can be compared and contrasted. In this way, common goals can be identified and forged.

In terms of the self-development of groups, Young (1990) makes an important distinction between empowerment and autonomy, one that provides a useful critique of Giddens' (1994) representation of such concepts. Young argues that (group) autonomy is a concept that emphasizes the right to keep others out, whereas empowerment aims to include more people – especially members of oppressed groups – who participate in making a wider range of decisions. One illustration of group empowerment is the school council where teachers, parents, administrators, students and community representatives share decisions on school policy and practice, including issues around quality and equality, representation and participation.

Making group life more democratic and empowering also builds 'equity' which goes beyond the more common usage of 'equality', a distinction we raised in Chapter 2. Conventionally, equality means treating all individuals in the same way and giving everyone the same opportunity. For example, many people think that simply being able to go to school means that all students have an equal opportunity to succeed academically. LouAnne Johnson, the teacher in *Dangerous Minds* (discussed in Chapter 6), is illustrative of this view. From this position, the educational process is understood as a free competition among individuals, much like exchanges in the marketplace.

In western capitalist societies, however, students of different social classes and racial groups are not usually provided with the same quality of schooling. As well, students enter schools with very unequal social backgrounds and resources, which in turn influence their performance. As discussed in Chapters 7 and 8 in particular, the social and economic geography of student circumstances is such that they provide good indicators of future success and failure. The lesson is, if students from marginalized groups do not receive specific attention, they will be held back, while the materially advantaged are likely to advance. Equity, therefore, requires that in order for everyone to be able to participate fully in social life, members of oppressed groups, at times, require different treatment.

Working together to make it work: democratizing institutional life

A third arena in democratic and just schooling is concerned with its institutional life. Again, we pose three dispositions as central to what could be termed *a democracy of systems and routines*. Rather than the generalizations and uniformity of many systems, we suggest that democratizing the institutional 'life styles' (Giddens 1994: 14) of schooling requires tendencies towards

- social reflexivity
- responsiveness
- devolved responsibility.

A disposition for reflexivity involves an ongoing commitment to rethinking and reworking accepted wisdom. Yet, all too often, schooling is characterized by traditional patterns of operation that are generalized across systems. While these can be efficient, they frequently lack sensitivity and flexibility. The irony of institutional life disposed towards such generalities and efficiencies is that uniform practices do not tend to produce uniform outcomes. As argued in Chapter 2 (note, particularly, the example regarding Andrew), treating everyone as if they are the same – the dominant perspective on fairness – does not deliver fair outcomes. This reality of informal segregation within formally unsegregated schools (Connell 1994) is well documented: children from poor and minority families receive lower scores on tests, leave school earlier and are less likely to go to college/university than children from middle-class white families. As Connell (1994: 129) notes: 'The evidence of socially unequal outcomes continues to mount; it is one of the most firmly established facts about western-style educational systems in all parts of the world'.

How, then, should teachers and schools respond to the evidence of these outcomes for students, particularly if they value a democratization of educational institutions? Connell's (1993) proposal is to adopt an approach that he calls 'curricular justice'. The logic of this approach is that rather than generalizing the perspective of the advantaged, which (re)produces disadvantages, Connell (1994: 52) 'attempts to generalize the point of view of the disadvantaged . . . [not] separate it off'; a responsiveness he describes as 'a new geography of the problem' (1994: 26). Curricula informed by these (re)arrangements would most likely produce quite a different account of the relationships between schooling and work, for example, but at the same time retain what is needed by students to participate in the workforce. Similar curricula adjustments would account for issues of gender and race, and the relations between dominant and marginalized cultures generally. As a consequence, sources of knowledge would also be expanded. In designing curricula, teachers would invite input from local people for whom matters such as social class, racism and sexism are already an issue and who are organizing for change.

In order to address these issues properly, teachers should be centrally involved in designing and adopting curricula. Top-down administrative directives for teachers to simply distribute a received curriculum, militates against collaborative, internally motivated processes. Highly bureaucratic administrations and excessive standardization must be challenged in order to give teachers opportunities to shape the conditions and outcomes of their work. For instance, responsibility to make decisions – not simply to be held accountable for decisions made elsewhere – on school budgets, scheduling, safety, peer review, teacher counselling, teacher retention and improvement, should be devolved to a level where they include teachers *alongside* administrators and relevant others. As Giddens (1994: 123) argues, 'a "responsibility-based organization" recognizes that reflexivity produces a return to the need for local knowledge'.

Community representatives, for instance, including those who are most marginalized, must also be drawn into the process of educational decision-making. While local communities must not be considered the sole arbiter of educational needs, democratic schooling requires that we formulate routines and mechanisms for progressive public debate and involvement around educational objectives and control. We must be clear, however, about the nature of community (see below) and community participation. While appearing to be community based, for example, calls for 'parental choice' in effect result in greater choice for the powerful and wealthy, abrogating democratic principles such as broad-based public deliberation and participation (see Whitty *et al.* 1998). Instead, committees involving teachers, administrators, parent communities and students can be formed to raise student achievement, develop responsibility and accountability systems and strengthen the links between the different cultures represented within the school. By working together, representatives from these different groups could strengthen their capacity to improve low-performing schools and overcome some of the challenges they confront.

Seeing the big picture: democratizing community life

Then, there is a fourth arena of 'communal life' that embraces *a democracy of scale* and within which democratic dispositions for just schooling include

- all of the above dispositions, writ large
- multiple collectives
- multiple connections.

Strong community ties is an ideal for many individuals and groups. We, however, agree with Young (1990) that the ideal of community – understood as similarity – may not be an appropriate vision of a democratic polity. This is because the meanings attached to 'community' tend to be utopian and, in practice, calls for community are often calls for homogeneity or exclusion of others. Yet democratizing community life means, in part, that within and outside of schools, individual and group differences are affirmed. Affirmation means allowing for difference without excluding or marginalizing others. Further, and perhaps more importantly, from 'identity' and 'difference' politics we have learned that we have the potential to be aware of our own history and to use that history self-critically. Thus, while cultural histories and communal symbolism must be acknowledged as integral parts of present arrangements, heterogeneous collectivity in common undertakings may be more important. This can lead us to see the ties we share with others and to building larger and more comprehensive forms of solidarity, but still in forms that respect difference.

Public schools must ensure that all students and parents feel that they belong and that they are respected. Further, all members of a school's community should feel that they can contribute to the quality of life in the school and that they are valued by the school. Indeed, community representatives, when involved in various school functions and departments, can provide students with a wide diversity of adults in their lives who have experiences from which the entire school community can learn.

An example here should illustrate what we mean. In early Zapotec Indian communities in southern Mexico, individual teachers were integrated into the communities where they taught, by serving them in a variety of ways on a wide range of social issues. For instance, teachers combined their efforts with those of their communities to have new roads built and to build health clinics. Through such projects, teachers and parents developed strong working relationships with one another. While these teachers were native bilingual teachers, teachers in more modern contexts can still learn from these experiences and also work with communities of colour, for example, to help reduce the distance between themselves and their students.

Such experiences can teach teachers to look at issues from perspectives different from their own. Working closely with diverse community members can help teachers better see themselves as not only teachers but also as parents, members of ethnic groups, children of workers, or newcomers. In turn, this contributes to weakening barriers of misunderstanding between professionals and non-professionals and to broadening the concept of 'expertise', as teachers permit themselves to learn from parents and community representatives (Giddens 1994: 121). In this way, teachers might also view themselves as learners, which is a requisite if they are not only to identify with their students as they struggle with new material and perspectives, but also to understand their students' lives, backgrounds and histories, and incorporate this knowledge into their pedagogy (Densmore 1998).

At the level of groups, broad alliances between teachers, local communities and the labour movement need to be developed in order to build a democratic culture that welcomes participation in schools, neighbourhoods, cities and regions (Walker and Barton 1989). Through these alliances, each group can put issues before the public that otherwise might not receive much attention. In addition, collaborative work of this sort gives all of us practice in voicing our concerns, taking other points of view into consideration, and problem-solving. Teachers have opportunities for interaction with the community where different traditions are brought into regular contact. As Burbules (1993: 29) notes, the reason for celebrating group differences is based on the ability of different groups to interact in a way that enriches and invigorates each other's lives.

Broad alliances of this sort can provide resources for the poor to mobilize around educational issues; resources that they do not have on their own. An example of this process occurred in indigenous regions of Mexico in the late 1970s when strikes by bilingual teachers were strongly supported by their communities and led to the formation of a democratic current within the teachers' union. The impetus for this movement originated from the teachers' participation in organizing improvements – such as higher wages and better living conditions – for farmers and other workers. This current called for an alternative pedagogy, one that involved parents and communities more intimately in the education process. In sum, collective activity provides opportunities for people to expand their intellectual and imaginative abilities, to use the new knowledge acquired from this work to help solve problems, to develop more self- and collective respect, and to become more socially responsible.

Conclusion

Our purpose in this chapter has been to suggest ways in which teachers, schools and communities might develop more democratic practices. We have sought to show how education, as it confronts pressing social and economic concerns, might prepare youth to make our (collective) personal and public lives more just and more democratic. Because schools are, to some extent, both funded and governed locally, and because of the myth surrounding their role in upward social and economic mobility, they are often the target of reform proposals. In considering reforms, including those that teachers might generate themselves, it is important not to lose sight of the cultural processes at work in schooling.

Schooling creates and reinforces meanings related to personal identity and control over students' futures. Critically, all humans have potential and abilities that are too often thwarted by undemocratic conditions under which they live. By exercising a radical democracy, students, teachers and parents are capable together of producing and creating far more than they could under a more conventional liberal form. Yet it is most likely that achieving radical democracy and a recognitive social justice in schools will require a dramatic transformation of the way we make our living and live together. Its achievement would enable each individual to realize their full potential and provide for our existence in ways that do not depend upon the exploitation of others. If, in some small way, we have contributed to the realization of these ideals and dispositions, our efforts in writing this book will have been worthwhile.

Questions for discussion/research

- How can teachers cultivate a school environment based on participatory democracy?
- In what ways can teachers work more closely with non-educators on mutual concerns?
- What is the relationship between teaching practice, culture and identity formation?
- What structural changes are needed in schools for democratic educational practice?

Suggested readings

Apple, M. (1993) *Official Knowledge: Democratic Education in a Conservative Age*. New York: Routledge, Chapter 7.

Connell, R.W. (1993) *Schools and Social Justice*. Leichhardt, NSW: Pluto, Chapter 4.

Smyth, J., Hattam, R. and Lawson, M. (eds) (1998) *Schooling for a Fair Go*. Leichhardt, NSW: Federation Press, Chapter 2.

Notes

3 Language games

1 In this chapter references to language refer specifically to English and its use as the medium of instruction in schools in western societies, although we suspect that the issues discussed have points of similarity with other languages and contexts.

2 This is much like the clusters of stars from Greek mythology, connected to form such figures as Archtrus (the bear), Orion (the hunter) and Pleiades (the seven daughters of Atlas).

3 A more contemporary analogy would draw on digitized technologies based on 'zeros' and 'ones'.

4 A more recent equivalent of this dominance of English can be seen in the Organization for Economic Cooperation and Development (OECD 1999) survey of Internet sites linked to 'secure servers' and engaged in 'e-commerce'. The survey found that at least 78 per cent of these sites were in English or, depending on the way the sites are defined, the figure was as high as 96 per cent.

5 Three blind men chance upon an elephant. The first man bumps into the elephant's broad flank and concludes: 'An elephant is very much like a wall'. The second man grabs the elephant's tail and reasons: 'This elephant is very similar to a rope'. The third man finds the trunk and proclaims: 'You're both wrong, an elephant is just like a hose'. One reading of this Indian parable is that there is danger in losing sight of the bigger picture by focusing on (de)tails!

6 See the discussion in Chapter 6 regarding metonymy.

7 See Delpit (1992) for a good discussion of this dilemma in relation to teaching practice.

8 The story is told in Greek mythology of Oedipus who, while passing near Thebes, is confronted by the Sphinx, a beast with the (winged) body of a lion and the head of a woman. To be spared from death, Oedipus must solve the riddle: 'Who am I? I walk on four legs in the morning, two legs at noon, and three legs in the evening.' Oedipus replies: 'The creature is a man, of course. He crawls on hands and knees in the morning, walks on two legs at noon and supports himself with a stick in the evening of his days.'

9 We acknowledge here that the term 'critical' is used in a variety of ways in the academic literature and in contexts of practice. Along with Lankshear *et al.* (1997: 40–1), we contend that this has often led to the term having 'too little' *and* 'too much' meaning and, therefore, an uncertain interpretation. Following Agger (1992), we adopt an 'overtly political' construction of what is critical that is expressed in its dialectical treatment of language, as discussed.

4 Language strategies

1 Theorists often distinguish between these two 'set plays' – those that establish frameworks and those that challenge boundaries – by referring to the first as strategies and to the second as tactics. While these distinctions are informative they can also set up unnecessary and empirically difficult separations that distract from language users' purposes. Throughout this chapter we have chosen, therefore, to refer to both of them as strategies.

2 In part, this is how we read Gee's (1990) distinction between Discourse (first letter capitalized) and discourse (no capitalization) – as a way of accounting for ideology embedded in discourse.

3 A similar schema representing the relationships between text, discourse and ideology first appeared in Gale (1999b). Explanations here of this schema also draw on that article.

4 These questions of what, how and why are adapted from Kenway's (1990: 24) approach to the analysis of policy.

5 The first and third of this second set of questions have their origins in Taylor *et al.*'s (1997: 39) additions to Kenway's list of policy questions, with the exception that 'what now?' is expressed in the original as 'what are the consequences?'

6 *Subject(ivity)* and *object(ivity)* might also be usefully understood in similar terms, although this would require a much fuller account than is possible here.

7 Some in the literature refer to 'cultural texts' to emphasize this broader under-standing that is not always reflected in narrower conceptions of literary texts. To reiterate, it is cultural texts to which we refer in this chapter.

8 See Evans (1974) for a similar discussion (and diagrams) of how teachers 'read' the various arrangements of texts in the principal's or head teacher's office.

9 Homonyms provide another form of textual comparison, that is, words of a similar form but with different meanings, and hence are not included in this discussion of meaning making.

10 See Kenway (1987) for a discussion of the politics of signification related to private schooling.

5 Getting a good education

1 See Chapter 9 for a discussion of the democratization of these life worlds.

6 (Re)structuring teacher–student relations

1 Our critique in this chapter relates to the teaching and classroom practices of the on-screen teacher depicted in the film *Dangerous Minds*. We are aware that the producers of this film claim that it is based on a real account. However, we do not wish in any way to suggest that our critique relates to the real LonAnne Johnson and her teaching, which we have not witnessed. Indeed, we suspect that the film may not accurately portray the realities of Johnson's classroom, an issue we return to at the end of the chapter.

2 Giddens' (1994: 120) comments here that such 'mass emotional identification . . . is the very antithesis of a dialogic democracy'.

3 See Chapter 4 for a discussion of such ordinary but critical incidents, based on Foucault's techniques of power.

7   Representing (self and) others

1 See Goldthorpe (1996) for a good discussion on the relationships between IQ, effort, and merit. Chapter 2 also provides a brief account of these issues.
2 See Whitty *et al.* (1998) for an insightful look at school choice in the current economic and political context. See also Gewirtz *et al.* (1995).

8   Thinking differently about gender, race and social class

1 We are not referring here to cases of fraud, where white artists have painted blak art and have passed this off as the work of a Black artist. Clearly, this is something we would not support.

9   (Re)constructing practice

1 In this respect, we think that teachers informed by a structuralist approach to language (described in Chapter 3) get it 'half right' in rethinking their roles in the education process.
2 See Green (1998) for a critique of teacher authority and identity.

References

Agger, B. (1992) *Cultural Studies as Critical Theory*. London: Falmer Press.

Agger, B. (1998) *Critical Social Theories: An Introduction*. Boulder, CO: Westview Press.

Altbach, P. and Lomotey, K. (eds) (1991) *The Racial Crisis in American Higher Education*. Albany, NY: State University of New York Press.

Anyon, J. (1980) Social class and the hidden curriculum of work, *Journal of Education*, 162(1): 67–92.

Anyon, J. (1981) Social class and school knowledge, *Curriculum Inquiry*, 11(1): 3–42.

Apple, M. (1986) *Teachers and Texts: A Political Economy of Class and Gender Relations in Education*. Boston, MA: Routledge and Kegan Paul.

Apple, M. (1989) Equality and the politics of commonsense, in W. Secada (ed.) *Equity in Education*. London: Falmer Press.

Apple, M. (1993) *Official Knowledge: Democratic Education in a Conservative Age*. New York: Routledge.

Apple, M. (1996) *Cultural Politics and Education*. Buckingham: Open University Press.

Apple, M. and Beane, J. (eds) (1999) *Democratic Schools: Lessons from the Chalkface*. Buckingham: Open University Press.

Apple, M. and Christian-Smith, L. (eds) (1991) *The Politics of the Textbook*. New York: Routledge.

Aronowitz, S. and Giroux, H. (1985) *Education under Siege*. South Hadley, MA: Bergin and Garvey.

Baldwin, J.D. and Baldwin, J.I. (1990) *Behaviour Principles in Everyday Life*. Englewood Cliffs, NJ: Prentice-Hall.

Ball, S. (1990) *Politics and Policy Making in Education: Explorations in Policy Sociology*. London: Routledge.

Ball, S. (1994) *Education Reform: A Critical and Post-structural Approach*. Buckingham: Open University Press.

Banks, J. (1988) *Multiethnic Education: Theory and Practice*, 2nd edn. Newton, MA: Allyn & Bacon.

Banton, M. (1998) *Racial Theories*, 2nd edn. Cambridge: Cambridge University Press.

Barnes, D. and Shemilt, D. (1974) Transmission and interpretation, *Educational Review*, 26(June): 213–28.

Barnes, D., Britton, J. and Rosen, H. (1971) *Language, the Learner and the School*. Harmondsworth: Penguin.

Barthes, R. (1972) *Mythologies*. London: Jonathan Cape.

Bastian, A., Fruchter, N., Gittell, M., Greer, C. and Haskins, K. (1986) *Choosing Equality: The Case for Democratic Schooling*. Philadelphia, PA: Temple University Press.

Baudrillard, J. (1981) *For a Critique of the Political Economy of the Sign* (trans. C. Levin). St Louis, MO: Telos Press.

Beilharz, P. (1989) Social democracy and social justice, *Australian and New Zealand Journal of Sociology*, 25(1): 85–99.

Berlin, I. (1969) *Four Essays on Liberty*. Oxford: Oxford University Press.

Bernstein, B. (1971) On the classification and framing of educational knowledge, in M. Young (ed.) *Knowledge and Control: New Directions for the Sociology of Education*. London: Collier-Macmillan.

Bessant, B. (1983) *Schooling in the Colony and State of Victoria*. Bundoora, Vic.: Centre for Comparative and International Studies in Education, La Trobe University.

Bourdieu, P. (1978) Sport and social class, *Social Science Information*, 17: 819–40.

Bourdieu, P. (1984) *Distinction*. Cambridge, MA: Harvard University Press.

Bourdieu, P. (1990) *In Other Words: Essays Toward a Reflexive Sociology*. Cambridge: Polity Press.

Bourdieu, P. (1997) The forms of capital, in A. Halsey, H. Lauder, P. Brown and A.S. Wells (eds) *Education: Culture, Economy and Society*. Oxford: Oxford University Press.

Bourdieu, P. (1998) *Practical Reason: On the Theory of Action*. Cambridge: Polity Press.

Bourdieu, P. and Passeron, J. (1977) *Reproduction in Education, Society and Culture*. London: Sage.

Bourdieu, P. and Wacquant, L. (1992) The purpose of reflexive sociology (the Chicago workshop), in P. Bourdieu and L. Wacquant (eds) *An Invitation to Reflexive Sociology*. Cambridge: Polity Press.

Bowe, R., Ball, S. and Gold, A. (1992) *Reforming Education and Changing Schools: Case Studies in Policy Sociology*. London: Routledge.

Bowles, S. and Gintis, L. (1976) *Schooling in Capitalist America: Educational Reform and the Contradictions of Economic Life*. London: Routledge and Kegan Paul.

Brah, A. (1992) Difference, diversity and differentiation, in J. Donald and A. Rattansi (eds) *Race, Culture and Difference*. London and Newbury Park, CA: Sage.

Brint, S. (1998) *Schools and Societies*. Thousand Oaks, CA: Pine Forge Press.

Burbules, N. (1993) *Dialogue in Teaching: Theory and Practice*. New York: Teachers College Press.

Carnoy, M. and Levin, H.M. (1985) *Schooling and Work in the Democratic State*. Stanford, CA: Stanford University Press.

Carnoy, M. and Levin, N. (1976) *The Limits of Educational Reform*. New York: David McKay.

Carnoy, M., Castells, M., Cohen, S. and Cardoso, F. (1993) *The New Global Economy in the Information Age: Reflections on Our Changing World*. University Park, PA: Pennsylvania State University Press.

Carr, W. and Hartnett, A. (1996) *Education and the Struggle for Democracy: The Politics of Educational Ideas*. Buckingham: Open University Press.

Cazden, C. (1988) *Classroom Discourse: The Language of Teaching and Learning*. Portsmouth, NH: Heinemann.

Chomsky, N. (1966) *Cartesian Linguistics: A Chapter in the History of Rationalist Thought*. New York: Harper and Row.

Chomsky, N. (1972) *Language and Mind*. New York: Harcourt Brace Jovanovich.

Christensen, C. and Rizvi, F. (eds) (1996) *Disability and the Dilemmas of Education and Justice*. Buckingham: Open University Press.

Christie, F. (1990) The changing face of literacy, in F. Christie (ed.) *Literacy for a Changing World: A Fresh Look at the Basics*. Melbourne, Vic.: Australian Council for Educational Research (ACER).

Comber, B. (1998) Problematising 'background': (re)constructing categories in educational research, *Australian Educational Researcher*, 25(3): 1–21.

Comber, B., Nixon, H., Badger, L. and Hill, S. (1994) *Literacy, Diversity and Schooling*. Adelaide, SA: University of South Australia.

Commission on Social Justice (1998) What is social justice?, in J. Franklin (ed.) *Social Policy and Social Justice*. Cambridge: Polity Press.

Conant, J. (1940) Education for a classless society: the Jeffersonian tradition, *The Atlantic*, 165(May): 593–602.

Connell, R.W. (1993) *Schools and Social Justice*. Leichhardt, NSW: Pluto.

Connell, R.W. (1994) Poverty and education, *Harvard Educational Review*, 64(2, Summer): 125–49.

Connell, R.W. (1995) *Masculinities*. St Leonards, NSW: Allen & Unwin.

Connell, R., Ashenden, D., Kessler, S. and Dowsett, G. (1982) *Making the Difference: Schools, Families and Social Division*. Sydney: Allen & Unwin.

Cornford, I. (1998) Schooling and vocational preparation: is a revolution *really* taking place? *Australian Journal of Education*, 42(2): 169–82.

Corry, D. (1998) The role of the public sector and public expenditure, in J. Franklin (ed.) *Social Policy and Social Justice*. Cambridge: Polity Press.

Corson, D. (ed.) (1991) *Education for Work, Background to Policy and Curriculum*. Clevedon: Multilingual Matters.

Corson, D. (1993) *Language, Minority Education and Gender: Linking Social Justice and Power*. Clevedon: Multilingual Matters.

Corson, D. (1998) *Changing Education for Diversity*. Buckingham: Open University Press.

Cosin, B. (1972) *Ideology*. Milton Keynes: Open University Press.

Cox, R. (1980) Social forces, states and world orders' millennium, *Millennium: Journal of International Studies*, 10(2): 126–55.

Dale, R. (1989) *The State and Education Policy*. Milton Keynes: Open University Press.

Dale, R. and Esland, G. (1977) *Mass Schooling*. Milton Keynes: Open University Press.

Dalton, M. (1995) The Hollywood curriculum: who is the 'good' teacher? *Curriculum Studies*, 3(1): 23–44.

Davies, I. (1969) Education and social science, *New Society*, 13(345, 8 May): 710–11.

Deem, R. (1978) *Women and Schooling*. London: Routledge and Kegan Paul.

Deem, R. (ed.) (1981) *Schooling for Women's Work*. London: Routledge and Kegan Paul.

Delbridge, A. and Bernard, J. (eds) (1994) *The Compact Macquarie Dictionary*. Sydney, NSW: Macquarie Library.

Delgado-Gaitan, C. (1990) *Literacy for Empowerment: The Role of Parents in Children's Education*. London: Falmer Press.

Delors, J. (1996) *Learning: The Treasure Within. Report to UNESCO of the International Commission on Education for the Twenty-First Century*. Paris: UNESCO Publishing.

Delpit, L. (1992) Acquisition of literate discourse: bowing before the master? *Theory into Practice*, 31(4): 296–302.

Densmore, K. (1998) The teacher and the community: a case study of teacher–community relations among Zapotec and Mixtec Indians of Oaxaca, Mexico, *Journal of Curriculum Studies*, 30(1, January–February): 61–85.

Derewianka, B. (1990) *Exploring how Texts Work*. Rozelle, NSW: Primary English Teaching Association (PETA).

Dewey, J. (1915) *The School and Society*, 2nd edn. Chicago: Chicago University Press.

Dixon, J. (1975) *Growth Through English: Set in the Perspective of the Seventies*. Oxford: Oxford University Press.

Doughty, P., Pearce, J. and Thornton, G. (1972) *Exploring Language*. London: Schools Council Publications.

Evans, K. (1974) The head and his territory, *New Society*, 30(629, 24 October): 199–201.

Fairclough, N. (1992a) The appropriacy of 'appropriateness', in N. Fairclough (ed.) *Critical Language Awareness*. London: Longman.

Fairclough, N. (1992b) *Discourse and Social Change*. Cambridge: Polity Press.

Farber, P. and Holm, G. (1994) A brotherhood of heroes: the charismatic educator in recent American movies, in P. Farber, E. Provenzo Jr and G. Holm (eds) *Schooling in the Light of Popular Culture*. Albany, NY: State University of New York Press.

Farber, P., Provenzo Jr, E. and Holm, G. (eds) (1994) *Schooling in the Light of Popular Culture*. Albany, NY: State University of New York Press.

Featherstone, M. (1989) In pursuit of the postmodern: an introduction, *Theory, Culture and Society*, 5(2–3): 195–216.

Floud, J. and Halsey, A. (1961) English secondary schools and the supply of labour, in A. Halsey, J. Floud and C. Anderson (eds) *Education, Economy and Society*. New York: Free Press.

Fordham, S. and Ogbu, J.U. (1986) Black students' school success: coping with the 'burden' of 'acting white', *Urban Review*, 18(3): 176–206.

Foucault, M. (1972) *The Archaeology of Knowledge*. London: Tavistock.

Foucault, M. (1978) *The History of Sexuality: An Introduction*, Vol. 1. Harmondsworth: Penguin.

Foucault, M. (1980) *Power/Knowledge*. New York: Harvester Wheatsheaf.

Foucault, M. (1981) The order of discourse, in R. Young (ed.) *Untying the Text: A Post-structuralist Reader*. London: Routledge and Kegan Paul.

Foucault, M. (1983) The subject and power, in H. Dreyfus and P. Rabinow (eds) *Michel Foucault: Beyond Structuralism and Hermeneutics*, 2nd edn. Chicago: University of Chicago Press.

Foucault, M. (1991) *Remarks on Marx: Conversations with Duccio Trombadori* (trans. R. Goldstein and J. Cascaito). New York: Columbia University.

Fraser, N. (1995) From redistribution to recognition: dilemmas of justice in a 'post-socialist' age, *New Left Review*, 212(July): 68–93.

Fraser, N. (1997) *Justice Interruptus: Critical Reflections on the 'Post-socialist' Condition*. New York: Routledge.

Freebody, P. and Ludwig, C. (1995) *Everyday Literacy Practices in and out of Schools in Low Socio-economic Urban Communities*, Vols 1 and 2. Brisbane, Qld: Centre for Literacy Education Research, Griffith University.

Freebody, P. and Luke, A. (1990) Literacies programs: debates and demands in cultural context, *Prospect: Australian Journal of ESL*, 5(3): 7–16.

Freire, P. (1972) *Pedagogy of the Oppressed*. Harmondsworth: Penguin.

Freire, P. and Macedo, D. (1987) *Literacy: Reading the Word and the World*. London: Routledge.

Frow, J. (1991) The order of discourse, in R. Young and H. Tiffin (eds) *Past the Last Post: Theorizing Post-colonialism and Post-modernism*. New York: Harvester Wheatsheaf.

Fuller, M. (1981) Black girls in a London comprehensive school, in R. Deem (ed.) *Schooling for Women's Work*. London: Routledge and Kegan Paul.

Gale, T. (1994) University entrance in Queensland: post World War II challenges to the influence of the University of Queensland, *History of Education Review*, 23(1): 38–52.

Gale, T. (1999a) Fair contest or elite sponsorship? Entry settlements in Australian higher education, *Higher Education Policy*, 12(1): 69–91.

Gale, T. (1999b) Policy trajectories: treading the discursive path of policy analysis, *Discourse: Studies in the Cultural Politics of Education*, 20(3): 393–407.

Gee, J. (1990) *Social Linguistics and Literacies: Ideology in Discourses*. London: Falmer Press.

Gee, J., Hull, G. and Lankshear, C. (1996) *The New Work Order: Behind the Language of the New Capitalism*. Sydney: Allen & Unwin.

Gewirtz, S., Ball, S. and Bowe, R. (1995) *Markets, Choice and Equity in Education*. Buckingham: Open University Press.

Gibson, M.A. and Bhachu, P.K. (1988) Ethnicity and school performance: a comparative study of South Asian pupils in Britain and America, *Ethnic and Racial Studies*, 11(3): 239–62.

Giddens, A. (1990) *The Consequences of Modernity*. Cambridge: Polity Press.

Giddens, A. (1994) *Beyond Left and Right: The Future of Radical Politics*. Cambridge: Polity Press.

Gillborn, D. (1995) *Racism and Antiracism in Real Schools: Theory, Policy, Practice*. Buckingham: Open University Press.

Gilroy, P. (1990) The end of anti-racism, *New Community*, 17(1): 71–83.

Giroux, H. (1983) *Theory and Resistance in Education*. Granby, MA: Bergin and Garvey.

Giroux, H. (1989) *Schooling for Democracy: Critical Pedagogy in the Modern Age*. London: Routledge.

Giroux, H. (1997) Rewriting the discourse of racial identity: towards a pedagogy and politics of whiteness, *Harvard Educational Review*, 67(2): 285–320.

Goldthorpe, J.H. (1996) Problems of 'meritocracy', in R. Erikson and J.O. Jonsson (eds) *Can Education be Equalized? The Swedish Case in Comparative Perspective*. Boulder, CO: Westview Press.

Gore, J. (1998a) Disciplining bodies: on the continuity of power relations in pedagogy, in T. Popkewitz and M. Brennan (eds) *Foucault's Challenge: Discourse, Knowledge, and Power in Education*. New York: Teachers College Press.

Gore, J. (1998b) Micro-level techniques of power in the classroom production of class, race, gender and other relations. Paper presented to the Annual Conference of the Australian Association for Research in Education (AARE), Adelaide, 30 November–3 December.

Grace, G. (1985) Judging teachers: the social and political contexts of teacher evaluation, *British Journal of Sociology of Education*, 6(1): 3–16.

Gramsci, A. (1971) *Selections from the Prison Notebooks of Antonio Gramsci* (ed. and trans. Q. Hoare and G. Smith). London: Lawrence and Wishart.

Green, B. (1995) Post-curriculum possibilities: English teaching, cultural politics, and the postmodern turn, *Journal of Curriculum Studies*, 27(4): 391–409.

Green, B. (1997) Keynote address: literacy, information and the learning society. Paper presented to the Joint Conference of the Australian Association for the Teaching of English, the Australian Literacy Educators' Association and the Australian School Library Association, Darwin, 8–11 July.

Green, B. (1998) Born-again teaching? Governmentality, 'grammar', and public schooling, in T. Popkewitz and M. Brennan (eds) *Foucault's Challenge: Discourse, Knowledge and Power in Education*. New York: Teachers College Press.

Griffiths, M. and Troyna, B. (eds) (1995) *Antiracism, Culture and Social Justice in Education*. Stoke-on-Trent: Trentham Books.

Guppy, P. and Hughes, M. (1998) *The Development of Independent Reading: Reading Support Explained*. Buckingham: Open University Press.

Halliday, M. (1973) *Explorations in the Functions of Language*. London: Edward Arnold.

Halliday, M. (1975) *Learning How to Mean: Explorations in the Development of Language.* London: Edward Arnold.

Halliday, M. and Hasan, R. (1976) *Cohesion in English.* London: Longman.

Halliday, M. and Hasan, R. (1985) *Language, Context and Text: Aspects of Language in a Social-Semiotic Perspective.* Geelong, Vic.: Deakin University Press.

Hamilton, D. (1989) *Towards a Theory of Schooling.* London: Falmer Press.

Harris, K. (1979) *Education and Knowledge.* London: Routledge and Kegan Paul.

Harvey, D. (1990) *The Condition of Postmodernity: An Enquiry into the Origins of Cultural Change.* Oxford: Blackwell.

Harvey, L. (1990) *Critical Social Research.* London: Unwin Hyman.

Heath, S.B. (1983) *Ways with Words: Language, Life and Work in Communities and Classrooms.* Cambridge: Cambridge University Press.

Henry, M. and Taylor, S. (1994) New pathways? Post-compulsory schooling, TAFE and mass higher education, *Australian Universities' Review*, 37(2): 29–33.

Henry, M. and Taylor, S. (1995) Equity and the AVC pilots in Queensland: a study in policy refraction, *Australian Educational Researcher*, 22(1): 85–106.

Henry, M., Knight, J., Lingard, R. and Taylor, S. (1988) *Understanding Schooling: An Introductory Sociology of Australian Education.* London: Routledge.

Hicks, E. (1981) Cultural Marxism: nonsynchrony and feminist practice, in L. Sargent (ed.) *Women and Revolution.* Boston, MA: South End Press.

Hodge, B. (1981) *Communication and the Teacher.* Melbourne, Vic.: Longman Cheshire.

hooks, b. (1989) *Talking Back.* Boston, MA: South End Press.

Howe, K. (1996) Educational ethics, social justice and children with disabilities, in C. Christensen and F. Rizvi (eds) *Disability and the Dilemmas of Education and Justice.* Buckingham: Open University Press.

Isaacs, P. (1996) Disability and the education of persons, in C. Christensen and F. Rizvi (eds) *Disability and the Dilemmas of Education and Justice.* Buckingham: Open University Press.

Jameson, F. (1983) Postmodernism and consumer society, in H. Foster (ed.) *Postmodern Culture.* London: Pluto.

Jameson, F. (1991) *Postmodernism, or the Cultural Logic of Late Capitalism.* Durham, NC: Duke University Press.

Jenkins, R. (1994) Rethinking ethnicity: identity, categorization and power, *Ethnic and Racial Studies*, 17(2): 197–223.

Johnston, K. (1990) Dealing with difference, *Education Links*, 38: 26–9.

Kenway, J. (1987) Left right out: Australian education and the politics of signification, *Journal of Education Policy*, 2(3): 189–203.

Kenway, J. (1990) *Gender and Education Policy: A Call for New Directions.* Geelong, Vic.: Deakin University Press.

Kenway, J. and Willis, S. (eds) (1990) *Hearts and Minds: Self-esteem and the Schooling of Girls.* London: Falmer Press.

Kenway, J., Blackmore, J. and Willis, S. (1996) Pleasure and pain: beyond feminist authoritarianism and therapy in the curriculum, *Curriculum Perspectives*, 16(1): 1–13.

Kenway, J., Willis, S., with Blackmore, J. and Rennie, L. (1997) *Answering Back: Girls, Boys and Feminism in Schools.* St Leonards, NSW: Allen & Unwin.

King, N. (1983) 'The teacher must exist before the pupil': The Newbolt report on the teaching of English in England, 1921, *Literature and History*, 13(1): 14–37.

Kirk, R. (1989) Against meritocracy and equality, in H. Holtz, I. Marcus, J. Dougherty, J. Michaels and R. Peduzzi (eds) *Education and the American Dream: Conservatives, Liberals and Radicals Debate the Future of Education.* New York: Bergin and Garvey.

Kliebard, H.M. (1986) *The Struggle for the American Curriculum: 1893–1958.* Boston, MA: Routledge and Kegan Paul.

Knight, T. (1998) Public education: Northland Secondary College versus the State, *International Journal of Inclusive Education*, 2(4): 295–308.

Kogan, M. (1979) Different frameworks for education policy-making and analysis, *Educational Analysis*, 1(2): 5–14.

Korndorffer, W. (1991) Vocational skills training in transition education: successful practice in New Zealand?, in D. Corson (ed.) *Education for Work, Background to Policy and Curriculum.* Clevedon: Multilingual Matters.

Kozol, J. (1991) *Savage Inequalities.* New York: Crown.

Kristeva, J. (1986) World dialogue and novel, in T. Moi (ed.) *The Kristeva Reader.* Oxford: Basil Blackwell.

Kuhn, T. (1970) *The Structure of Scientific Revolutions*, 2nd edn. Chicago: University of Chicago Press.

Labov, W. (1987) Are black and white vernaculars diverging? *American Speech*, 65: 5–12.

Lankshear, C., with Gee, J., Knobel, M. and Searle, C. (1997) *Changing Literacies.* Buckingham: Open University Press.

Lauder, H. (1993) *Democracy, the Economy and the Marketisation of Education.* Wellington, NZ: Victoria University Press.

Lawton, D. (1984) *Theory and Practice of Curriculum Studies.* London: Routledge and Kegan Paul.

Lazerson, M. (1977) *Parents, Teachers and Children: Prospects for Choice in American Education.* San Francisco, CA: Institute for Contemporary Studies.

Lenzo, K. (1995) Validity and self-reflexivity meet post-structuralism: scientific ethos and the transgressive self, *Educational Researcher*, 52(1): 17–23.

Little, G. (1985) Standards and curriculum, unpublished paper. Canberra: Curriculum Development Centre.

Lomotey, K. (1990) *Going to School: The African-American Experience.* Albany, NY: State University of New York Press.

Luke, A., Lingard, B., Green, B. and Comber, B. (2000) The abuses of literacy: educational policy and the construction of crisis, in J. Marshall and M. Peters (eds) *Education Policy.* Oxford: Edward Elgar.

Lummis, C.D. (1996) *Radical Democracy.* Ithaca, NY: Cornell University Press.

Lyotard, J. (1984) *The Postmodern Condition: A Report on Knowledge* (trans. G. Bennington and B. Massumi). Manchester: Manchester University Press.

McCarthy, C. (1990) *Race and Curriculum: Social Inequality and the Theories and Politics of Difference in Contemporary Research in Schooling.* Lewes: Falmer Press.

Macdonnell, D. (1986) *Theories of Discourse.* Oxford: Blackwell.

MacIntyre, S. (1985) *Winners and Losers.* Sydney: Allen and Unwin.

Mackie, R. (ed.) (1981) *Literacy and Revolution: The Pedagogy of Paulo Freire.* New York: Continuum.

McLaren, P. (1997) Multiculturalism and the postmodern critique: toward a pedagogy of resistance and transformation, in A. Halsey, H. Lauder, P. Brown and A.S. Wells (eds) *Education: Culture, Economy, and Society.* Oxford: Oxford University Press.

Marginson, S. (1993) *Education and Public Policy in Australia.* Cambridge: Cambridge University Press.

Martin, J. (1985) *Factual Writing: Exploring and Challenging Social Reality.* Geelong, Vic.: Deakin University Press.

Marx, K. and Engels, F. (1976) *The German Ideology*. Moscow: Progress.

May, S. (1994) *Making Multicultural Education Work*. Clevedon: Multilingual Matters.

Mayor, B. and Pugh, A.K. (1987) *Language, Communication and Education*. Milton Keynes: Open University Press.

Meekosha, H. and Jakubowicz, A. (1996) Disability, participation, representation and social justice, in C. Christensen and F. Rizvi (eds) *Disability and the Dilemmas of Education and Justice*. Buckingham: Open University Press.

Meier, K., Stewart, J. and England, R.E. (1989) *Race, Class and Education: The Politics of Second Generation Discrimination*. Madison, WI: University of Wisconsin Press.

Mills, S. (1997) *Discourse*. London: Routledge.

Nieto, S. (1992) *Affirming Diversity: The Sociopolitical Context of Multicultural Education*, 2nd edn. White Plains, NY: Longman.

Norris, N. (1991) The trouble with competence, *Cambridge Journal of Education*, 21(3): 331–41.

Nozick, R. (1976) *Anarchy, State and Utopia*. Oxford: Blackwell.

Oakes, J. (1985) *Keeping Track: How Schools Structure Inequality*. New Haven, CT: Yale University Press.

O'Donnell, C. (1984) *The Basis of the Bargain: Gender, Schooling and Jobs*. Sydney: Allen & Unwin.

Orenstein, P. (1994) *Schoolgirls, Young Women, Self-esteem and the Confidence Gap*. New York: Anchor.

Organization for Economic Cooperation and Development (OECD) (1999) *OECD Communications Outlook 1999*. Paris: OECD.

Perry, T. and Delpit, L. (eds) (1997) *The Real Ebonics Debate: Power, Language and the Education of African-American Children*. Boston, MA: Beacon Press.

Persell, C. (1997) Social class and educational equality, in J. Banks and C. McGee Banks (eds) *Multicultural Education: Issues and Perspectives*, 3rd edn. Boston, MA: Allyn & Bacon.

Pettman, J. (1992) *Living in the Margins: Racism, Sexism and Feminism in Australia*. Sydney: Allen & Unwin.

Popkewitz, T. and Brennan, M. (eds) (1998) *Foucault's Challenge: Discourse, Knowledge and Power in Education*. New York: Teachers College Press.

Preston, N. and Symes, C. (1992) *Schools and Classrooms: A Cultural Analysis of Education*. Melbourne, Vic.: Longman Cheshire.

Rawls, J. (1971) *A Theory of Justice*. Oxford: Oxford University Press.

Raynor, J. (1972) *The Curriculum in England*. Milton Keynes: Open University Press.

Ricoeur, P. (1981) The model of the text: meaningful action considered as a text, in J.B. Thompson (ed.) *Hermeneutics and the Human Sciences: Essays on Language, Action and Interpretation*. Cambridge: Cambridge University Press.

Rizvi, F. (1993) Children and the grammar of popular racism, in C. McCarthy and W. Crichloe (eds) *Race, Identity and Representation in Education*. New York: Routledge. Rizvi, F. (1994) Devolution and education: three contrasting perspectives, in R. Martin, J. McCollow, L. McFarlane *et al.* (eds) *Devolution, Decentralisation and Recentralisation: The Structure of Schooling*. Melbourne, Vic.: Australian Education Union.

Rizvi, F. and Lingard, B. (1996) Disability, education and the discourses of justice, in C. Christensen and F. Rizvi (eds) *Disability and the Dilemmas of Education and Justice*. Buckingham: Open University Press.

Roberts, P. (1997) The consequences and value of literacy: a critical reappraisal, *Journal of Educational Thought*, 31(1): 45–67.

Roberts, P. (1998) Extending literate horizons: Paulo Freire and the multidimensional world, *Educational Review*, 50(2): 105–14.

Rury, J. and Mirel, J. (1997) The political economy of urban education, in M. Apple (ed.) *Review of Research in Education No. 22*. Washington, DC: American Educational Research Association.

Ryan, A. (ed.) (1993) *Justice*. Oxford: Oxford University Press.

Sabel, C. (1984) *Work and Politics: The Division of Labor in Industry*. New York: Cambridge University Press.

Sadker, M. and Sadker, D. (1994) *Failing at Fairness: How America's Schools Cheat Girls*. New York: Charles Scribner's Sons.

Sarup, M. (1986) *The Politics of Multiracial Education*. London: Routledge and Kegan Paul.

Saussure, F. (1983) *Course in General Linguistics* (trans. R. Harris). London: Duckworth.

Seddon, T. (1994) *Context and Beyond: Reframing the Theory and Practice of Education*. London: Falmer Press.

Seidler, V. (1989) *Rediscovering Masculinity: Reason, Language and Sexuality*. London: Routledge.

Sharp, R. (1980) The culture of the disadvantaged: three views, *School and Community News*, 4(2): 45–59.

Shilling, C. (1993) *The Body and Social Theory*. London: Sage.

Shor, I. (1993) Education is politics, in P. McLaren and P. Leonard (eds) *Paulo Freire: A Critical Encounter*. London: Routledge.

Smith, B. (1991) Crime and the classics: the humanities and government in the nineteenth century Australian University, in I. Hunter (ed.) *Accounting for the Humanities: The Language of Culture and the Logic of Culture*. Brisbane, Qld: Institute for Cultural Policy Studies, Griffith University.

Smith, D. (1990) *The Conceptual Practices of Power: A Feminist Sociology of Knowledge*. Boston, MA: Northeastern University Press.

Smyth, J., Hattam, R. and Lawson, M. (eds) (1998) *Schooling for a Fair Go*. Leichhardt, NSW: Federation Press.

Snook, I. (1991) Unemployment and the schools, in D. Corson (ed.) *Education for Work, Background to Policy and Curriculum*. Palmerston North, NZ: Dunmore Press.

Speak, M. (1992) The children's view, in Sports Development Board (ed.) *Children in Sports*. Hong Kong: Sports Development Board.

Spender, D. (1982) *Invisible Women: The Schooling Scandal*. London: Writers and Readers.

Spring, J. (1972) *The Rise and Fall of the Corporate State*. Boston, MA: Beacon Press.

Spring, J. (1997) *Deculturalization and the Struggle for Equality: A Brief History of the Education of Dominated Cultures in the United States*, 2nd edn. New York: McGraw-Hill.

Stewart, C. (1997) Words of warning, *Weekend Australian Review*, 22 February.

Takaki, R. (1993) *A Different Mirror: A History of Multicultural America*. Boston, MA: Little, Brown.

Taylor, S. and Henry, M. (1994) Equity and the new post-compulsory education and training policies in Australia: a progressive or regressive agenda? *Journal of Education Policy*, 9(2): 105–27.

Taylor, S., Rizvi, F., Lingard, B. and Henry, M. (1997) *Educational Policy and the Politics of Change*. London: Routledge.

Thompson, J.B. (1984) *Studies in the Theory of Ideology*. Cambridge: Polity Press.

Thompson, J.B. (1991) *Language and Symbolic Power*. Cambridge: Polity Press.

Tripp, D. (1993) *Critical Incidents in Teaching: Developing Professional Judgement*. London: Routledge.

Tripp, D. (1998) Critical incidents in action inquiry, in G. Shacklock and J. Smyth (eds) *Being Reflexive in Critical Educational and Social Research*. London: Falmer Press.

Troyna, B. (1993) *Racism and Education*. Buckingham: Open University Press.

Troyna, B. and Vincent, C. (1995) The discourses of social justice in education, *Discourse: Studies in the Cultural Politics of Education*, 16(2): 149–66.

Tyack, D. (1974) *The One Best System: A History of American Urban Education*. Cambridge, MA: Harvard University Press.

Unger, R. (1987) *Social Theory: Its Situation and its Task*. Cambridge: Cambridge University Press.

Walker, S. and Barton, L. (1989) *Politics and the Processes of Schooling*. Milton Keynes: Open University Press.

Wallace, M. (1991) Multiculturalism and oppositionality, *Afterimage*, October: 6–9.

Walzer, M. (1983) *Spheres of Justice*. Oxford: Blackwell.

Wenner, J. (1990) Culture, gender and self esteem: teaching Indo-Chinese students, in J. Kenway and S. Willis (eds) *Hearts and Minds: Self-esteem and the Schooling of Girls*. London: Falmer Press.

Whitty, G., Power, S. and Halpin, D. (1998) *Devolution and Choice in Education: The School, the State and the Market*. Buckingham: Open University Press.

Wilkinson, C. (1982) *Communicating in the Classroom: Language, Thought and Culture*. New York: Academic Press.

Williams, R. (1961) *The Long Revolution*. London: Chatto and Windus.

Williams, R. (1989) The idea of a common culture, in R. Gable (ed.) *Resources of Hope: Culture, Democracy, Socialism*. London: Verso.

Williams, T., Long, M., Carpenter, P. and Hayden, M. (1993) *Entering Higher Education in the 1980s*. Canberra: Australian Government Printing Service.

Willis, P. (1977) *Learning to Labour: How Working Class Kids Get Working Class Jobs*. Farnborough: Saxon House.

Wirth, A.G. (1991) Issues in the vocational-liberal studies controversy (1900–1917): John Dewey vs the social efficiency philosophers, in D. Corson (ed.) *Education for Work, Background to Policy and Curriculum*. Clevedon: Multilingual Matters.

Wittgenstein, L. (1953) *Philosophical Investigations* (trans. G. Anscombe). Oxford: Basil Blackwell.

Wouters, C. (1986) Formalization and informalization: Changing tension balances in civilizing processes, *Theory, Culture and Society*, 3(2): 1–18.

Wouters, C. (1987) Developments in the behavioural codes between the sexes: The formalization of informalization in the Netherlands 1930–85, *Theory, Culture and Society*, 4: 405–27.

Wyn, J. (1990) Working class girls and educational outcomes: is self esteem an issue?, in J. Kenway and S. Willis (eds) *Hearts and Minds: Self-esteem and the Schooling of Girls*. London: Falmer Press.

Yates, L. (1997) In the brave new world of competitive schools and postmodern research, how do we tell stories about class? Paper presented to the Australian Association for Research in Education (AARE) Conference, Brisbane, 30 November –4 December.

Young, I.M. (1990) *Justice and the Politics of Difference*. Princeton, NJ: Princeton University Press.

Index

text, 55–6
  contexts (connecting texts), 62–3
  intertextuality, 59–62
  making sense of, 57–65
Thompson, J.B., 58, 63, 64, 65
Thorndike, E., 79
time, 97–8
Torres Strait Islanders, 120–1
totalization, 71
traditional language perspective, 32–7
Tripp, D., 1, 3, 106
Troyna, B., 134, 136
trust, active, 146–8

unemployment, 80
UNESCO: *International Commission on Education for the Twenty-First Century*, 88
Unger, R., 30, 46
United States, 79, 117
  racial differences, 133–5
universal common interests, 145
urban schools, 137

violence, 142
vocational education, 75, 78–84, 88–9

Wacquant, L., 91
Walker, S., 153

Wallace, M., 1
Walzer, M., 12, 13
Wenner, J., 131, 132
Whitty, G., 152
whole language pedagogies, 38–41
Wilkinson, C., 31
Williams, R., 74, 75, 76, 79, 86
Willis, S., 130, 131
Wittgenstein, L., 32
work
  education as preparation for, 75, 78–84, 88–9
  meaningful, 85
Wouters, C., 103

Yates, L., 138, 139
Young, I.M., 86, 105, 122, 145, 152
  classroom relations, 106–7
  critical language perspective, 46, 51
  difference, 20, 118
  domination, 23–4
  group autonomy and empowerment, 150
  oppression, 21, 141–2
  social justice, 18, 19, 26, 28, 144, 146

Zapotec Indian communities, 153